Lecture Notes in Computer Science 12380

Abdelkader Hameurlain · A Min Tjoa ·
Philippe Lamarre · Karine Zeitouni (Eds.)

Transactions on Large-Scale Data- and Knowledge-Centered Systems XLIV

Special Issue on Data Management – Principles, Technologies, and Applications

 Springer

Editors-in-Chief
Abdelkader Hameurlain
IRIT, Paul Sabatier University
Toulouse, France

A Min Tjoa
Vienna University of Technology
Vienna, Austria

Guest Editors
Philippe Lamarre
INSA Lyon, LIRIS
Villeurbanne Cedex, France

Karine Zeitouni
University of Versailles
Saint-Quentin-en-Yvelines
Versailles Cedex, France

ISSN 0302-9743   ISSN 1611-3349   (electronic)
Lecture Notes in Computer Science
ISSN 1869-1994   ISSN 2510-4942   (electronic)
Transactions on Large-Scale Data- and Knowledge-Centered Systems
ISBN 978-3-662-62270-4   ISBN 978-3-662-62271-1   (eBook)
https://doi.org/10.1007/978-3-662-62271-1

This Springer imprint is published by the registered company Springer-Verlag GmbH, DE
part of Springer Nature
The registered company address is: Heidelberger Platz 3, 14197 Berlin, Germany

Preface

This volume contains six fully revised selected papers from the 35th conference on Data Management – Principles, Technologies and Applications (BDA 2019), covering a wide range of very hot topics in the fields of data management. These topics concern big data, graph data streams, workflow execution in the cloud, privacy in crowd-sourcing, secure distributed computing, machine learning, and data mining for recommendation systems.

The papers were selected by the chairs of BDA 2019 among the best papers, and the authors were invited to submit a journal version. Each paper received three reviews from this special issue editorial board. Three papers in this special issue are extended versions of international conference papers published in DBPL 2019, DEXA 2019, and TrustCom 2019.

We would like to take this opportunity to express our sincere thanks to all the editorial board members of this special issue for their effort and their valuable contribution in raising the quality of the camera-ready version of the papers.

We are also grateful to the Editors-in-Chief, Abdelkader Hameurlain and A Min Tjoa, for giving us the opportunity to edit this special issue as part of TLDKS Journal series. Finally, we would like to thank Gabriela Wagner for her availability and her valuable work in the realization of this special issue.

July 2020   Philippe Lamarre
                                                                                             Karine Zeitouni

Organization

Editors-in-Chief

Abdelkader Hameurlain   Paul Sabatier University, IRIT, France
A Min Tjoa   Technical University of Vienna, IFS, Austria

Guest Editors

Philippe Lamarre   INSA Lyon, LIRIS, France
Karine Zeitouni   Université de Versailles-Saint-Quentin-en-Yvelines,
     Labratoire DAVID, France

Editorial Board

Reza Akbarinia   Inria, France
Sabeur Aridhi   University of Lorraine, France
Nicole Bidoit-Tollu   University of Paris-Saclay, France
Alexandru Costan   Inria, France
Laurent d'Orazio   University of Rennes 1, France
Cedric du Mouza   CNAM, France
Zoubida Kedad   Université de Versailles Saint-Quentin-en-Yvelines,
     France

Anne Laurent   University of Montpellier, France
Sofian Maabout   University of Bordeaux, France
Engelbert Mephu Nguifo   Université Clermont Auvergne, France
Benjamin Nguyen   INSA, France
Themis Palpanas   University of Paris, France
Fatiha Saïs   University of Paris-Saclay, France
Genoveva Vargas-Solar   CNRS, LIG, LAFMIA, France
Dan Vodislav   CY Cergy Paris University, France
Shaoyi Yin   Paul Sabatier University, France

Contents

Scalable Saturation of Streaming RDF Triples

Mohammad Amin Farvardin[1(✉)], Dario Colazzo[1], Khalid Belhajjame[1], and Carlo Sartiani[2]

[1] Université Paris-Dauphine, PSL, Research University,
Place du Maréchal de Lattre de Tassigny, 75016 Paris, France
{mohammad-amin.farvardin,dario.colazzo,
khalid.belhajjame}@lamsade.dauphine.fr
[2] Università degli Studi della Basilicata, Potenza, Italy
carlo.sartiani@unibas.it
https://www.dauphine.psl.eu,
https://www.unibas.it

Abstract. In the Big Data era, RDF data are produced in high volumes. While there exist proposals for reasoning over large RDF graphs using big data platforms, there is a dearth of solutions that do so in environments where RDF data are dynamic, and where new instance and schema triples can arrive at any time. In this work, we present the first solution for reasoning over large streams of RDF data using big data platforms. In doing so, we focus on the saturation operation, which seeks to infer implicit RDF triples given RDF Schema or OWL constraints. Indeed, unlike existing solutions which saturate RDF data in bulk, our solution carefully identifies the fragment of the existing (and already saturated) RDF dataset that needs to be considered given the fresh RDF statements delivered by the stream. Thereby, it performs the saturation in an incremental manner. Experimental analysis shows that our solution outperforms existing bulk-based saturation solutions.

1 Introduction

To take full advantage of semantic data and turn them into actionable knowledge, the semantic web community has devised techniques for processing and reasoning over RDF data (e.g. [4,23,27]). However, in the Big Data era, RDF data, just like many other kinds of data, are produced in high volumes. This is partly due to sensor data produced in the context of health monitoring and financial market applications, feeds of user-content provided by social network platforms, as well as long-running scientific experiments that adopt a stream-flow programming model [16]. This trend generated the need for new solutions for processing and reasoning over RDF datasets since existing state of the art techniques cannot cope with large volumes of RDF data.

Supported by PSL, University Dauphine-Paris.

A. Hameurlain et al. (Eds.) TLDKS XLIV, LNCS 12380, pp. 1–40, 2020.
https://doi.org/10.1007/978-3-662-62271-1_1

A typical and fundamental operation for reasoning about RDF data is *data saturation*. This operation involves a set D of RDF data triples and a set S of semantics properties, expressed in terms of either RDF Schema [5] and/or OWL, and aims at inferring the implicit triples that can be derived from D by using properties in S. Data saturation is crucial in order to ensure that RDF processing and querying actually work on the *complete* informative content of an RDF database, without ignoring implicit information. To deal with the problem of saturating massive RDF datasets, a few approaches exploiting big data paradigms (namely Map-Reduce [15]) and platforms, notably Hadoop and Spark (see e.g., [11,24]), have already been proposed. In [24] Urbani *et al.* presented WebPIE, a system for RDF data saturation relying on the Map-Reduce paradigm over Hadoop. In [11] Gu *et al.* presented the Cichlid system and showed how to speed up saturation by using Spark and its underlying Resilient Distributed Datasets (RDDs) abstraction. In [19,20] authors proposed a parallel reasoning method based on P2P self-organizing networks, while in [28] authors propose a parallel approach for RDF reasoning based on MPI. These approaches, however, assume that RDF datasets are fully available prior to the saturation, and as such, are not instrumented to saturate RDF data produced continuously in streams. Indeed, when RDF data are produced in streams, such systems must re-process the whole data collection in order to obtain triples entailed by the newly received ones. This is due to the fact that both initial and already obtained triples (by means of past saturation) can entail new triples under the presence of newly received instance/schema triples. A number of works have addressed the problem of incremental saturation [3,18,26,29], but these approaches, being mostly centralized, do not ensure a scalable, distributed, and robust RDF streaming saturation.

To overcome these limitations, in this work we present the first distributed technique for saturating *streams* of large RDF data, by relying on the Spark Streaming API, hence ensuring scalability and robustness. We present our approach in two steps. In the first one, we deal with streaming RDFS saturation in the presence of RDF Schema statements. The choice of focusing first on RDF Schema is motivated by the fact that, despite its simplicity, RDF Schema is rich enough to make the efficient saturation of streaming large RDF data far from being trivial. The main challenge here is to quickly process fresh data, that must be joined with past met data, whose volume can soon become particularly high in the presence of massive streams. To this end, unlike existing state-of-the-art solutions [11,24] for large-scale RDF saturation, upon the arrival of new RDF statements (both schema and instance triples) our solution *finely* identifies the subset of the existing (and already saturated) RDF dataset that needs to be considered. This is obtained by relying on a specific indexing technique we devised for our approach. Our indexing algorithm partitions triples into property and object triples, and creates distinct subindexes for each micro-batch; hash maps allow the system to quickly retrieve all triples having a given property or a given object.

In the second part of the presentation, we deal with OWL-Horst rules. In this case we show how our saturation technique, initially developed for RDFS only, can be easily adapted to OWL-Horst: indeed, here we have to deal with weaker constraints on rule application order as well as with the need of computing a fix point.

Finally, we validate our claims of efficiency and scalability through an extensive experimental evaluation, where we analyze the behavior of our algorithm on RDFS-based datasets as well as on OWL-based datasets.

Paper Outline. The paper is structured as follows. Section 2 presents preliminaries about RDF saturation and Spark Streaming, while Sect. 3 presents an overview of our technique on RDFS by means of examples. In Sect. 4, we describe our extension of our technique for the OWL-Horst rule set, while Sect. 5 is dedicated to the performance evaluation of our approach. Sections 6 and 7, respectively, discuss related works and future perspectives.

The work presented in this paper is an extension of a previous conference paper [8]. The material in Sect. 4, which examines incremental saturation considering OWL-Horst rules is new, as is the evaluation of the effectiveness of saturation in the presence of OWL-Horst rules reported in Sect. 5. We also added in Sect. 3.3 a proof showing the soundness of our solution given the ordering of RDFS rules that we consider.

2   Preliminaries

2.1   RDF and Semantic Data Reasoning

An RDF dataset is a set of triples of the form $s\ p\ o$, where s is an IRI[1] or a blank node that represents the subject, p is an IRI that represents the predicate, and o is an IRI, blank node or a literal, and it stands for the object. Blank nodes, denoted as $\_{:}b_i$, are used to represent unknown resources (IRIs or literals).

RDF Schema (or RDFS for short) provides the vocabulary for specifying the following relationships between classes and properties, relying on a simplified notation borrowed from [10]:

- *subclass relationship* $\prec_{sc}$: the triple $c_1 \prec_{sc} c_2$ specifies that c_1 is a subclass of c_2;
- *subproperty relationship* $\prec_{sp}$: the triple $p_1 \prec_{sp} p_2$ specifies that p_1 is a subproperty of p_2;
- *property domain* $\hookleftarrow_d$: the triple $p \hookleftarrow_d x$ specifies that the property p has as a domain x; and
- *property range* $\hookrightarrow_r$: the triple $p \hookrightarrow_r z$ specifies that the property p has as a range z.

---

[1] An IRI (*Internationalized Resource Identifier*) is just a URI exploiting Unicode in place of US Ascii as the character set, and is used in the semantic web community to identify resources.

For the sake of readability, in what follows we use simple strings instead of IRIs to denote predicates, subjects, and objects in triples. Also, we abbreviate the `rdf:type` predicate with the τ symbol.

Example 1. Figure 2 illustrates a set of RDF instance triples that we use as a running example, together with the equivalent graph representation. The graph describes the resource doi_1 that belongs to an unknown class, whose title is "Complexity of Answering Queries Using Materialized Views", whose author is "Serge Abiteboul" and having an unknown contact author. This paper is in the proceedings of an unknown resource whose name is "PODS′98". Lastly, the IRI edbt2013 is a conference and hasName, the property associating names to resources, is created by "John Doe".

Figure 1 lists schema triples. For example, it specifies that the class *posterCP* is a subclass of *ConfP*, that the property *hasContactA* is a sub-property of *hasAuthor*. It also specifies that the property *hasAuthor* has as domain *paper* and as range a literal.

$$
\begin{aligned}
S = \{ \; &\text{posterCP} \prec_{sc} \text{confP}, &&\_:b_0 \prec_{sc} \text{confP}, \\
&\text{confP} \prec_{sc} \text{paper}, &&\text{hasTitle} \hookleftarrow_d \text{confP}, \\
&\text{hasTitle} \hookrightarrow_r \text{rdfs:Literal}, &&\text{hasAuthor} \hookleftarrow_d \text{paper}, \\
&\text{hasAuthor} \hookrightarrow_r \text{rdfs:Literal}, &&\text{hasContractA} \prec_{sp} \text{hasAuthor}, \\
&\text{inProceesingOf} \hookleftarrow_d \text{confP}, &&\text{inProceesingOf} \hookrightarrow_r \text{conference}, \\
&\text{hasName} \hookleftarrow_d \text{conference}, &&\text{hasName} \hookrightarrow_r \text{rdfs:Literal}, \\
&\text{createdBy} \hookrightarrow_r \text{rdfs:Literal} \; \}
\end{aligned}
$$

Fig. 1. Instance and schema RDF triples.

$$
\begin{aligned}
G = \{ \; &doi_1 \; \tau \; \_:b_0, \quad doi_1 \; \textit{hasTitle} \; \text{"CAQU MV"}, \\
&doi_1 \; \textit{hasAuthor} \; \text{"SA"}, \quad doi_1 \; \textit{hasContactA} \; \_:b_1, \\
&doi_1 \; \textit{inProceedingsOf} \; \_:b_2, \; \_:b_2 \; \textit{hasName} \; \text{"PODS′98"}, \\
&\textit{hasName} \; \textit{createdBy} \; \text{"John Doe"}, \; \text{"edbt2013"} \; \tau \; \text{Conference} \; \}
\end{aligned}
$$

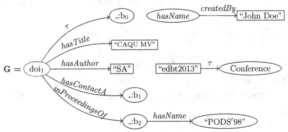

Fig. 2. RDF graph representation of a conference paper.

As in other works (e.g., [10, 11, 24]) we focus on the core rules of RDFS, the extension to other rules being trivial. In particular, we consider here rules 2, 3, 5, 7, 9, and 11 among the 13 RDFS rules illustrated in Table 1.

The realm of the semantic web embraces the Open World Assumption: facts (triples) that are not *explicitly* stated may hold given a set of RDFS triples expressing constraints. These are usually called *implicit* triples, and, in our work, we consider the problem of RDF saturation, i.e., given a set of RDFS rules, inferring all possible implicit triples by means of these rules applied on explicit triples, or, recursively, on implicit triples. For example, rule *rdfs2* in Table 1 states that, if a property p has a domain x, given a triple $s\ p\ o$, we can infer that s is of type x. Rule *rdfs9*, instead, specifies that, if s is of type x and x is a subclass of y, then we can infer that s is of type y.

Table 1. RDFS rules.

Rule	Condition	Consequence	Level
rdfs1	$s\ p\ o$	$\_{:}b\ \tau\ rdfs{:}Literal$	–
rdfs2	$p \hookleftarrow_d x,\ s\ p\ o$	$s\ \tau\ x$	Instance-level
rdfs3	$p \hookrightarrow_r x,\ s\ p\ o$	$o\ \tau\ x$	Instance-level
rdfs4	$s\ p\ o$	$s/o\ \tau\ rdfs{:}Resource$	–
rdfs5	$p \prec_{sp} q, q \prec_{sp} r$	$p \prec_{sp} r$	Schema-level
rdfs6	$p\ \tau\ rdf{:}Property$	$p \prec_{sp} p$	–
rdfs7	s p o, $p \prec_{sp}$ q	s q o	Instance-level
rdfs8	s τ rdfs:Class	s $\prec_{sc}$ rdfs:Resource	–
rdfs9	s τ x, x $\prec_{sc}$ y	s τ y	Instance-level
rdfs10	s τ rdfs:Class	s $\prec_{sc}$ s	–
rdfs11	x $\prec_{sc}$ y, y $\prec_{sc}$ z	x $\prec_{sc}$ z	schema-level
rdfs12	p τ rdfs:ContainerMembershipProperty	p $\prec_{sp}$ rdfs:member	–
rdfs13	o τ rdfs:Datatype	o $\prec_{sc}$ rdfs:Literal	–

In the remaining part of the paper, we will use the following notation to indicate derivations/inference of triples. A *derivation tree* is defined as follows.

$$T := t\ \mid\ \{T \mid T\} - rdfsX \rightarrow t$$

where the rule number X ranges over $\{2, 3, 5, 7, 9, 11\}$. A derivation tree can be empty, hence consisting of a given triple t, or can be of the form $\{T1 \mid T2\} - rdfsX \rightarrow t$, meaning that the tree derives t, by means of rule *rdfsX* whose premises are (matched to) the two triples given by T1 and T2, respectively. So, for instance we can have the following derivation tree T1 for the G and S previously introduced:

$$\{hasTitle \hookleftarrow_d confP \mid doi_1\ hasTitle\ ``CAQUMV"\} - rdfs2 \rightarrow doi_1\ \tau\ confP$$

Moreover, we can have the following derivation T2 relying on T1:

$$\{T1 \mid confP \prec_{\mathrm{sc}} paper\} - rdfs9 \rightarrow doi_1 \ \tau \ paper$$

In the following, given a set of instance RDF triples D and a set of schema triples S, we say that T is over D and S if the derivation tree uses triples in D and S as leaves. Moreover, we define the saturation of D over S as D extended with all the possible instance triples obtained by means of derivation (below, derivation trees are assumed to be over D and S):

$$D_S^* = D \ \cup \ \{t \mid \exists \{T1 \mid T2\} - rdfsX \rightarrow t \ with \ X \in \{2, 3, 7, 9\}\}$$

Notice above that, say, T2 can be a derivation tree totally over S, recursively applying rule 5 (or rule 11) thus deriving a triple in S^*, below defined.

$$S^* = S \ \cup \ \{t \mid \exists \{T1 \mid T2\} - rdfsX \rightarrow t \ with \ X \in \{5, 11\}\}$$

Above, in the S^* definition, please note that since $X \in \{5, 11\}$ the whole derivation tree consists of subsequent applications of rule 5 (or rule 11).

2.2 Spark and Spark Streaming

Spark [30] is a widely used in-memory distributed cluster computing framework. It provides the means for specifying DAG-based data flows using operators like `map`, `reduceByKey`, `join`, `filter`, etc. over data collections represented by means of *Resilient Distributed Datasets* (RDDs). For our purposes, we use the streaming capabilities of Spark whereby data come into micro-batches that need to be processed within a time-interval (also referred to as a window).

In Spark, the data to be processed are mapped into RDDs, where an RDD is an immutable collection of objects (e.g, <key, value> pairs); RDDs are partitioned and distributed over the Spark cluster.

Spark essentially works by applying operations to RDDs. These operations can be divided into *transformations* and *actions*. Transformations are lazy operations that return a new RDD, and are evaluated only when an action (e.g., `count`, `collect`) is invoked. Typical transformations are $map()$, that applies a given function to all the objects in a RDD, and $filter()$, which applies a predicate to the input data (e.g., `rdd.map(x => x + x)`, `rdd.filter(x => x != 3)`).

3 Streaming RDF Saturation

Our goal is to support the saturation of RDF streams by leveraging on Spark stream processing capabilities. Using Spark, an RDF stream is discretized into a series of timestamped micro-batches that come (and are, therefore, processed) at different time intervals. In our work, we assume that a micro-batch contains a set of instance RDF triples, but may also contain schema (i.e., RDFS) triples.

Consider, for example, an RDF stream composed of the following series of micro-batches $[mb_i, \ldots, mb_n]$, where $i > 0$. A first approach for saturating such a stream using a batch-oriented solution would proceed as follows: when a micro-batch mb_i arrives, it unions mb_i with the previous instance dataset (including triples obtained by previous saturation) and then the resulting dataset is totally re-saturated.

On the contrary, our approach allows for RDF saturation in a streaming fashion, by sensibly limiting the amount of data re-processing upon the arrival of a new micro-batch. To this aim our saturation approach leverages on a novel indexing scheme for RDF triples, as well as on a few heuristics and optimization techniques.

3.1 Indexing Scheme

Our triple indexing structure allows the system to quickly retrieve a triple given its object or its property. This structure, which is stored on HDFS, comprises two root HDFS directories, called o and p.

Assume that a new micro-batch mb_i arrives at time t. At mb_i arrival time, the indexing algorithm creates a new subdirectory t inside o, as well as a new subdirectory t inside p. On o/t the algorithm stores triples having as predicate rdf:type, and, therefore, providing information about the type of a resource; inside o/t triples are further partitioned into files according to their actual object, so that triples with the same object are stored in the same file. Notice that triples with the rdf:type predicate are used in the premises of *rdfs9*. Given a schema triple of the form $y \prec_{sc} z$, our indexing approach allows for the fast retrieval of the files in the o directories of the micro-batches that have as an object the resource y, and therefore can be used to trigger *rdfs9*.

On p/t the algorithm stores the remaining instance triples of mb_i i.e., those that do not have rdf:type as a predicate. As in the previous case, triples inside p/t are partitioned according to their predicate, so that triples with the same predicate are stored in the same file.

Our indexing scheme also exploits two hash maps, stored in RDDs persisted in main memory, that each map each object o_i to the corresponding HDFS files, as well as each property p_i to the HDFS files storing the matching triples; these hash maps contain no mapping for objects and properties without triples. By means of this kind of indexing, we can optimize application of rules *rdfs2*, *rdfs3* and *rdfs7* to infer new instance triples as we can inspect the previously described hash maps in order to retrieve only files containing triples with properties needed by these 3 rules.

To illustrate, assume for example that a new micro-batch mb_i arrives at a given time instant t, and that it contains the schema triple t_{sc}: $s_1 \prec_{sc} s_2$. Such schema triple can contribute to the inference of new schema triples (i.e., by means of *rdfs11*) as well as new instance triples by means of *rdfs9*. Since the indexing mechanism we designed is sought for the inference of instance triple, let us focus on *rdfs9*. To identify the instance triples that can be utilized together with the schema triple t_{sc}, we need to examine existing instance triples. Our indexing mechanism allows us to sensibly restrict the set of triples that need to be examined, as the hash map indexing the files under the o directories enables the fast recovering of files containing triples with s_1 as an object resource, and that can be combined with the schema triple t_{sc} to trigger *rdfs9*. The indexing on files in p directories is exploited in a similar manner in order to efficiently recover files containing *instance* triples with a given property, so as to use included triples to trigger *rdfs2/3/7*, under the arrival of a correspondent schema triple in the stream. To illustrate our approach more in detail, consider the following example.

Example 2. We assume that we have the initial schema **S** of Fig. 1 and that we saturate it by obtaining **S'** as indicated below.

$$\mathbf{S'} = \mathbf{S} \cup \{hasContactA \hookrightarrow_r rdfs{:}Literal, \quad \_{:}b_0 \prec_{sc} paper\}$$

This operation is fast and centralized, as the initial schema is always relatively small in size. Our approach then proceeds according to the following steps.

1. The saturated schema **S'** is broadcast to each task, that can access **S'** with no further network communication.
2. Then available micro-batches are processed. For the sake of simplicity, we make here the (unnatural) assumption that each micro-batch consists of only one triple. The stream of micro-batches is in Table 2.

Table 2. Instance triples.

mb	Subject	Predicate	Object
1	doi_1	τ	$\_{:}b_0$
2	doi_1	$hasTitle$	"CAQU MV"
3	doi_1	$hasAuthor$	"SA"
4	doi_1	$hasContactA$	$\_{:}b_1$
5	doi_1	$inProceedingsOf$	$\_{:}b_2$
6	$\_{:}b_2$	$hasName$	"PODS'98"

3. The first received micro-batch triggers *rdfs9* so that we have the derivation of two new triples:

$$\{doi_1 \; \tau \; \_{:}b_0 \mid \_{:}b_0 \prec_{sc} confP\} - rdfs9 \rightarrow doi_1 \; \tau \; confP$$
$$\{doi_1 \; \tau \; \_{:}b_0 \mid \_{:}b_0 \prec_{sc} paper\} - rdfs9 \rightarrow doi_1 \; \tau \; paper$$

The received triple plus the two derived ones are then stored according to our indexing strategy. As already said, triples are grouped by their objects when having the rdf:type property, so as to obtain the following file assignment, knowing that t_1 is the time stamp for the current micro-batch:

Table 3. Saturated streaming triples.

mb_i	Received triple(s)	Schema-triple	Entails($E.$) & Received($R.$)	Stored path
1	doi_1 τ _:b_0	_:b_0 $\prec_{sc}$ confP, _:b_0 $\prec_{sc}$ paper	$E.$ doi_1 τ confP, $E.$ doi_1 τ paper, $R.$ doi_1 τ _:b_0	$o/t_1/file_1$, $o/t_1/file_2$, $o/t_1/file_3$
2	doi_1 *hasTitle* "CAQU MV"	*hasTitle* $\hookrightarrow_d$ *confP*	$E.$ doi_1 τ confP, $R.$ doi_1 *hasTitle* "CAQU MV"	$o/t_2/file_1$, $p/t_2/file_1$ $p/t_2/file_1$
3	doi_1 *hasAuthor* "SA"	hasAuthor $\hookrightarrow_d$ paper	$E.$ doi_1 τ paper, $R.$ doi_1 *hasAuthor* "SA"	$o/t_3/file_1$, $p/t_3/file_1$
4	doi_1 *hasContactA* _:b_1	no inference	$R.$ doi_1 *hasContactA* _:b_1	$p/t_4/file_1$
5	doi_1 *inProceedingOf* _:b_2	inProceeingOf $\hookrightarrow_d$ confP, inProceedingOf $\hookrightarrow_r$ conference	$E.$ doi_1 τ confP, $E.$ _:b_2 τ conference, $R.$ doi_1 *inProceedingOf* _:b_2	$o/t_5/file_1$, $o/t_5/file_2$, $p/t_5/file_1$
6	_:b_2 *hasName* "PODS′98"	hasName $\hookrightarrow_d$ conference	$E.$ _:b_2 τ conference, $R.$ _:b_2 *hasName* "PODS′98"	$o/t_6/file_1$, $p/t_6/file_1$

$$NST = \{ \textbf{\textit{paper}} \prec_{sc} \textbf{\textit{publication, hasContactA}} \prec_{sp} \textbf{\textit{hasAuthor}}$$
$$posterCP \prec_{sc} publication, confP \prec_{sc} publication,$$
$$\text{_:}b_0 \prec_{sc} publication, hasContactA \hookrightarrow_d paper \}$$

Fig. 3. *N*ewly received and inferred *S*chema *T*riples (*NST*).

$$doi_1 \ \tau \ confP \ \Rightarrow o/t_1/file_1,$$
$$doi_1 \ \tau \ paper \ \Rightarrow o/t_1/file_2,$$
$$doi_1 \ \tau \ \text{_:}b_0 \Rightarrow o/t_1/file_3$$

4. The processing goes on by deriving new instance triples for the micro-batches from 2 to 6, as indicated in Table 3, which also indicates how instance triples are stored/indexed.

Now assume that in micro-batch 7 we have the followed RDF schema triples:

$$paper \ \prec_{sp} \ publication, \quad hasContractA \ \prec_{sp} \ hasAuthor$$

So we have now three steps: **i)** infer the new schema triples by considering the already present schema triples, **ii)** broadcast these schema triples minus the already existing/broadcast schema triples (Fig. 3), to enable tasks to locally access them, **iii)** re-process previously met/inferred instance triples by taking into consideration the new schema.

Consider for instance $\{hasContactA \prec_{sp} hasAuthor\}$ as new schema triple. This schema triple triggers *rdfs7*. Therefore, our indexing tells us that *only* file $p/t_4/file_1$ (Table 3, line 4) needs to be loaded to infer new triples, that, of course, will be in turn stored according to our indexing strategy.

As we will see in our experimental analysis, the pruning of loaded files ensured by our indexing will entail fast incremental saturation. Also, note that our app-

Algorithm 1. Incremental RDFS Indexing Algorithm

1: // mb'_i is indicated as instance and implicit triples from received mb'_i
2: **Input:** Saturated mb'_i
3: // The information of mb'_i keeps as two RDDs in memory.
4: **Output:** *oIndexingRDD, pIndexingRDD*
5: **Begin**
6:     // Get a fixed timestamp to save the mb'_i triples.
7:     val *fts* = System.currentTimeMillis.toString

8:     // The mb'_i triples partitions by their *object* where their *predicate* is rdf:type.
9:     val *oPartition* = mb'_i.**filter**(_._2.**contains**(*"rdf-syntax-ns#type"*)).
10:         **map**(t ⇒ (t._3, t._1)).**partitionBy**(number of different *object*).
11:         **mapPartitions**(_.**map**(t ⇒ (t._2, t._1)))

12:     // The mb_i' triples partitions by their *predicate* where their *predicate* is NOT rdf:type.
13:     val *pPartition* = mb'_i.**filter**(!_._2.**contains**(*"rdf-syntax-ns#type"*)).
14:         **map**(t ⇒ (t._2, t)).**partitionBy**(number of different *predicate*).
15:         **mapPartitions**(_.**map**(_._2))

16:     // The *oPartitions* and *pPartitions* store on HDFS at fixed timestamp under *o* and *p* sub-
        directory paths respectively.
17:     *oPartition*.**saveAsTextFile**(*outputPath* + *"o/"* + *fts* + *"/data/"*)
18:     *pPartition*.**saveAsTextFile**(*outputPath* + *"p/"* + *fts* + *"/data/"*)

19:     // *oIndexingRDD* is a HashTable which keeps the *object* of instance triple as key and their
        physical paths as value.
20:     *oIndexingRDD* ∪= *oPartition*.**mapPartitionsWithIndex**((*index,iterator*) ⇒{
21:         *iterator*.**map**(t ⇒ (t._2, *fts* + *"-"* + *index* + *"_"*)) }).**mapPartitions**(
22:         _.**map**(t ⇒ (t,1))).**reduceByKey**(_+_).**mapPartitions**(_.**map**(_._1))

23:     // *pIndexingRDD* is a HashTable which keeps the *predicate* of instance triple as key and
        their physical paths as value.
24:     *pIndexingRDD* ∪= *pPartition*.**mapPartitionsWithIndex**((*index,iterator*) ⇒{
25:         *iterator*.**map**(t ⇒ (t._2, *fts* + *"-"* + *index* + *"_"*)) }).**mapPartitions**(
26:         _.**map**(t ⇒ (t,1))).**reduceByKey**(_+_).**mapPartitions**(_.**map**(_._1))

27:     return *oIndexingRDD* & *pIndexingRDD*
28: **End**

roach tends to create a non-negligible number of files, but fortunately without compromising efficiency thanks to distribution.

The indexing algorithm (Algorithm 1) is responsible for storing on HDFS at the intended paths, but also for collecting the object/predicate of triples and their paths for indexing variable. We focus here on the algorithm for indexing, which is central to our contribution. Central to the efficiency of the solution presented in the previous section is the technique that we elaborated for incrementally indexing the new instance triples that are asserted or inferred given a new micro-batch.

Algorithm 1 takes as input new instance triples that are asserted or inferred given the last micro-batch mb'. It filters the instances triples to create two RDDs. The first RDD is used for storing object-based triples (*line 9–11*). Since the predicate of object-based triples is rdf:type, we only store *subject* and *object* of object-based triples. The second RDD is used for predicate-based triples (*line 13–15*). Notice that the triples of the two RDDs are grouped based on their object and predicate, respectively, by utilizing RDD partitioning. The Spark method *partitionBy*() takes as an argument the number of partitions to be created. In the case of the RDD used for storing object-based triples, we use the number of different objects that appear in the triples as an argument. In the case of the RDD used for storing predicate-based triples, we use the number of different predicates that appear in the triples. It is worth mentioning here that we could have used the method *sortBy()* provided by Spark for RDDs instead of *partitionBy()*. However, *sortBy()* is computationally more expensive as it requires a local sort.

Besides grouping the RDDs containing the triples, the algorithm creates two auxiliary lightweight hash structures to keep track of the partitions that store triples with a given object (*line 20–22*) and predicate (*line 24–26*), respectively. Such memory-based hash structures act as indexes. They are lightweight memory-based structures that are utilized during the saturation to quickly identify partitions that contain a given object and predicate, respectively. Note that all the steps of the algorithm, with the exception of the very first one (line 7), are processed in a parallel manner.

3.2   Heuristics and Optimization Techniques

To improve the performance and the scalability of RDF streaming saturation, our indexing scheme alone is not sufficient. Therefore, we also adopt the rule application strategy of Cichlid, and devised new optimization techniques. We will briefly recall the Cichlid strategy, and then focus on our novel techniques.

Rule Application Order. While the outcome of the saturation operation is orthogonal to the order in which the rules are applied, the time and resources consumed by such an operation are not. Because of this, the authors of Cichlid (and WebPIE before them) identified a number of optimisations that influence the rule application order with the view to increasing the efficiency of the saturation. In what follows, we discuss the main ones.

1. *RDF Schema is to be saturated first.* The size of the RDF schema[2] in an RDF graph is usually small, even when saturated. It is usually orders of magnitudes smaller than the size of the remaining *instance* triples. This suggests that the schema of the RDF graph is to be saturated first. By saturating the schema of an RDF graph we mean applying rules that produce new triples describing the vocabulary used in an RDF graph. Furthermore, because the size of the schema is small, schema saturation can be done in a centralized fashion. In this respect, the RDFS rules presented in Table 1 can be categorised into two disjoint categories: schema-level and instance-level RDFS rules. Schema-level RDFS rules (*rdfs5* and *rdfs11*) designate the rules that produce triples describing the vocabulary (classes, properties, and their relationships). Instance-level triples, on the other hand, specify resource instances of the classes in the RDF vocabularies and their relationships. Each rule is

---

[2] By schema, we mean the RDF triples that describe the vocabulary of an RDF graph, i.e., classes, properties, and their constraints.

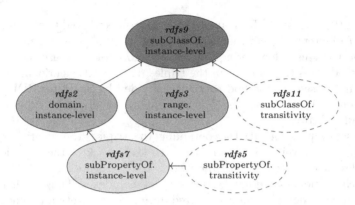

Fig. 4. The optimized order of execution for RDFS. Dashed ellipses show the schema-level entailment, while the solid ellipses are for the Instance-level entailment. The white colour ellipse has no dependency prerequisite with other RDFS. The lighter ellipses come first. (Color figure online)

made up of two premises and one conclusion, each of which is an RDF triple. While premises of schema-level rules are schema triples, premises of instance-level rules are a schema triple and an instance triple. Also, instance-level rules entail an RDF instance triple, while schema-level rules entail an RDF schema triple.

2. *Dependencies between rules.* When determining the rule execution order, the dependencies among rules must be taken into account too. In particular, a rule R_i precedes a rule R_j if the conclusion of R_i is used as a premise for rule R_j. For example *rdfs7* has a conclusion that is used as a premise for rules *rdfs2* and *rdfs3*. Therefore, *rdfs7* should be applied before *rdfs2* and *rdfs3*.

By taking (1) and (2) into consideration, the authors of Cichlid established the order of application of rules illustrated in Fig. 4.

Rule Pruning for Schema Saturation. Given a new micro-batch $\mathtt{mb_i}$, we filter all the schema triples contained in it. Note that, in the general case, it is not likely that these new schema triples trigger all the saturation rules, i.e., it is not the case that the new micro-batch includes all kinds of RDFS triples at once - i.e., *subPropertyOf, domain, range,* and *subClassOf.* Therefore, for saturating the schema at the level of the new micro-batch we first filter new schema triples, and then obtain the set of new schema triples

$$NST = Transitive\ Closure\ (new\ received\ schema\ \cup\ past\ schema) - past\ schema$$

The Saturation operation is local and only triggers rules that do need to be applied, in the right order. Table 4 illustrates the rules to be activated given some matching schema triple: the number 1 indicates the availability of a matching schema triple, and 0 indicates it is not. For example, if a schema triple specifying the domain of a property exists, then this triggers rule 2. All possible cases are

Table 4. The 1 and 0 indicate for the availability of that particular schema rules in mb_i. $X \rightarrow Y$ means: the output of rule X used as an input of rule Y.

	subPropertyOf	domain	range	subClassOf	Saturation order
1	1	1	1	1	$R7 \rightarrow (R2, R3) \rightarrow R9$
2	1	1	1	0	$R7 \rightarrow (R2, R3)$
3	1	1	0	1	$R7 \rightarrow R2 \rightarrow R9$
4	1	1	0	0	$R7 \rightarrow R2$
5	1	0	1	1	$R7 \rightarrow R3 \rightarrow R9$
6	1	0	1	0	$R7 \rightarrow R3$
7	1	0	0	1	$R7, R9$
8	1	0	0	0	$R7$
9	0	1	1	1	$(R2, R3) \rightarrow R9$
10	0	1	1	0	$R2, R3$
11	0	1	0	1	$R2 \rightarrow R9$
12	0	1	0	0	$R2$
13	0	0	1	1	$R3 \rightarrow R9$
14	0	0	1	0	$R3$
15	0	0	0	1	$R9$
16	0	0	0	0	$-$

indicated in Table 4, and Saturation selects one line of this table, depending on the kind of schema predicates met in the new schema triples. This avoids triggering useless rules.

Once saturation for mb_i schema triples is done in this optimized fashion, obtained triples (i.e., *NST*) are merged with the existing RDFS schema for a second-pass of global schema saturation, taking into account triples deriving from both mb_i and the pre-existing schema.

Efficiently Saturate Existing Instance Triples by Leveraging on our Incremental Indexing Scheme. Given the new schema triples that are provided by the micro-batch mb_i or inferred in (1), we need to scan existing instances triples to identify those that, if combined with the new schema triples, will trigger RDFS rules in Table 1. This operation can be costly as it involves examining all the instance triples that have been provided and inferred micro-batches received before mb_i. To alleviate this problem, we exploit the incremental indexing scheme of the previous section; this technique allows for the fast retrieval of the instance triples that will likely trigger the RDFS rules given some schema triples. Once retrieved, such instances triples are used together with the new schema triples to generate new instance triples. Notice here that we cannot infer new schema triples. This is because the rules for inferring new schema triples require two schema triples as a premise (see Table 1).

Incremental Loading. As we previously observed, our indexing technique may lead to the creation of a huge number of files on HDFS, which in turn may increase the risk of a failure when Spark must so many files at once. Therefore, we addressed this reliability issue by loading the index files incrementally (i.e., 150 files per time), until all files have been loading, and then by *unioning* the tuples inside them.

Saturate New Instance Triples. The instance triples inferred in (2) need to be examined as they may be used to infer new instance triples. Specifically, each of those triples is examined to identify the RDFS rule(s) to be triggered. Once identified, such rules are activated to infer instance triples. The instance triples in mb_i as well as those inferred in (2) and (3) are stored and indexed using the technique described in Sect. 3.1.

3.3   Streaming Saturation Algorithm

The overall streaming saturation algorithm is shown in Algorithm 2, and commented hereafter.

Given a micro-batch mb_i, we first perform schema saturation if mb_i contains schema triples (*lines 12, 13*). The related instance triples are retrieved based on mb_{NST} (*line 14*). Given newly inferred schema triples, instance triples are retrieved and examined to identify cases where new instance triples may be inferred (*line 15*). The obtained schema triples (i.e., mb_{NST}) are added and broadcast within the initial schema RDD (*line 17, 18*). The inferred triples, if any, are merged with instance triples of mb_i (i.e., mb_{ins}) and saturation is applied to them. In the next step, the received and inferred instance triples are combined and obtained duplicates, if any, are removed (*line 22*). In the last step, the instance triples from the previous step are saved and indexed using our method (*line 24–25*).

Soundness and Completeness. We deal now with the proof of soundness and completeness of our approach.

We need the following lemma, which is at the basis of soundness and completeness of our system as well as of WebPIE [24] and Cichlid [11], and reflects rule ordering expressed in Fig. 4. To illustrate the lemma, assume we have $D = \{s \ \tau \ c_1\}$ while the schema includes four triples of the form $c_i \prec_{\text{sc}} c_{i+1}$, for $i = 1 \ldots 4$. Over D and S we can have the tree T1 corresponding to:

$$\{c_1 \prec_{\text{sc}} c_2 \mid c_2 \prec_{\text{sc}} c_3\} - rdfs11 \rightarrow c_1 \prec_{\text{sc}} c_3$$

Algorithm 2. Overall Algorithm for Saturating RDF Stream

1: **Input:** MB $\leftarrow [mb_1, \cdots, mb_n]$ // a stream of micro-batches.
2: **Output:** Schemas $\leftarrow [Sch_1, \cdots, Sch_n]$ // Sch_i represents the schema triples obtained as a result of saturating the micro-batches MB = $[mb_1, \cdots mb_i]$.
3: **Output:** Datasets $\leftarrow [DS_1, \cdots, DS_n]$ // DS_i represents the instance triples obtained as a result of saturating the micro-batches MB = $[mb_1, \cdots mb_i]$.
4: **Output:** IndexInformation $\leftarrow [oIndex, pIndex]$ // oIndex and pIndex keeps object- and predicate-based information respectively.
   Begin
5:   $D_{ins} \leftarrow \emptyset$ // Initialize a dataset for instance triples
6:   $D_{sc} \leftarrow \emptyset$ // Initialize a dataset for schema triples
7:   $br \leftarrow$ if D_{sc} exist then **TransitiveClosure** and **broadcast** them
8:   **do** {
        // Separate schema from instance triples in mb
9:      $(mb_{sch}, mb_{ins}) \leftarrow$ **SeparatingTriples**(mb_i)

10:     $if\,(mb_{sch} \neq \emptyset$ **then**) {
11:        // Retrieve the already saturated instance triples and re-saturate them based on combination of received and existing RDFS triples
12:        $mb'_{sch} \leftarrow$ (**TransitiveClosure** ($mb_{sch} \cup D_{sc}$)) - D_{sc}
13:        $mb_{NST} \leftarrow$ **broadcast**(mb'_{sch})
14:        $D'_{ins} \leftarrow$ Retrieve instance triples to be saturated by using mb_{NST}
15:        $mb'_i \leftarrow$ **Saturate**(D'_{ins}, mb_{NST})

16:        // Combine received and existing RDFS triples and re-broadcast them
17:        $D_{sc} \leftarrow mb_{NST} \cup D_{sc}$
18:        $br \leftarrow$ **broadcast**(D_{sc}) // The total schema so far received.
19:     }

20:     // Saturate the received instance triples with total RDFS triples
21:     $mb_{imp} \leftarrow$ **Saturate**($mb_{ins} \cup mb'_i$, br)
22:     $mb''_i \leftarrow (mb_{ins} \cup mb_i' \cup mb_{imp})$.distinct

23:     // The following two lines are handled by **Indexing Algorithm**
24:     Save mb''_i in the HDFS
25:     $[oIndex, pIndex] \cup \leftarrow$ **indexing**(mb''_i)
26: } **while**(is there an incoming micro-batch mb?)
27: **End**

A more complex tree is T2 defined in terms of T1:

$$\{s\ \tau\ c_1 \mid T1\} - rdfs9 \rightarrow s\ \tau\ c_3$$

Imagine now we have T3 defined as

$$\{c_3 \prec_{sc} c_4 \mid c_4 \prec_{sc} c_5\} - rdfs11 \rightarrow c_3 \prec_{sc} c_5$$

We can go on by composing our derivation trees, obtaining T4:

$$\{T2 \mid T3\} - rdfs9 \rightarrow s \; \tau \; c_5$$

Note that the above tree T4 includes two applications of $rdfs9$. At the same time we can have the tree T5

$$\{T1 \mid T3\} - rdfs11 \rightarrow c_1 \prec_{\mathrm{sc}} c_5$$

enabling us to have the tree T4' which is equivalent to T4, having only one application of rule 9, and consisting of

$$\{s \; \tau \; c_1 \mid T5\} - rdfs9 \rightarrow s \; \tau \; c_3$$

As shown by this example, and as proved by the following lemma, repeated applications of instance rules $\{2, 3, 7, 9\}$ can be collapsed into only one, provided that this rule is then applied to an instance triple and to a schema triple in S^*, obtained by repeated applications of schema rules 5 and 11. This also proves that it is sound to first saturate the schema S and then applying instance rules $\{2, 3, 7, 9\}$ (each one at most once) over schema rules in S^*.

Lemma 1. *Given an RDF dataset D of instance triples and a set S of RDFS triples, for any derivation tree T over D and S, deriving $t \in D_S^*$, there exists an equivalent T' deriving t, such that each of the instance rules $\{2, 3, 7, 9\}$ are used at most once, with rule 7 applied before either rule 2 or 3, which in turn is eventually applied before 9 in T'. Moreover, each of these four rules is applied to a S^* triple.*

Proof. To prove the above lemma, we examine the dependencies between the rules $\{2, 3, 5, 7, 9, 11\}$. A rule $\mathbf{r}$ depends on a rule $\mathbf{r'}$ where possibly $\mathbf{r}$ and $\mathbf{r'}$ are the same rule, if the activation of $\mathbf{r'}$ produces a triple that can be used as a premise for the activation of $\mathbf{r}$. This examination of rule dependencies reveals that:

- Rule 5 depends on itself only;
- Rule 11 depends on itself only;
- Rule 7 depends on rule 5: indeed, rule 7 uses as a premise triples of the form $p \prec_{\mathrm{sp}} q$, which are produced by the activation of rule 5;
- Rules 2 and 3 depend on rule 7: both rules 2 and 3 use as a premise triples of the form spo, which are given in prior and produced by rule 7;
- Rule 9 depends on rules 2, 3 and all given triples in prior with τ as a predicate: both rules produce triples of the form $p \; \tau \; x$, a premise for activating rule 9. It also depends on rule 5.

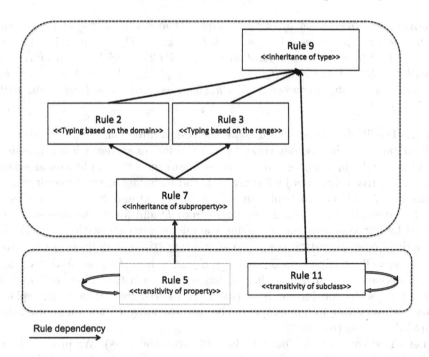

Fig. 5. RDFS rule dependencies.

Figure 5 depicts the obtained rule dependency graph. With the exception of rule 5 and 11, the graph is acyclic, meaning that the saturation can be performed in a single pass. Furthermore, the dependency graph shows that in order for the saturation to be made in a single pass schema rules 5 and 11 need to be first (transitively) applied to saturate the schema, followed by the instance rules. Rule 7 is the first instance rule to be executed, followed by the instance rules 2 and 3 (which can be applied simultaneously or in any order), before applying at the end rule 9. That said, we need to prove now that for an arbitrary derivation tree T there exists an equivalent derivation tree T' as described in the lemma thesis. This follows from the fact that if (*) T contains more than one rule $rdfsX$ with $X \in \{2, 3, 7, 9\}$, then it must be because of subsequent applications of rule 9 (resp. rule 7) each one applied to a schema triple eventually derived by rule 11 (resp. rule 5), exactly as depicted by the example just before the lemma. As shown by the example, this chain of rule 9 (resp. rule 7) applications can be contracted so as to obtain a unique application of rule 9 (resp. rule 7) applied to a schema triple in S^*, obtained by subsequent applications of rule 11 (resp. rule 9). So, in the case (*) holds, the just described rewriting for chains of rule 9 (resp. rule 7) can be applied to T in order to obtain T'.   □

Given the above lemma, we can now present the theorem stating the soundness of our approach.

Theorem 1. *Given a set of instance triples D and schema triples S, assume the two sets are partitioned in n micro-batches $mb_i = D_i \cup S_i$ with $i = 1 \ldots n$. We have that there exists a derivation tree $\{T1 \mid T2\} - rdfsX \rightarrow t$ over D and S, with $t \in D_S^*$, if and only if there exists $j \in \{1, \ldots, n\}$ such t is derived by our system when mb_j is processed, after having processed micro-batches mb_h with $h = 1 \ldots j - 1$.*

Proof. The 'if' direction (soundness) is the easiest direction. We prove this case by induction on j. In case one triple t is derived by our system when processing the micro-batch mb_1, then we can see that in Algorithm 2 this triple is obtained by a derivation tree calculated by `Saturate()`, and including at the leaves instance triples in D_1 and schema triples in S_1^*. As $D_1 \subseteq D$ and $S_1^* \subseteq S^*$, we have that this derivation tree can derive t also from D and for S. Assume now t is derived by our system when processing the micro-batch mb_j with $j > 1$. Triple t is derived by a derivation tree T possibly using triples t' derived in mb_h with $h < j$, as well as triples in D_j and $(\bigcup_1^j S_i)^*$. By induction we have that for each t' derived at step $h < j$ there exists a derivation tree T' over D and S deriving t'. So to conclude it is sufficient to observe that, if in T we replace leaves corresponding to triples t' with the corresponding T', then we obtain the desired derivation tree for t.

Let's now consider the 'only-if' direction (completeness). We proceed by a double induction, first on n, the number of micro-batches, and then on the size of the derivation tree T deriving t. Assume $n = 1$; this means that we only process one micro-batch. By Lemma 1 we have that there exists an equivalent T' for t, satisfying the properties stated in the lemma, and hence that can be produced by our algorithm, as we first saturate the schema and then apply instance rules in sequence 7-2-9 or 7-3-9, as in T'.

Assume now $n > 1$. We proceed by induction on the derivation tree $T = \{T1 \mid T2\} - rdfsX \rightarrow t$. The base case is that both T1 and T2 are simple triples t1 and t2 in D and S respectively. In this case let j be the minimal index ensuring that both triples have been met in processed micro-batches mb_h, with $h \leq j$. This j exists by hypothesis, and we have that either t1 or t2 is in mb_j. Assume it is t1, a schema triple and that t2 has been met in mb_s with $s < j$. Then by means of our index we recover t2 (line 14) and saturation for the step j in line 21 builds T to derive the triple t.

Assume now that both T1 and T2 do not consist of a simple triple (the case when only one of T1 and T2 is a triple is similar). By Lemma 1, we have that there exists an equivalent $T' = \{T1' \mid T2'\} - rdfsY \rightarrow t$ such that instance rules are used a most once (in the order of Fig. 4), where each rule uses a schema triple in S^*. This means that, w.l.o.g, T2' is a schema triple t2' in S^*. By hypothesis $(S = \bigcup_1^n S_i)$, we have that there exists mb_h such that t2 is obtained by schema saturation (which is globally kept in memory) and that there exists mb_s in which t1 is derived and indexed by our algorithm. Now consider $j = max(s, h)$. At step j both t1 (indexed) and t2 (in the main memory) are available to our algorithm, which can hence produce $\{t1 \mid t2\} - rdfsY \rightarrow t$.

The remaining cases are similar.   □

4   Extension to Streaming OWL-Horst Saturation

This section is devoted to RDF streaming saturation in the presence of OWL-Horst ontology [13]. For space reason, we do not present OWL-Horst in detail, and assume the reader is already familiar with it.

In recent years, OWL-Horst has gained consistent attention by both research and industrial communities, as it represents a good balance between expressivity and computational tractability. The rules are reported in Table 5, and, as it can be seen, OWL-Horst is much more expressive than RDFS. However, the techniques we have developed for RDFS saturation still remain effective in the context of OWL-Horst rules, but the transposition is not direct, and we had to take particular care of the integration of RDFS and OWL-Horst saturation in the presence of streaming instance and schema data. However, for each single OWL-Horst rule the extension of our RDFS approach is almost direct, validating the effectiveness of our previously introduced indexing technique.

As already observed in [11], an important difference wrt RDFS saturation is that for OWL-Horst it is not possible to identify an ordering in rule application which is as fine grained as that for RDFS (Fig. 5). That said, a careful analysis that distinguishes the setting where new schema triples are considered from the setting where new instance triples are considered, allows us to establish some partial ordering among the rules. Specifically, given some new schema triples, which come with a new micro-batch, the examination of rules dependencies allows us to identify three groups of rules that may be triggered: G_1^{sh}, G_2^{sh} and G_3^{sh}, each of which is composed of the following rules:

- $G_1^{sh} = \{\text{OWL} - \text{Horst}(9, 10, 12_{(a,b)}, 13_{(a,b)}) + \text{RDFS}(5, 11)\}$
- $G_2^{sh} = \{\text{RDFS}(7, 2, 3, 9)\}$
- $G_3^{sh} = \{\text{Rules}(14_{(a,b)}, 3, 8_{(a,b)}, 15, 16, 4, 1, 2)\}$

The first group contains OWL-Horst rules together with the two RDFS rules that produce schema triples, viz RDFS5 and RDFS11. The OWL-Horst in the group can be applied in any order once, however RDFS rules 5 and 7 need to be applied multiple times until a fix-point is reached. The second group G_2^{sh} contains RDFS rules that use as premise triples that are produced by the rules in G_1^{sh}. The third group G_3^{sh}, on the other hand, is independent of the other two groups. The above analysis suggests the following order of application of rules given newly acquired schema triples: the rules in group G_1^{sh} need to be applied before applying those in group G_2^{sh}, whereas the rules in the third group G_3^{sh} can applied in parallel to those in G_1^{sh} and G_2^{sh}.

The analysis of rule dependencies considering newly acquired or inferred instance triples is less conclusive since we cannot escape the iterative application of rules. That said, we identified the following groups of rules, which are exploited in the saturation algorithm shown in Fig. 6:

- $G_1^{ins} = \{\text{RDFS}(7, 2, 3, 9)\}$
- $G_2^{ins} = \{\text{OWL} - \text{Horst}(14_{(a,b)}, 3, 8_{(a,b)})\}$

Table 5. OWL-Horst rule set. Schemas are indicated by *italic* font.

No	Condition	Consequence
1	*p τ owl:FunctionalProperty* u p v, u p w	v owl:sameAs w
2	*p τ owl:InverseFunctionalProperty* v p u, w p u	v owl:sameAs w
3	*p τ owl:SymmetricProperty* v p u	u p v
4	*p τ owl:TransitiveProperty* u p w, w p v	u p v
5a	u p v	u owl:sameAs u
5b	u p v	v owl:sameAs v
6	v owl:sameAs w	w owl:sameAs v
7	v owl:sameAs w, w owl:sameAs u	v owl:sameAs u
8a	*p owl:inverseOf q*, v p w	w q v
8b	*p owl:inverseOf q*, v q w	w p v
9	*v τ owl:Class*, v owl:sameAs w	$v \prec_{sc} w$
10	*p τ owl:Property*, p owl:sameAs q	$p \prec_{sp} q$
11	u p v, u owl:sameAs x, v owl:sameAs y	x p y
12a	*v owl:equivalentClass w*	$v \prec_{sc} w$
12b	*v owl:equivalentClass w*	$w \prec_{sc} v$
12c	$v \prec_{sc} w$, $w \prec_{sc} v$	*v owl:equivalentClass w*
13a	*v owl:equivalentProperty w*	$v \prec_{sp} w$
13b	*v owl:equivalentProperty w*	$w \prec_{sp} v$
13c	$v \prec_{sp} w$, $w \prec_{sp} v$	*v owl:equivalentProperty w*
14a	*v owl:hasValue w, v owl:onProperty p*, u p v	u τ v
14b	*v owl:hasValue w, v owl:onProperty p* u τ v	u p v
15	*v owl:someValuesFrom w, v owl:onProperty* *p* u p x, x τ w	u τ v
16	*v owl:allValuesFrom u, v owl:onProperty p* w τ v, w p x	x τ u

- $G_3^{ins} = \{\text{OWL} - \text{Horst}(15, 16, 4)\}$
- $G_4^{ins} = \{\text{OWL} - \text{Horst}(15, 16, 4)\}$
- $G_5^{ins} = \{\text{OWL} - \text{Horst}(1, 2, 7, 11)\}$

The first group G_1^{ins} contains RDFS rules that need to be applied in the order specified. The remaining groups contain OWL-Horst rules that can be applied once in any order (except for step B5). The rules in the second group G_2^{ins} are independent of those in the first group G_1^{ins} and they can produce in parallel with the first group G_1^{ins}. The rules in G_3^{ins} depends on those in the first G_1^{ins} and the second G_2^{ins} groups, in the sense that the triples produced by these can be used as a premise by the rules in G_1^{ins}. Also, the rules in G_1^{ins} depends on those in G_3^{ins}. Notice that this introduces a loop between the three first groups. The rules in the forth group G_4^{ins} depend on those triples that are produced by the last two schema groups (G_2^{sch} and G_3^{sch}) and the first three instance groups (G_1^{ins}, G_2^{ins}, and G_3^{ins}) plus those triples that are received by the current micro-batch. Since the rules in the fourth group G_4^{ins} needs two instance triples to trigger the rules, thus, the objective of the fourth group G_4^{ins} is to find the complement part of the received instance triples from DS' by assuming that both schema triples plus one of the instance triples exist. The analysis of the rules in the fifth group, G_5^{ins}, reveals that these depend on the rules in the first four groups, whereas none of the rules in the first four groups depend on the rules in G_5^{ins}, as already assumed by Cichlid [11]. It is worth recalling that *sameAs* saturation, performed by G_5^{ins}, needs to be dealt with in a careful way in order to avoid a blow up in triple creation. We use the approach introduced by WebPIE [24] and then re-used by Cichlid [11], which we do not describe here again and which, in a nutshell, creates and manages in an efficient way a *sameAsTable* in which, for instance, if a, b, c, and d are the same according to the sameAs relation, then those resources will be stored in a unique line of the table, essentially containing one equivalence class induced by sameAs. Also observe that we could imagine that OWL-Horst rule 11 could trigger again other rules, say rule 14_a. Actually, as shown in [11,24], these triggered rules would produce triples already inferred by our step B5. For instance, if rule 11 produces $x \tau y$ where (*) x and y are, respectively, sameAs u and v (already used by rule 14a in the premise $u \tau v$), then if we assume rule 14_a produces again (once re-triggered) a triple by using $x \tau y$, that triple would be $x p y$. Since step B5 takes as input $u p v$ (produced in step B2 by rule 14_a), we have that $x p y$ is produced by step B5 due to (*), so there is no need to trigger rule 14_a again.

The above analysis allowed us to design an algorithm, which is depicted in Fig. 6, for efficiently saturating RDF streams considering both RDFS and OWL-Horst. It is worth observing that the rule ordering in our solution is similar to that proposed by Cichild [11], with the notable difference that we strive to perform the saturation incrementally.

As shown in Fig. 6, when a new micro-batch arrives, first a simple filtering separates new instance triples from new schema triples. Our algorithm first performs step A, in which saturation for new schema rules is performed, by also taking into account the previously inferred *schema* triples. Note that this step is needed in order to avoid inferring many times the same triples starting from newly arrived schema triples. The idea is to infer the new schema and perform a first wave of instance triple derivation in terms of the new schema, only once (as we will see in Step B, newly derived instance triples will be considered for fix point computation).

In step A, first the driver saturates the new schema rules in sub step A1.1 dedicated to the derivation of new RDFS triples, and in which, first, OWL-Horst rules that can produce premises for RDFS rules 5 and 11 are applied, and then these last ones are applied. In A1.1, once the new schema triples are derived, these ones plus the new schema triples in the current micro-batch (the old schema rules are not used here) are used for RDFS instance triple saturation, as happened for our algorithm for RDFS saturation (Sect. 3). The novelty in step A is that now we have step A2 applying OWL-Horst rules for instance triple derivation, by using new schema triples plus the old ones, and by using our indexing approach to retrieve needed instance triples derived in the past (stored on HDFS). For instance, for rule 2, once the indicated schema triple identifies a property p, then we use this to retrieve, by means of our indexing scheme, only the triples having p as property and then we perform the join required by the second and third premise (note that such kind of joins does not occur for RDFS saturation). In this way the number of triples involved in the join operation is sensibly reduced. To summarize, step A is totally along the lines of our algorithm for RDFS saturation: we obtain new schema triples and use them to infer new instance triples, that are then used in step B, which we comment below.

Step B follows step A and takes as input: the newly received instance triples in the current micro-batch, plus the instance triples derived in step A, plus the new global RDFS-OWL schema triples still computed and broadcast in step A. The main part of step B consists of a loop for iterating saturation until a fix point is reached. The body of the iteration consists of three subsequent steps: a first one concerning RDFS rules for instance triple derivation (step B1), followed by OWL-Horst derivation (step B2) involving rules that could be triggered by RDFS derivation in step B1; in case these two steps produce new triples, then step B3 uses those triples for applying OWL-Horst rules 15, 16 and 4. Once the fix point of the loop is reached, step B4 needs to fetch instance triples from HDFS by using our indexing technique, once in the driver the existence of schema triples to trigger rules (e.g., rule 15) is detected. In case B4 produces new instance triples, then (step B5) uses those triples as well for applying OWL-Horst rules 1,2,7 and 11 . Their application requires the system to fetch instance triples through our indexes, plus the indexing of newly inferred triples.

Regarding the implementation of individual rules, we distinguish the following kinds of rules:

1. Rules that take one or two schema triples and produce a schema triple, e.g., OWL-Horst rules $12_{(a,b,c)}$.
2. Rules that take one schema triple and one or two instance triples and produce an instance triple, e.g., OWL-Horst rules 4 and $8_{(a,b)}$.
3. Rules that take one instance triple and produce one instance triple.
4. Rules that take two schema triples and two instance triples and produce an instance triple, namely OWL-Horst rules 15 and 16.

Algorithm 3. OWL-Horst *Rule 15* (Step A2)

1: **Input:** mb_{sch} – Received schema triples
2: **Input:** op' and sv' – Two datasets that represent schema triples with *owl:onProperty* and
   owl:someValuesFrom as predicate respectively except those they received by the current mb
3: **Output:** *results* – reasoning results
4: **Begin**
5:    // *Extract* owl:onProperty *and* owl:someValuesFrom *schema from* mb_{sch}
6:    val $new\_op =$
       $\text{mb}_{\text{sch}}.\textbf{filter}(\text{t} \Rightarrow \text{t.\_2.equals}(\text{``owl:onProperty''})).\text{map}(\text{t} \Rightarrow (\text{t.\_1, t.\_3})).\text{collect.toSet}$
7:    val $new\_sv =$
       $\text{mb}_{\text{sch}}.\textbf{filter}(\text{t} \Rightarrow \text{t.\_2.equals}(\text{``owl:someValuesFrom''})).\text{map}(\text{t} \Rightarrow (\text{t.\_1, t.\_3})).\text{collect.toSet}$

     // *Rule 15 won't trigger if there is no new schema triple arrives*
8:    if(new_op.isEmpty && new_sv.isEmpty) **then**
9:        **return** empty

     // *Keep those schema triples if the second match of schema is arrived too.*
10:   val $op_1 = $ findMatches(new_op, new_sv)
11:   val $sv_1 = $ findMatches(new_sv, new_op)

     // *Also find other matches among the previous schema based on the current schemas*
12:   val $op_2 = $ findMatches(op', new_sv)
13:   val $sv_2 = $ findMatches(sv', new_op)

14:   val op $ = (op_1$.toSeq $++$ op_2.toSeq)
15:   val sv $ = (sv_1$.toSeq $++$ sv_2.toSeq)

     // *There is a guarantee that for every new op, at least, a new and/or old sv/sv' exists and*
     // *so on for every new sv too*
16:   if((op_1.toSeq $++$ op_2.toSeq).isEmpty || (sv_1.toSeq $++$ sv_2.toSeq).isEmpty) **then**
17:       **return** empty

     // *Retrieve related instance triples from DS' by relying on indexing information*
18:   val $pTriples = $ Fetch triples from *predicate_based* paths of DS' based on the op
19:   val $oTriples = $ Fetch triples from *object_based* paths of DS' based on the sv

     // *Saturation process among the fetched triples*
20:   val $in_{15} = pTriples.\textbf{map}(\text{t} \Rightarrow ((\text{op.value(t.\_2), t.\_3}), \text{t.\_1}))$
21:   val $t_{15} = oTriples.\textbf{map}(\text{t} \Rightarrow ((\text{sv.value(t.\_2), t.\_1}), \text{Nil}))$
22:   $results = in_{15}.\textbf{join}(t_{15}).\text{map}(\text{t} \Rightarrow (\text{t.\_2.\_1, t.\_1.\_1}))$

23:   **return** *results*
24: **End**

Rules in (1) and (2) can be implemented similarly to the RDFS rules presented earlier. Rules in (3) can be implemented straightforwardly since they involve a single instance triple. Rules in (4), however, need to be processed differently. For this reason, we focus on detailing the processing of Rule 15. Other rule in (4) can be implemented similarly.

For the sake of clarity, we recall rule 15 definition.

Schemas: v *owl:someValuesFrom* w, v *owl:onProperty* p
Instances: u p x, x *rdf:type* w
Result: $\Rightarrow$ u *rdf:type* v

This rule is processed differently depending on whether it is triggered given a newly acquired schema triple (see Box A2 in Fig. 6), given an instance triple (see Box B3 in Fig. 6), or based on received a new instance triple (see Box B4 in Fig. 6). Algorithm 3 details the processing of rule 15 (Fig. 6 Step A2), when

---

Algorithm 4. OWL-Horst *Rule 15* (Step B3)

1: **Input:** mb_{inst} – Instance Triples of micro-batch
2: **Input:** $op'Swap$ and $sv'Swap$ – Two datasets that represent schema triple with $owl{:}onProperty$
   and $owl{:}someValuesFrom$ as predicate respectively. i.e., Swap means (Object, Subject)
3: **Output:** *results* – Reasoning results
4: **Begin**
   // *Extract the given triples and types based on the entire (so far) received schema.*
5:   val *potential_Triples* = mb_{inst}.**filter**(t $\Rightarrow$ $op'Swap$.value.contains(t._2))
6:   val *potential_Types* =
       mb_{inst}.**filter**(t $\Rightarrow$ t._2.equals("*rdf:type*") && $sv'Swap$.value.contains(t._3))

7:   val tr_{15} = *potential_Triples*.**map**(t $\Rightarrow$ (($op'Swap$.value(t._2), t._3), t._1))
8:   var ty_{15} = *potential_Types*.**map**(t $\Rightarrow$ (($sv'Swap$.value(t._2), t._1), Nil)).persist
9:   val r_{15} = tr_{15}.**join**(ty_{15}).**map**(t $\Rightarrow$ (t._2._1, t._1._1))

10:   **return** r_{15}
11: **End**

---

given corresponding new schema triples. It starts by retrieving the two kinds of schema triples that are necessary for triggering the rule, namely *onProperty* triples and *someValuesFrom* triples (*lines 6–7*). If such triples exist, then the algorithm tries to find their match. For example, if a newly acquired triple is an onProperty triple, e.g., (v_1 owl:onProperty p_1), then the algorithm attempts to find a matching triples, e.g., (v_1 owl:someValuesFrom w), from received and already existing schema, and vice versa (*lines 10–13*). For every matching pair of someValuesFrom and onProperty triples (*lines 14–15*), the algorithm retrieves instance triples that can be used for triggering the rule using our index (*lines 18–19*), and, inferring implicit triples (*lines 20–22*) accordingly as specified by the rule.

Algorithm 4 details the processing of rule 15 given the received and inferred instance triples. This algorithm relies on received instance triples and total schema. The algorithm starts by retrieving the required instance triples from the received and inferred instance triples (*lines 5–6*) and triggers the rule by considering the schema triples that were present before and along the given micro-batch (*lines 7–9*). The inferred results (*line 10*) will be used into another round of saturation process if the previous round of the saturation process infers new triples. Otherwise, the saturation process jumps out of the loop and goes to the next saturation step (Step B4).

Algorithm 5. OWL-Horst *Rule 15* (Step B4)

1: **Input:** $\text{mb}_{\text{inst/inf}}$ – Instance and inferred triples based on the current mb_i.
2: **Input:** *Tsch* – The total schema that received so far
3: **Output:** *results* – Reasoning results
4: **Begin**
   // Extract the respective schema triples from the total schema
5: val $sv_{set} = Tsch.\textbf{filter}(\text{t} \Rightarrow \text{t.\_2.equals}(\textit{"owl:someValuesFrom"})).\textbf{map}(\text{t} \Rightarrow (\text{t.\_1, t.\_3}))$
6: val $op_{set} = Tsch.\textbf{filter}(\text{t} \Rightarrow \text{t.\_2.equals}(\textit{"owl:onProperty"})).\textbf{map}(\text{t} \Rightarrow (\text{t.\_1, t.\_3}))$

   // Choose all someValuesFrom if exists any related onProperty for that and vice versa.
7: val $svs = \textbf{findMatches}(sv_{set}, op_{set})$
8: val $ops = \textbf{findMatches}(op_{set}, sv_{set})$

   // Assuring that both schemas exist
9: if(svs.isEmpty || ops.isEmpty) **return** empty

   // Broadcast the svs and ops and the swap version of them, i.e.,(Object, Subject)
10: val $sv_{br} = \textbf{broadcast}(svs.\textbf{toMap})$
11: val $op_{br} = \textbf{broadcast}(ops.\textbf{toMap})$

12: val $svSwap_{br} = \textbf{broadcast}(svs.\textbf{map}(\text{t} \Rightarrow (\text{t.\_2, t.\_1})).\textbf{toMap})$
13: val $opSwap_{br} = \textbf{broadcast}(ops.\textbf{map}(\text{t} \Rightarrow (\text{t.\_2, t.\_1})).\textbf{toMap})$

   // Filter types, find triples with a matching signature, fetch triples from disk, saturation process
14: val *CandidatedTypes* =
     $\text{mb}_{\text{inst/inf}}.\textbf{filter}(\text{t} \Rightarrow svSwap_{br}.\text{value.contains}(\text{t.\_3}) \&\& \text{t.\_2.equals}(\textit{"rdf:type"}))$
15: val $vs_1 = CandidatedTypes.\textbf{map}(\text{t} \Rightarrow svSwap_{br}.\text{value}(\text{t.\_2})).\textbf{distinct}$
16: val $ps_1 = vs_1.\textbf{map}(\text{t} \Rightarrow op_{br}.\text{value}(\text{t})).\text{collect.toList}$
17: val $relatedPs = $ Fetch triples from predicate-based paths based on ps_1

18: val $tr_{15\_1} = relatedPs.\textbf{map}(\text{t} \Rightarrow ((opSwap_{br}.\text{value}(\text{t.\_2}), \text{t.\_3}), \text{t.\_1}))$
19: val $ty_{15\_1} = CandidatedTypes.\textbf{map}(\text{t} \Rightarrow ((svSwap_{br}.\text{value}(\text{t.\_2}), \text{t.\_1}), Nil)).\text{persist}$
20: val $r_{15\_1} = tr_{15\_1}.\textbf{join}(ty_{15\_1}).\textbf{map}(\text{t} \Rightarrow (\text{t.\_2.\_1, t.\_1.\_1}))$

   // Filter types, find triples with a matching signature, fetch types from disk, saturation process
21: val *CandidatedTriples* $= \text{mb}_{\text{inst/inf}}.\textbf{filter}(\text{t} \Rightarrow opSwap_{br}.\text{value.contains}(\text{t.\_2}))$
22: val $ps_2 = CandidatedTriples.\textbf{map}(\text{t} \Rightarrow opSwap_{br}.\text{value}(\text{t.\_2})).\textbf{distinct}$
23: val $vs_2 = ps_2.\textbf{map}(\text{t} \Rightarrow sv_{br}.\text{value}(\text{t})).\text{distinct.collect.toList}$
24: val $relatedTs = $ Fetch types from object-based paths based on vs_2

25: val $tr_{15\_2} = newP.\textbf{map}(\text{t} \Rightarrow ((opSwap_{br}.\text{value}(\text{t.\_2}), \text{t.\_3}), \text{t.\_1}))$
26: val $ty_{15\_2} = relatedTs.\textbf{map}(\text{t} \Rightarrow ((svSwap_{br}.\text{value}(\text{t.\_2}), \text{t.\_1}), Nil))$
27: val $r_{15\_2} = tr_{15\_2}.\textbf{join}(ty_{15\_2}).\textbf{map}(\text{t} \Rightarrow (\text{t.\_2.\_1, t.\_1.\_1}))$

   // Return the results of both phases
28: **return** $r_{15\_1}.\textbf{union}(r_{15\_2})$
29: **End**

Algorithm 5 aims at finding one of the bipartite instance triples of rule 15 from the already existing triples (DS') received through previous micro-batches. In this step, the necessary condition is the existence of both schema triples and at least one of the instance triple. In this regard, we suppose that both necessary schema triples exist, and one of the related instance triples received and/or inferred via current micro-batch. Therefore as a first step, we extract the related schema triple (*owl:onProperty* and *owl:someValuesFrom*), that are required for rule 15, among the schema triples received up to this moment of the process (*lines 5–6*). As we said, just a complete set of the schema triples is eligible to trigger. For this purpose, the algorithm makes use of the **findMatches**() subroutine to find those matches for every intended schema triple which for *owl:onProperty* triples returns corresponding *owl:someValuesFrom* triples and vice-versa (*lines 7–8*). In the next step, by considering that both schema triples exist (*line(9)*), we examine the provided instance triples with the selected schema triples to pick those instances that both schema triples exist for them. For this purpose, we broadcast the collected schema triples via *broadcast* operation (*lines 10–13*). Then, we pick those triples from the $mb_{inst/inf}$ when they have *rdf:type* as a predicate with the same object as the collected *someValuesFrom* objects (*line 14*). We extract all corresponding *owl:onProperty* schema triples based on the *owl:someValuesFrom* schema and the candidate triples –those with *rdf:types* as predicate– (*lines 15–16*). In the following, by utilizing the indexing information, we fetch the related triples among the predicate-based triples from the disk DS' (*line 17*), those triples that have the same predicate as the *owl:onProperty*'s object. It is worth mentioning that the number of distinct objects and predicates in datasets is small enough to fit in memory. For example, the examined dataset in this section contains only 116 different distinct objects and 83 different predicates for object- and predicate-based triples, respectively. Finally, we apply the saturation process between the chosen schema triples, the candidate *rdf:type* triples, and their corresponding predicate-based triples fetched from the disk DS' (*lines 18–20*). So far, we have done a complete informative saturation for every triple with *rdf:type* as a predicate that we got and inferred via the current $mb_{inst/inf}$. The Algorithm 5, *lines 21–24*, is dedicated to the same process (*lines 14–20*) except to find the right *rdf:type* triples with corresponding objects. For this purpose, we fetch those triples from the object-based triples located on the disk, in DS'. Finally, we apply the saturation process between over the selected and fetched triples by considering both matched schema triples. Finally, the results of the saturation processes (i.e., r_{15}_1 and r_{15}_2) are concatenated and returned (*line 28*).

5   Evaluation

The saturation method we have just presented[3] lends itself, at least in principle, to outperform state of the art techniques, notably Cichlid, when dealing with streams of RDF data. This is particularly the case when the information about the RDF schema or OWL-Horst ruleset is also obtained in a stream-based fashion.

To validate this claim and to understand to which extent our method outperforms its competitors, we performed an empirical evaluation on real-life RDF datasets. The results of this evaluation are shown in the next sections.

5.1   Datasets

We used for our experiments three RDF datasets for RDFS saturation that are widely used in the semantic web community: DBpedia [2], LUBM [12], and dblp[4]

---

[3] https://git.lamsade.fr/afarvardin/RDFInStream.

[4] Computer science bibliography (https://dblp.uni-trier.de/faq/What+is+dblp.html).

Since these three datasets do not have any OWL-Horst schema triples, we choose a portion of UniProt[7] for OWL-Horst saturation

These datasets are not stream-based datasets, and therefore we had to partition them into micro-batches to simulate a setting where the data are received in a streamed manner. We make in our experiments the assumption that a substantial part of the data is received initially and that micro-batches arrive then in a streaming fashion. We consider this to be a realistic assumption, in those scenarios where a substantial part of the data is known initially, and new triples arrive as time goes by. In what follows, and for space sake, we report on the experiments we ran against DBpedia for RDFS and UniProt for OWL-Horst saturation.

Using DBpedia, we created three stream-based datasets DBpedia-100, DBpedia-200, and DBpedia-300. They are composed of initial chunks that contain 100, 200, and 300 million instance triples respectively, and a series of 15 micro-batches, each composed 160K triples plus between 64 and 2500 schema triples. For the initial chunk we reserve 25% of schema triples, while the remaining ones are spread over the micro-batches as indicated above. Regarding saturation using OWL-Horst ruleset, we used the *UniProt* dataset, which contains 320 million triples and occupies 49.6 GB. For evaluation purposes, we partition the Uniprot datasets into micro-batches. In doing so, we set the size of micro-batches to 512 MB. The schema triples of Uniprot (549 triples) are divided equally between the micro-batches. Thus, each micro-batch has a range of [5–6] schema triples.

5.2   Experiment Setup

In the case of RDFS saturation, for each of the above datasets, we ran our saturation algorithm initially for the first chunk, and then incrementally for each remaining micro-batch. For comparison purposes, for each of the above datasets, we ran the Cichlid algorithm on the initial chunk, and then on each of the micro-batches. Given that Cichlid is not incremental, for each micro-batch, we had to consider the previous micro-batches and the initial chunk as well as the current micro-batch.

Alike RDFS datasets in the OWL-Horst dataset, every micro-batch contains schema triples. Therefore, Cichlid needs to reload every past micro-batches by receiving a new micro-batch.

We performed our experiments on a cluster with 4 nodes (and 8 nodes (check the extended version [9])), connected with 1 Gbps Ethernet. One node was reserved to act as the master node and the remaining 3 nodes as worker nodes. Each node has a Xeon O2.4 GHz processor, 48 GB memory, and 33 TB Hadoop file system, and runs Linux Debian 9.3, Spark 2.1.0, Hadoop 2.7.0, and Java 1.8.

For each dataset we ran our experiment 5 times, and reported the average running time.

5.3   Results

Saturation Considering RDF Schema Rules

Figures 7 shows the results obtained when saturating 300 million triples from the DBpedia dataset. The x-axis represents the initial chunk and the micro-batches that composed the dataset. For the initial chunk, the y-axis reports the time required for its saturation. For each of the following micro-batches, the y-axis reports the time required for saturating the dataset composed of the current micro-batch, the previous micro-batches, and the initial chunk put together.

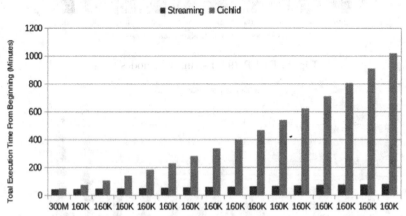

Fig. 7. DBpedia 300 million triples - run on 4 nodes.

The figure shows that the time required by Cichlid for saturating the stream increases substantially as the number of micro-batches increases, and is significantly higher than the one required by our algorithm. Specifically, the saturation takes more than 1000 min given the last micro-batch, that is 22 times the amount of time required to saturate the first micro-batch, namely 45 min. On the other hand, our incremental algorithm takes almost the same time for all micro-batches. Specifically, it takes 41 min given the first micro-batch, and 78 min given the last micro-batch.

We obtained similar trends using other datasets: the dblp dataset (see Fig. 8), and the LUBM dataset (see Fig. 9); these datasets have smaller sizes wrt to the DBpedia one (190M and 69M, respectively).

Streaming Incremental RDFS (DBLP 190M - 4 nodes)

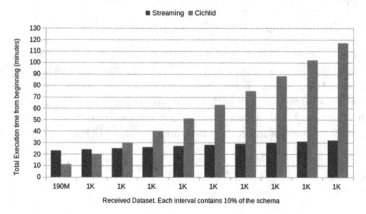

Fig. 8. DBLP 190M - run on 4 nodes.

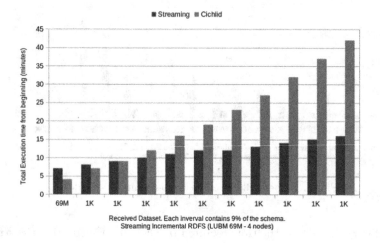

Fig. 9. DBLP 190M - run on 4 nodes.

The good performance of our algorithm is due to its incremental nature, but also to its underlying indexing mechanism. To demonstrate this, Fig. 10 illustrates for DBpedia, and for each micro-batch, the number of triples that are fetched using the index as well as the total number of triples that the saturation algorithm would have to examine in the absence of the indexing structure (that requires the whole amount of triples to be loaded). As it can be observed, the number of triples fetched by the index is a small fraction of the total number of triples that compose the dataset.

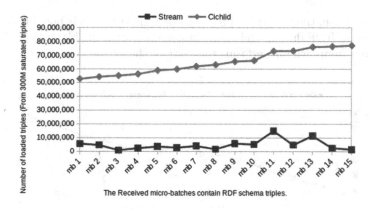

Fig. 10. DBpedia 300M - retrieved triples when receiving new schema triples.

Micro-Batch Size. So far, we have considered that the size of the micro-batch is specified *a priori*. Ultimately, the size of the micro-batch depends, at least partly, on the time interval, the resource we have (cluster configuration). To investigate this point, we considered a DBpedia instance of 25.4 GB and run 7 different incremental saturations. In saturation i, for $i = 1 \ldots 7$, the size of the micro-batch is $i*100$ MB, resulting in n_i microbatches, in which the whole set of schema triples have been evenly distributed over the n_i microbatches. We used for this experiment a cluster with 4 nodes, 11 executors, 4 cores per executor, and 5 GB memory per executor.

Figure 11 illustrates the average time required for performing the saturation given a micro-batch (blue line), and the average time required for the index management (red line). Regarding the saturation, the figure shows that micro-batches with different sizes require different times for processing. For example, the time required for processing a 100 MB micro-batch is smaller compared to the time required for processing micro-batches with larger sizes. The increase is not steady. In particular, we observe that micro-batches with 400 MB and 500 MB require the same processing time. This means the cluster could process a bigger chunk of data within the given time-interval. We can also conclude that the cluster was idle for some time when processing 400 MB micro-batches.

Regarding the index management time (red line), our experiment shows that it is significantly small with respect to the saturation time, and it costs in the worse case less than half a minute. Besides the time-interval, the configuration of the cluster impacts stream saturation. As shown in Fig. 11, 500 MB micro-batches require the same time as 400 MB micro-batches for maintaining the index.

Concerning global execution time (for all micro-batches), experiments showed that, when the number of micro-batches decreases, this time can decrease in some cases (this happens in particular for $i \in \{1, 2, 3\}$, see [9] for details, Table 5).

To summarize, the results we presented here show that it is possible to saturate streams of RDF data in an incremental manner by using big data platforms, and that our approach outperforms the state of the art.

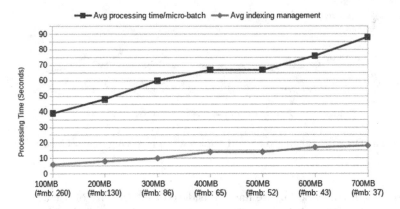

Fig. 11. Average processing and indexing management time/micro-batch. (Color figure online)

Saturation Considering RDF Schema and OWL-Horst Rules

Figure 12 shows the execution time required by our incremental streaming method and the execution time required by the state of the art, i.e., Cichlid, to saturate the UniProt dataset. The figure also shows for both approaches the exponential trendline. The x-axis represents the received micro-batches, each one composed of instance triples, 512 MB, and a few schema triples, i.e., 5 to 6 schema triple (Table 6) per micro-batch. The y-axis reports the execution time required for saturation of each micro-batch in seconds.

Figure 12 shows that the time required by Cichlid to saturate the dataset (depicted using a red line) increases substantially as the number of micro-batches does. Furthermore, Cichlid fails to saturate the dataset starting from the 18th micro-batch. This is in contrast to our incremental solution (depicted using a blue line), which manages to efficiently saturate the dataset given the received micro-batches. Specifically, we observe that the time required for saturation varies slightly between micro-batches, and is far smaller than the time required by Cichlid, especially in later iterations.

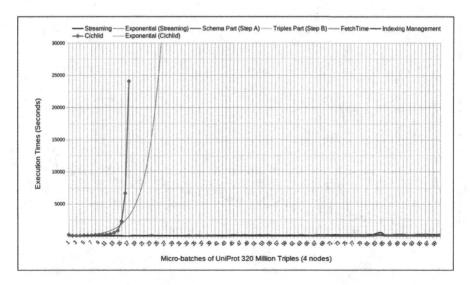

Fig. 12. UniProt 320 million triples - comparison with Cichlid (4 nodes).

Table 6. Types and numbers of schema triple per micro-batch in Fig. 12.

μ_b	Schemas
$\mu_b 0$	owl($onProperty \rightarrow 1$), rdfs($domain \rightarrow 2$, $range \rightarrow 1$, $subClassOf \rightarrow 2$)
$\mu_b 1$	owl($allValuesFrom \rightarrow 1$), rdfs($domain \rightarrow 1$, $range \rightarrow 2$, $subClassOf \rightarrow 2$)
$\mu_b 2$	owl($onProperty \rightarrow 1$), rdfs($range \rightarrow 2$, $subPropertyOf \rightarrow 1$, $subClassOf \rightarrow 2$)
$\mu_b 3$	owl($allValuesFrom \rightarrow 1$), rdfs($domain \rightarrow 3$, $subClassOf \rightarrow 2$)
$\mu_b 4$	rdfs($domain \rightarrow 1$, $range \rightarrow 2$, $subClassOf \rightarrow 3$)
$\mu_b 5$	owl($onProperty \rightarrow 1$), rdfs($range \rightarrow 1$, $domain \rightarrow 1$, $subPropertyOf \rightarrow 1$, $subClassOf \rightarrow 2$)
$\mu_b 6$	owl($inverseOf \rightarrow 1$, $allValuesFrom \rightarrow 1$), rdfs($range \rightarrow 2$, $subClassOf \rightarrow 2$)
$\mu_b 7$	owl($onProperty \rightarrow 1$, $equivalentClass \rightarrow 1$), rdfs($range \rightarrow 1$, $domain \rightarrow 2$, $subClassOf \rightarrow 1$)
$\mu_b 8$	owl($onProperty \rightarrow 1$, $equivalentClass \rightarrow 1$), rdfs($range \rightarrow 1$, $domain \rightarrow 1$, $subClassOf \rightarrow 2$)
$\mu_b 9$	owl($onProperty \rightarrow 1$), rdfs($domain \rightarrow 1$, $subClassOf \rightarrow 3$)
$\mu_b 10$	owl($onProperty \rightarrow 1$), rdfs($range \rightarrow 2$, $subClassOf \rightarrow 3$)
$\mu_b 11$	rdfs($range \rightarrow 2$, $domain \rightarrow 1$, $subClassOf \rightarrow 3$)
$\mu_b 12$	owl($equivalentClass \rightarrow 1$), rdfs($domain \rightarrow 3$, $subClassOf \rightarrow 2$)
$\mu_b 13$	owl($onProperty \rightarrow 2$), rdfs($range \rightarrow 1$, $domain \rightarrow 2$, $subClassOf \rightarrow 1$)
...	...
$\mu_b 82$	owl($hasValue \rightarrow 1$), rdfs($range \rightarrow 1$, $domain \rightarrow 1$, $subPropertyOf \rightarrow 1$, $subClassOf \rightarrow 1$)
$\mu_b 83$	rdfs($range \rightarrow 1$, $domain \rightarrow 2$, $subPropertyOf \rightarrow 1$, $subClassOf \rightarrow 2$)
...	...
$\mu_b 100$	owl($allValuesFrom \rightarrow 1$), rdfs($domain \rightarrow 2$, $range \rightarrow 1$, $subClassOf \rightarrow 2$)

Figures 12 illustrates that using Cichlid, the saturation of the first 17 micro-batches takes 1086 min, while our solution takes 15mn to process those batches. Our solution takes 257 min (which is still far smaller than the time required by Cichlid to process the initial 17 micro-batches) to process the entire dataset, which consists of 100 micro-batches.

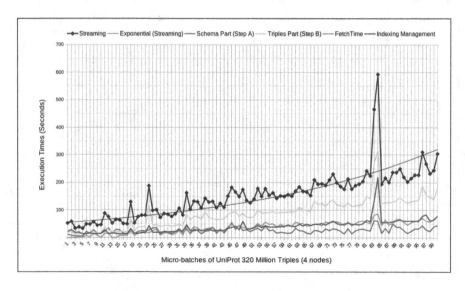

Fig. 13. UniProt 320 million triples - incremental streaming (4 nodes).

Figure 13 illustrates the time required for each step of our incremental solution using 4 nodes. The blue line illustrates the total time required to process each micro-batch. The green line illustrates the time required to process the schema (Step A in Fig. 6). The yellow line illustrates the time required to process the instance triples within the micro-batch (Step B in Fig. 6). The purple line illustrates the time required for index management, which consists of partitioning, compressing (using a default Spark compressor, i.e., *gzip*), storage time, in addition to collecting data information for our indexing technique from the saturated micro-batch. Finally, the gray line illustrates the time required to detect and retrieve data from the existing dataset DS' (this time is embedded in both steps A and B). The figure shows that the total fetching time (the gray line) for the entire process is 61 min. That is 23.7% of the total processing time, which is 257 min.

On average, our indexing technique takes 37 s to detect and fetch the necessary triples from DS' (stored on disk) when new schema triples are received. Notice that in Fig. 13, we have a spike on the micro-batch 84 (mb_{84}). To find out the reason for this leap, we compared what happens during the saturation of micro-batch 82 (mb_{82}), which takes 224 s, with what happens during the saturation of micro-batch mb_{84}, which takes instead 593 s.

– *Fetching time:* The fetching time for mb_{84} is 87 s, while it is 51 s for the mb_{82}. That time corresponds to the retrieval of almost 111 and 31 million potential RDF triples (object- and predicate-based triples) from DS' for mb_{84} and mb_{82}, respectively. Those triples are retrieved from 1075 files for mb_{84}, and 964 files for mb_{82}, respectively. We, therefore, conclude that the fetching time is not the main reason for the difference in processing the two micro-batches.

Furthermore, given the growing volume of data to be fetched, we can observe that our fetching algorithm retrieves them in a reasonable time.

- *Step A:* This step for mb_{84} takes 60 s (including the required fetching times), while it takes 25 s for mb_{82}.
- *Step B:* The time required in Step B, including fetching time for this step, is 314 s for mb_{84}, while it is 142 s for mb_{82}.
- *Indexing Management:* The indexing management time for mb_{84} is 219 s. This time is divided into 187 and 32 s for partitioning, indexing, and saving the data into object- and the predicate-based triples, respectively. The indexing management time for mb_{82} is 58 s that consists of 27 and 31 s for the object- and predicate-based triples, respectively. Concerning this step, we observed that the dominant execution time belongs to object-based triples.
- *Fixpoint:* On the other hand, both mbes used four iterations to reach a fixpoint. In the mb_{84}, we 110 K predicate-based triples 660K object-based triples per partition (i.e., there are 44 partitions in 4 nodes) that are required to saturate in every iteration. These numbers for mb_{82} 111 K predicate-based triples 36 K object-based triples in every iteration. To a considerable extent, this explains the difference in the processing time required for saturating data in mb_{84} compared to time needed for mb_{82}.

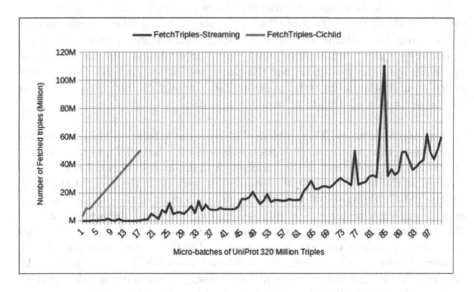

Fig. 14. Fetches triples per mb. UniProt 320 million triples.

We also recorded the number of triples that are retrieved by a given new micro-batch using our incremental method and compared it with the number of triples that are retrieved by Cichlid. Figure 14 depicts the results. It shows that our method retrieves far smaller numbers of triples compared with the Cichlid.

This can be explained by the fact that our method utilizes indexing structures designed to retrieve only the triples that are likely to yield the activation of a saturation rule.

It is worth noting that for mb_{84}, we fetch 111 million triples (around one-third of the whole dataset) from the already existing dataset DS'. Thanks to the *incremental loading* of our indexing data structures, our approach can fetch a massive number of triples successfully in a reasonable time by utilizing a relatively small cluster.

6   Related Work

RDF Saturation Using Big data Platforms. To the best of our knowledge, the first proposal to use big data platforms, and MapReduce in particular, to scale the saturation operation is [17], but the authors did not present any experimental result. Other works then addressed the problem of large-scale RDF saturation by exploiting big data systems such as Hadoop and Spark, (see e.g., [11,24,25]). For example, Urbani *et al.* [24,25] proposed a MapReduce-based distributed reasoning system called WebPIE. In doing so, they identified the order in which RDFS rules can be applied to efficiently saturate RDF data. Moreover, they specified for each of the RDFS rule how it can be implemented using map and/or reduce functions, and executed over the Hadoop system. Building on the work by Urbani *et al.*, the authors of Cichlid [11] implemented RDF saturation over Spark using, in addition to map and reduce, other transformations that are provided by Spark, such as filter, union, etc. Cichlid has shown that the use of Spark can speed up saturation wrt the case when Hadoop is used. Our solution builds on and adapts the techniques proposed by WebPie and Cichlid to cater for the saturation of streams of massive RDF data.

Incremental Saturation. The problem of incremental saturation of RDF data has been investigated by a number of proposals (see e.g., [3,6,10,24,26]). For example, Volz *et al.* investigated the problem of maintenance of entailments given changes at the level of the RDF instances as well as at the level of the RDF schema [26]. In doing so, they adapted a previous state of the art algorithm for incremental view maintenance proposed in the context of deductive database [22]. Barbieri *et al.* [3] builds on the solution proposed by Volz *et al.* by considering the case where the triples are associated with an expiration date in the context of streams (e.g., for data that are location-based). They showed that the deletion, in this case, can be done more efficiently by tagging the inferred RDF triples with an expiration date that is derived based on the expiration dates of the triples used in the derivation. While Volz *et al.* and Barbieri *et al.* [3] seek to reduce the effort required for RDF saturation, they do not leverage any indexing structure to efficiently perform the incremental saturation. As reported by Volz *et al.* in the results of their evaluation study, even if the maintenance was incremental, the inference engine ran out of memory in certain cases. Regarding, Barbieri *et al.* [3], they considered in their evaluation a single transitive rule (Sect. 5 in [3]), and did not report on the size of the dataset used, nor the micro-batch size.

Chevalier *et al.* proposed Slider, a system for RDF saturation using a distributed architecture [6]. Although the objective of Slider is similar to our work, it differs in the following aspects. First, in Slider, each rule is implemented in a separate module. We adopt a different approach, where rules are broken into finer operations (map, reduce, union, etc.). This creates opportunities for sharing the results of processing at a finer level. For example, the result of a map can be used by multiple rules, thereby reducing the overall processing required. Second, Slider utilizes vertical partitioning [1] for indexing RDF triples. This indexing structure is heavy since it creates a table for each property in the RDF. While such an indexing structure proved its efficiency in the context of RDF querying, it is heavy when it comes to RDF saturation. Indeed, we know in the context of RDF saturation the inference rules that can be triggered, and therefore can tune the indexing structure needed for this purpose, which we did in our solution.

Guasdoué *et al.* proposed an incremental solution for saturating RDF data [10]. The incrementality comes from the fact that only rules that have a premise triple that is newly asserted or derived are triggered. We adopt a similar approach to Guasdoué *et al.*. However, we utilize an indexing structure to fetch existing triples that have been asserted/derived when processing previous micro-batches. Moreover, Guasdoué *et al.* apply the rules in an arbitrary order, whereas in our work, we order the rules in a way to minimize the number of iterations required for saturating the RDF data.

The authors of WebPie [24] briefly touched on the problem of incrementally saturating RDF data. In doing so, they time-stamped the RDF tuples to distinguish new and old tuples. An inference rule R is then activated only if the timestamp associated with one of its premises is new, i.e., greater than the last time the saturation was performed. We proceed similarly in our work. However, unlike our work, WebPie does not leverage any indexing structures when querying the existing triples to identify those that may be used to activate a given rule R.

To sum up, compared with the existing state of the art in incremental saturation of RDF, we leverage a lightweight indexing structure, a fine-tuned ordering of the execution of the rules, as well as the use of a Big Data platform, namely Spark, to efficiently saturate large micro-batches of RDF data.

Indexing Structures for RDF Data. The indexing mechanism we proposed here is comparable to those proposed by Weiss et al. [29], by Schätzle *et al.* [21] and by Kaoudi [14] et al. for efficiently evaluating SPARQL queries. For example, Weiss *et al.* developed Hexastore, a centralized system that maintains six indexes for all triple permutations, namely spo, sop, pso, pos, osp, and ops. For example, using spo indexing a subject s_i is associated with a sorted list of properties $\{p_1^i, \ldots, p_n^i\}$. Moreover, each property is associated with a sorted list representing the objects. While this approach allows for efficiently evaluating SPARQL queries, it is expensive in terms of memory usage and index maintenance. According to the authors, Hexastore may require 5 times the size the storage space required for storing an RDF dataset due to the indexes. The solution developed by Schätzle *et al.* [21], on the other hand, is meant for distributed evaluation of SPARQL queries using Hadoop. To do so, they uses an indexing scheme named ExtVP, which precompute semi-join reductions between all properties. As shown by the authors, the computation of such indexes is heavy, e.g., it requires 290 s to index 100 million triples. To alleviate this, we proposed here an index that is aimed at speeding up RDF saturation, as opposed to any SPARQL query, and that is amenable to incremental maintenance.

7   Conclusion and Future Work

In this paper we presented a solution for incrementally saturating streams of massive RDF datasets considering RDFS rules and OWL-Horst rules. In our solution, we strive to cater for the incremental processing of the saturation operation. To do so, we make use of an indexing scheme that allows us to retrieve only the instance triples that are necessary for saturation given a newly arrived micro-batch. We have shown that our approach and techniques are effective for both RDFS and OWL-Horst rules and outperform the state of the art solution, viz Cichlid. As future work, we would like to extend our algorithm for query answering problem, for which we believe that our technique could still entail possible optimizations.

References

1. Abadi, D.J., Marcus, A., Madden, S., Hollenbach, K.J.: Scalable semantic web data management using vertical partitioning. In: Proceedings of the 33rd International Conference on Very Large Data Bases, University of Vienna, Austria, 23–27 September 2007, pp. 411–422. ACM (2007). http://www.vldb.org/conf/2007/papers/research/p411-abadi.pdf
2. Auer, S., Bizer, C., Kobilarov, G., Lehmann, J., Cyganiak, R., Ives, Z.: DBpedia: a nucleus for a web of open data. In: Aberer, K., et al. (eds.) ASWC/ISWC -2007. LNCS, vol. 4825, pp. 722–735. Springer, Heidelberg (2007). https://doi.org/10.1007/978-3-540-76298-0_52
3. Barbieri, D.F., Braga, D., Ceri, S., Valle, E.D., Grossniklaus, M.: Incremental reasoning on streams and rich background knowledge. In: The Semantic Web: Research and Applications, 7th Extended Semantic Web Conference, ESWC 2010, Heraklion, Crete, Greece, 30 May–3 June 2010, Proceedings, Part I, pp. 1–15 (2010). https://doi.org/10.1007/978-3-642-13486-9_1
4. Bizer, C., Heath, T., Berners-Lee, T.: Linked data-the story so far. Int. J. Semant. Web Inf. Syst. **5**(3), 1–22 (2009)
5. Brickley, D., Guha, R.: RDF Schema 1.1. Technical report W3C (2014). W3C Recommendation
6. Chevalier, J., Subercaze, J., Gravier, C., Laforest, F.: Slider: an efficient incremental reasoner. In: Proceedings of the 2015 ACM SIGMOD International Conference on Management of Data, Melbourne, Victoria, Australia, 31 May–4 June 2015, pp. 1081–1086 (2015). https://doi.org/10.1145/2723372.2735363

7. Consortium, T.U.: UniProt: a worldwide hub of protein knowledge. Nucleic Acids Res. **47**(D1), D506–D515 (2018). https://doi.org/10.1093/nar/gky1049
8. Farvardin, M.A., Colazzo, D., Belhajjame, K., Sartiani, C.: Streaming saturation for large RDF graphs with dynamic schema information. In: Proceedings of the 17th ACM SIGPLAN International Symposium on Database Programming Languages, DBPL 2019, Phoenix, AZ, USA, 23 June 2019, pp. 42–52. ACM (2019). https://doi.org/10.1145/3315507.3330201
9. Farvardin, M.A., Colazzo, D., Belhajjame, K., Sartiani, C.: Streaming saturation for large RDF graphs with dynamic schema information, February 2019. https://www.lamsade.dauphine.fr/~afarvardin/submissions/2019/technical-paper.pdf
10. Goasdoué, F., Manolescu, I., Roatiş, A.: Efficient query answering against dynamic RDF databases. In: Proceedings of the 16th International Conference on Extending Database Technology, pp. 299–310. ACM (2013)
11. Gu, R., Wang, S., Wang, F., Yuan, C., Huang, Y.: Cichlid: efficient large scale RDFS/OWL reasoning with spark. In: 2015 IEEE International Parallel and Distributed Processing Symposium (IPDPS), pp. 700–709. IEEE (2015)
12. Guo, Y., Pan, Z., Heflin, J.: LUBM: a benchmark for OWL knowledge base systems. J. Web Sem. **3**(2–3), 158–182 (2005)
13. ter Horst, H.J.: Completeness, decidability and complexity of entailment for RDF schema and a semantic extension involving the owl vocabulary. Web Semant: Sci. Serv. Agents WWW **3**(2–3), 79–115 (2005)
14. Kaoudi, Z., Miliaraki, I., Koubarakis, M.: RDFS reasoning and query answering on top of DHTs. In: Sheth, A., et al. (eds.) ISWC 2008. LNCS, vol. 5318, pp. 499–516. Springer, Heidelberg (2008). https://doi.org/10.1007/978-3-540-88564-1_32
15. Leskovec, J., Rajaraman, A., Ullman, J.D.: Mining of Massive Datasets. Cambridge University Press, Cambridge (2014)
16. Liew, C.S., Atkinson, M.P., Galea, M., Ang, T.F., Martin, P., Hemert, J.I.V.: Scientific workflows: moving across paradigms. ACM Comput. Surv. (CSUR) **49**(4), 66 (2017)
17. Mika, P., Tummarello, G.: Web semantics in the clouds. IEEE Intell. Syst. **23**(5), 82–87 (2008)
18. Motik, B., Nenov, Y., Piro, R.E.F., Horrocks, I.: Incremental update of datalog materialisation: the backward/forward algorithm. In: Proceedings of the Twenty-Ninth AAAI Conference on Artificial Intelligence, 25–30 January 2015, Austin, Texas, USA, pp. 1560–1568 (2015). http://www.aaai.org/ocs/index.php/AAAI/AAAI15/paper/view/9660
19. Mühleisen, H., Dentler, K.: Large-scale storage and reasoning for semantic data using swarms. IEEE Comp. Int. Mag. **7**(2), 32–44 (2012)
20. Oren, E., Kotoulas, S., Anadiotis, G., Siebes, R., ten Teije, A., van Harmelen, F.: Marvin: Distributed reasoning over large-scale semantic web data. J. Web Semant. **7**(4), 305–316 (2009)
21. Schätzle, A., Przyjaciel-Zablocki, M., Skilevic, S., Lausen, G.: S2RDF: RDF querying with SPARQL on spark. PVLDB **9**(10), 804–815 (2016). https://doi.org/10.14778/2977797.2977806. http://www.vldb.org/pvldb/vol9/p804-schaetzle.pdf
22. Staudt, M., Jarke, M.: Incremental maintenance of externally materialized views. In: VLDB, pp. 75–86. Morgan Kaufmann (1996)
23. Stocker, M., Sirin, E.: Pelletspatial: a hybrid RCC-8 and RDF/OWL reasoning and query engine. In: OWLED, vol. 529 (2009)
24. Urbani, J., Kotoulas, S., Maassen, J., Van Harmelen, F., Bal, H.: Webpie: a web-scale parallel inference engine using mapreduce. Web Semant.: Sci. Serv. Agents WWWb **10**, 59–75 (2012)

25. Urbani, J., Kotoulas, S., Oren, E., van Harmelen, F.: Scalable distributed reasoning using MapReduce. In: Bernstein, A., et al. (eds.) ISWC 2009. LNCS, vol. 5823, pp. 634–649. Springer, Heidelberg (2009). https://doi.org/10.1007/978-3-642-04930-9_40

26. Volz, R., Staab, S., Motik, B.: Incrementally maintaining materializations of ontologies stored in logic databases. J. Data Semant. **2**, 1–34 (2005). https://doi.org/10.1007/978-3-540-30567-5_1

27. Wang, X.H., Zhang, D.Q., Gu, T., Pung, H.K.: Ontology based context modeling and reasoning using owl. In: Proceedings of the Second IEEE Annual Conference on Pervasive Computing and Communications Workshops, 2004, pp. 18–22. IEEE (2004)

28. Weaver, J., Hendler, J.A.: Parallel materialization of the finite RDFS closure for hundreds of millions of triples. In: Bernstein, A., et al. (eds.) ISWC 2009. LNCS, vol. 5823, pp. 682–697. Springer, Heidelberg (2009). https://doi.org/10.1007/978-3-642-04930-9_43

29. Weiss, C., Karras, P., Bernstein, A.: Hexastore: sextuple indexing for semantic web data management. PVLDB **1**(1), 1008–1019 (2008). https://doi.org/10.14778/1453856.1453965. http://www.vldb.org/pvldb/1/1453965.pdf

30. Zaharia, M., et al.: Resilient distributed datasets: a fault-tolerant abstraction for in-memory cluster computing. In: NSDI, pp. 15–28. USENIX Association (2012)

Efficient Execution of Scientific Workflows in the Cloud Through Adaptive Caching

Gaëtan Heidsieck[1]([✉]) [iD], Daniel de Oliveira[2] [iD], Esther Pacitti[1] [iD],
Christophe Pradal[3] [iD], François Tardieu[4] [iD], and Patrick Valduriez[1] [iD]

[1] Inria & LIRMM, Univ. Montpellier, Montpellier, France
`gaetan.heidsieck@inria.fr`
[2] Institute of Computing, UFF, Rio de Janeiro, Brazil
[3] CIRAD & AGAP, Univ. Montpellier, Montpellier, France
[4] INRAE & LEPSE, Montpellier, France

Abstract. Many scientific experiments are now carried on using scientific workflows, which are becoming more and more data-intensive and complex. We consider the efficient execution of such workflows in the cloud. Since it is common for workflow users to reuse other workflows or data generated by other workflows, a promising approach for efficient workflow execution is to cache intermediate data and exploit it to avoid task re-execution. In this paper, we propose an adaptive caching solution for data-intensive workflows in the cloud. Our solution is based on a new scientific workflow management architecture that automatically manages the storage and reuse of intermediate data and adapts to the variations in task execution times and output data size. We evaluated our solution by implementing it in the OpenAlea system and performing extensive experiments on real data with a data-intensive application in plant phenotyping. The results show that adaptive caching can yield major performance gains, *e.g.*, up to a factor of 3.5 with 6 workflow re-executions.

Keywords: Adaptive caching · Scientific workflow · Cloud · Workflow execution

1 Introduction

In many scientific domains, *e.g.*, bio-science [18], complex experiments typically require many processing or analysis steps over huge quantities of data. They can be represented as scientific workflows (SWfs), which facilitate the modeling, management and execution of computational activities linked by data dependencies. As the size of the data processed and the complexity of the computation keep increasing, these SWfs become data-intensive [18], thus requiring execution in a high-performance distributed and parallel environment, *e.g.*, a large-scale virtual cluster in the cloud [17].

© Springer-Verlag GmbH Germany, part of Springer Nature 2020
A. Hameurlain et al. (Eds.) TLDKS XLIV, LNCS 12380, pp. 41–66, 2020.
https://doi.org/10.1007/978-3-662-62271-1_2

Most Scientific Workflow Management Systems (SWfMSs) can now execute SWfs in the cloud [23]. Some examples are Swift/T, Pegasus, SciCumulus, Kepler and OpenAlea [21]. Our work is based on OpenAlea [30], which is being widely used in plant science for simulation and analysis [29].

It is common for SWf users to reuse other SWfs or data generated by other SWfs. Reusing and re-purposing SWfs allows for the user to develop new analyses faster [14]. Furthermore, a user may need to execute a SWf many times with different sets of parameters and input data to analyze the impact of some experimental step, represented as a SWf fragment, *i.e.*, a subset of the SWf activities and dependencies. In both cases, some fragments of the SWf may be executed many times, which can be highly resource consuming and unnecessarily long. SWf re-execution can be avoided by storing the intermediate results of these SWf fragments and reusing them in later executions.

In OpenAlea, this is provided by a cache in memory, *i.e.* the intermediate data is simply kept in memory after the execution of a SWf. This allows for the user to visualize and analyze all the activities of a SWf without any recomputation, even with some parameter changes. Although cache in memory represents a step forward, it has some limitations, *e.g.*, it does not scale in distributed environments and requires much memory if the SWf is data-intensive.

From a single user perspective, the reuse of the previous results can be done by storing the relevant outputs of intermediate activities (intermediate data) within the SWf. This requires the user to manually manage the caching of the results that she wants to reuse. This can be difficult as the user needs to be aware of the data size, execution time of each task, *i.e.*, the instantiation of an activity during the execution of a SWf, or other factors that could allow deciding which data is best to be cached.

A complementary, promising approach is to reuse intermediate data produced by multiple executions of the same or different SWfs. Some SWfMSs support the reuse of intermediate data, yet with some limitations. VisTrails [7] automatically makes the intermediate data persistent with the SWf definition. Using a plugin [36], VisTrails allows SWf execution in HPC environments, but does not benefit from reusing intermediate data. Kepler [3] manages a persistent cache of intermediate data in the cloud, but does not take data transfers from remote servers into account. There is also a trade-off between the cost of re-executing tasks versus storing intermediate data that is not trivial [2,11]. Yuan et al. [34] propose an algorithm to determine what data generated by the SWf should be cached, based on the ratio between re-computation cost and storage cost at the task level. The algorithm is improved in [35] to take into account SWf fragments. Both algorithms are used before the execution of the SWf, using the provenance data of the intermediate datasets, *i.e.*, the metadata that traces their origin. However, these two algorithms are static and cannot deal with variations in tasks' execution times. In both cases, such variations can be very important depending on the input data, *e.g.*, data compression tasks can be short or long depending on the data itself, regardless of size. For instance, an image of a given resolution can contain more or less information.

In this paper, we propose an adaptive caching solution for efficient execution of data-intensive SWfs in the cloud. By adapting to the variations in tasks' execution times, our solution can maximize the reuse of intermediate data produced by SWfs from multiple users. Our solution is based on a new SWfMS architecture that automatically manages the storage and reuse of intermediate data. Cache management is involved during two main steps: SWf preprocessing, to remove all fragments of the SWf that do not need to be executed; and cache provisioning, to decide at runtime which intermediate data should be cached. We propose an adaptive cache provisioning algorithm that deals with the variations in task execution times and output data. We evaluated our solution by implementing it in OpenAlea and performing extensive experiments on real data with a complex data-intensive application in plant phenotyping.

This paper is a major extension of [16], with a detailed presentation of the Phenomal use case, an elaborated cost model, a more thorough experimental evaluation and a new section on related work.

This paper is organized as follows. Section 2 presents our real use case in plant phenotyping. Section 3 introduces our SWfMS architecture in the cloud. Section 4 describes our cost model. Section 5 describes our caching algorithm. Section 6 gives our experimental evaluation. Section 7 discusses related work. Finally, Sect. 8 concludes.

2 Use Case in Plant Phenotyping

In this section, we introduce in more details a real SWf use case in plant phenotyping that will serve both as a motivation for the work and as a basis for the experimental evaluation.

In the last decade, high-throughput phenotyping platforms have emerged to perform the acquisition of quantitative data on thousands of plants in well-controlled environmental conditions. These platforms produce huge quantities of heterogeneous data (images, environmental conditions and sensor outputs) and generate complex variables with *in-silico* data analyses. For instance, the seven facilities of the French Phenome project (https://www.phenome-emphasis. fr/phenome_eng/) produce each year 200 Terabytes of data, which are heterogeneous, multiscale and originate from different sites. Analysing automatically and efficiently such massive datasets is an open, yet important, problem for biologists [33].

Computational infrastructures have been developed for processing plant phenotyping datasets in distributed environments [27], where complex phenotyping analyses are expressed as SWfs. Thus, such analyses can be represented, managed and shared in an efficient way, where compute- and data-based activities are linked by dependencies [10]. Several workflow management systems use provenance to analyze and share executions and their results. These SWfs are data-intensive due to the high volume and the size of the data to process. They are computed using distributed computational infrastructures [27].

One scientific challenge in phenomics, *i.e.*, the systematic study of phenotypes, is to analyze and reconstruct automatically the geometry and topology

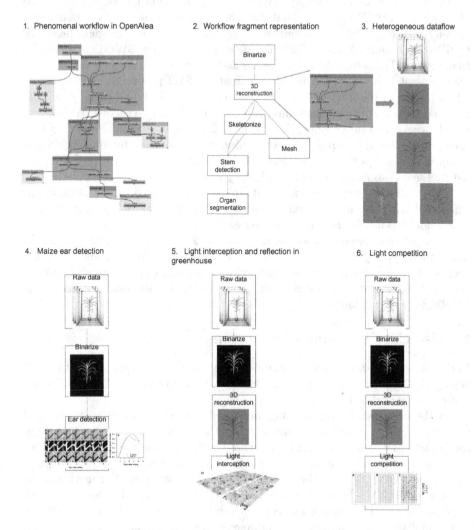

Fig. 1. Use cases in Plant Phenotyping. The different use cases are based on the OpenAlea SWfMS. 1) The Phenomenal SWf in the visual programming OpenAlea environment. Phenomenal SWf allows to reconstruct plants in 3D from thousands of images acquired in high-throughput phenotyping platform. The different colors represent different SWf fragments. 2) A conceptual view of the SWf with the different SWf fragments. 3) Heterogeneous raw and intermediate data such as raw RGB images, 3D plant volumes, tree skeleton, and segmented 3D mesh. 4) A SWf for maize ear detection reusing the *Binarize* SWf fragment. 5) A SWf reusing the *Binarize* and *3D reconstruction* SWf fragment to compute light interception and biomass production on a reconstructed canopy. 6) The previous SWf adapted to understand plant competition in various multi-genotype canopies.

of thousands of plants in various conditions observed from various sensors [32]. For this purpose, we developed the OpenAlea Phenomenal software package [4]. Phenomenal provides fully automatic SWfs dedicated to 3D reconstruction, segmentation and tracking of plant organs, and light interception to estimate plant biomass in various scenarios of climatic change [28].

Phenomenal is continuously evolving with new state-of-the-art methods, thus yielding new biological insights (see Fig. 1). A typical SWf is shown in Fig. 1.1. It is composed of different fragments, *i.e.*, reusable sub-workflows. In Fig. 1.2, the different fragments are for binarization, 3D reconstruction, skeletonization, stem detection, organ segmentation and mesh generation:

- The *Binarize* fragment separates plant pixels from the background in each image. It produces a binary image from a RGB one.
- The *3D reconstruction* fragment produces a 3D volume based on 12 side and 1 top binary images.
- The *Skeletonisation* fragment computes a skeleton inside the reconstructed volume.
- The *Mesh* fragment computes a 3D mesh from the volume and decimates it based on user parameters to reduce its size.
- The *Stem detection* fragment computes a main path in the skeleton to identify the main stem of cereal plants (*e.g.*, maize, wheat, sorghum).
- The *Organ segmentation* segments the different organs on the skeleton after removal of the main stem.

Other fragments such as greenhouse or field reconstruction, or simulation of light interception, can be reused.

Based on these different SWf fragments, different users can conduct different biological analyses using the same datasets (see Fig. 1.4, 1.5 and 1.6). Illustrated in Fig. 1.4, Brichet et al. [5] reuse the *Binarize* fragment to predict the flowering time in maize by detecting the apparition of the ear on maize plants.

In Fig. 1.5, the same *Binarize* fragment is reused and the *3D reconstruction* fragment is added to reconstruct the volume of the 1,680 plants in 3D. This SWf reuses the same *Binarize* segment to reconstruct the volume of the 1600 plants in 3D (*3D reconstruction* fragment) and compute the light intercepted by each plant placed in a virtual scene reproducing the canopy in the glasshouse [6,26]. Finally, in the SWf shown in Fig. 1.6, the previous SWf is reused by Chen et al. [8], but with different parameters to study the environmental versus the genetic influence of biomass accumulation.

These three studies have in common both the plant species (in our case maize plants) and share some SWf fragments. At least, scientists want to compare their results on previous datasets and extend the existing SWf with their own developed activities or fragments. To save both time and resources, they want to reuse the intermediate results that have already been computed rather than recompute them from scratch.

The Phenoarch platform is one of the Phenome nodes in Montpellier. It has a capacity of 1,680 plants with a controlled environment (*e.g.*, temperature, humidity, irrigation) and automatic imaging through time. The total size of the raw image dataset for one experiment is 11 Terabytes. It represents about 80000 time series of plants and about 1040000 images.

Currently, processing a full experiment with the Phenomenal SWf on local computational resources would take more than one month, while scientists require this to be done over night (12 h). Furthermore, they need to be able to restart an analysis by modifying parameters, fix errors in the analysis or extend it by adding new processing activities. Thus, we need to use more computational resources in the cloud including both large data storage that can be shared by multiple users.

3 Cloud SWfMS Architecture

In this section, we present the proposed SWfMS architecture that integrates caching and reuse of intermediate data in the cloud. We motivate our design decisions and describe our architecture in two ways: i) in terms of functional layers (see Fig. 2), which shows the different functions and components; and ii) in terms of nodes and components (see Fig. 3), which are involved in the processing of SWfs.

Our architecture capitalizes on the latest advances in distributed and parallel computing to offer performance and scalability [25]. We consider a distributed architecture with on premise servers, where raw data is produced (e.g., by a phenotyping experimental platform in our use case), and a cloud site, where the SWf is executed. The cloud site (data center) is a shared-nothing cluster, i.e., a cluster of server machines, each with processor, memory and disk. We adopt shared-nothing as it is the most scalable and cost-effective architecture for big data analysis.

In the cloud, metadata management has a critical impact on the efficiency of SWf scheduling as it provides a global view of data location, e.g., at which nodes some raw data is stored, and enables task tracking during execution [20]. We organize the metadata in three repositories: catalog, provenance database and cache index. The catalog contains all information about users (access rights, etc.), raw data location and SWfs (code libraries, application code). The provenance database captures all information about SWf execution. The cache index contains information about tasks and cache data produced, as well as the location of files that store the cache data. Thus, the cache index itself is small (only file references) and the cached data can be managed using the underlying file system. A good solution for implementing these metadata repositories is a key-value store, such as Cassandra (https://cassandra.apache.org), which provides efficient key-based access, scalability and fault-tolerance through replication in a shared-nothing cluster [1].

The raw data (files) are initially produced at some servers, e.g., in our use case, at the phenotyping platform and get transferred to the cloud site. The server associated with the phenotyping platform is using iRODS [31] to grant access to the data generated. The intermediate data is placed on the node that execute the task, and is produced and processed through memory. It is only written on disk if it is added to the cache. The cache data (files) are produced at the cloud site after SWf execution. A good solution to store these files in a cluster is a distributed file system like Lustre (http://lustre.org) which is used a lot in HPC as it scales to high numbers of files.

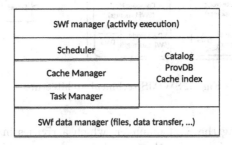

Fig. 2. SWfMS functional architecture

Figure 2 extends the SWfMS architecture proposed in [21], which distinguishes various layers, to support intermediate data caching. The SWf manager is the component that the user clients interact with to develop, share and execute SWfs, using the metadata (catalog, provenance database and cache index). It determines the SWf activities that need to be executed, and generates the associated tasks for the scheduler. It also uses the cache index for SWf preprocessing to identify the intermediate data to reuse and the tasks that need not be re-executed.

The scheduler exploits the catalog and provenance database to decide which tasks should be scheduled to cloud sites. The task manager controls task execution and uses the cache manager to decide whether the task's output data should be placed in the cache. The cache manager implements the adaptive cache provisioning algorithm described in Sect. 5. The SWf data manager deals with data storage, using a distributed file system.

Figure 3 shows how these components are involved in SWf processing, using the traditional master-worker model. There are three kinds of nodes, master, compute and data nodes, which are all mapped to cluster nodes at configuration time, e.g., using a cluster manager like Yarn (http://hadoop.apache.org). The master node includes the SWf manager, scheduler and cache manager, and deals with the metadata. The worker nodes are either compute or data nodes. The master node is lightly loaded as most of the work of serving clients is done by the compute and data nodes (or worker nodes), that perform task management and execution, and data management, respectively. Therefore, the master node is not a bottleneck. However, to avoid any single point of failure, there is a standby master node that can perform failover upon the master node's failure and provide high availability.

Let us now illustrate briefly how SWf processing works. User clients connect to the cloud site's master node. SWf execution is controlled by the master node,

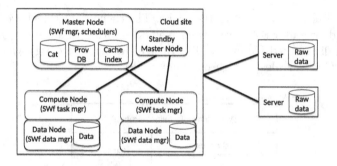

Fig. 3. SWfMS technical architecture

which identifies, using the SWf manager, which activities in the fragment can take advantage of cached data, thus avoiding task reexecution. The scheduler schedules the corresponding tasks that need to be processed on compute nodes which in turn rely on data nodes for data access. It also adds the transfers of raw data from remote servers that are needed for executing the SWf. For each task, the task manager decides whether the task's output data should be placed in the cache taking into account storage costs, data size, network costs. When a task terminates, the compute node sends to its master the task's execution information to be added in the provenance database. Then, the master node updates the provenance database and may trigger subsequent tasks.

4 Cost Model

In this section, we present our cost model. We start by introducing some terms and concepts. A SWf $W(A, D)$ is the abstract representation of a directed acyclic graph (DAG) of computational activities A and their data dependencies D. There is a dependency between two activities if one consumes the data produced by the other. An activity is a description of a piece of work and can be a computational script (computational activity), some data (data activity) or some set-oriented algebraic operator like map or filter [22]. The parents of an activity are all activities directly connected to its inputs. A task t is the instantiation of an activity during execution with specific associated input data. The input $In(t)$ of t is the data needed for the task to be computed, and the output $Out(t)$ is the data produced by the execution of t. Whenever necessary, for clarity, we alternatively use the term intermediate data instead of output data. Execution data corresponds to the input and output data related to a task t. For the same activity, if two tasks t_i and t_j have equal inputs, then they produce the same output data, i.e., $In(t_i) = In(t_j) \Rightarrow Out(t_i) = Out(t_j)$. A SWf's input data is the raw data generated by an experimental platform, e.g., a phenotyping platform.

Our approach focuses on the trade-off between execution time and cache size. In order to compare the execution time and cache size, we use a monetary cost approach, which we will also use in the experimental evaluation in Sect. 6. All the costs are compared at the task level and are expressed in USD. For a task t, the total cost of n executions according to the caching decision can be defined by:

$$Cost(t, n) = \omega_t * TimeCost(t, n) + \omega_c * CacheCost(t, n) \tag{1}$$

where $TimeCost(t, n)$ is the cost associated with the execution time and $CacheCost$ (t,n) is the cost associated with caching. They represent the amount of USD spent in order to obtain the output of a task, n times. ω_t and ω_c represent the weights of the two cost components, which are positive.

The execution time cost of a task depends on whether or not the output data of the task is added to the cache. If the output of t is not added to the cache, the execution time cost $Cost_{nocache}(t, n)$ is the sum of the costs associated with getting $In(t)$ and executing t, n times. Otherwise, i.e., $Out(t)$ is added to the cache, the execution time cost $Cost_{cache}(t, n)$ is composed of the cost of the first execution of t, the cost to provision the cache with $Out(t)$ and the cost of retrieving $Out(t)$, n-1 times. $TimeCost(t, n)$ can be defined by:

$$TimeCost(t, n) = \begin{cases} Cost_{nocache}(t, n), & \text{if Out(t) not in cache.} \\ Cost_{cache}(t, n), & \text{otherwise.} \end{cases} \tag{2}$$

During workflow execution, the execution time of each task t, denoted by $Time_{exec}(t)$, is stored in the provenance database. If t has already been executed, $Time_{exec}(t)$ is already known and can be retrieved from the provenance database. When t is re-executed, its execution time is recomputed and $Time_{exec}(t)$ is updated as the average of all execution times. The access times to read and write in the cache are $Time_{read}$ and $Time_{write}$. Here it will be applied to input $In(t)$ and output $Out(t)$ data. This time mostly dependent on the data size. $Cost_{nocache}(t, n)$ and $Cost_{cache}(t, n)$ are then given by:

$$Cost_{nocache}(t, n) = Cost_{cpu} * n * [Time_{read}(In(t)) + Time_{exec}(t)] \tag{3}$$

$$Cost_{cache}(t, n) = Cost_{nocache}(t, 1) + Cost_{cpu} * (n - 1) * Time_{read}(Out(t)) \tag{4}$$

where $Cost_{cpu}$ represents the average monetary cost to use virtual CPUs in one determined time interval.

The cost associated with the size of the cache can be defined by:

$$CacheCost(t, n) = Cost_{disk} * size(Out(t)) \tag{5}$$

where $Cost_{disk}$ represents the monetary cost of storing data in one specific time interval, determined by the user, and $size(Out(t))$ is the real size of the output data generated by t execution.

The caching decision depends on the trade-off between the execution time cost and the storage cost. For some tasks, the output data is either much bigger in size or much complex than their input data, in this case, it is more time consuming to retrieve data from the cache than re-executing the task (see Eq. 6). This is the case for most of the tasks on plant graph generation in our SWf's use case. In this case, no matter what is the storage cost, it is less costly to simply re-execute t. The output data generated is then not added to the cache.

$$Time_{read}(In(t)) + Time_{exec}(t) \leq Time_{read}(Out(t)) \qquad (6)$$

In other cases, $i.e.$, when it is time saving to retrieve the output data of a task t instead of re-executing t, the execution time cost and caching cost are compared. The output data of the task t is worth putting in the cache if for n executions of t, the cost of adding the data into the cache is smaller than the cost of an execution without cache, $i.e.$:

$$Cost_{cache}(t, n) + CacheCost(t, n) \leq Cost_{nocache}(t, n) \qquad (7)$$

From Eqs. (3), (4), (5) and (7), we can now get the minimal number of times denoted by $n_{min}(t)$, which the task t needs to be executed that it is cost effective to add its output into the cache. $n_{min}(t)$ is given by:

$$n_{min}(t) = 1 + \frac{Time_{write}(Out(t)) + \dfrac{Cost_{disk} * size(Out(t))}{Cost_{cpu}}}{Time_{read}(In(t)) + Time_{exec}(t) - Time_{read}(Out(t))} \qquad (8)$$

We introduce $p(t)$, the probability that t be re-executed. There is then a limit value $p_{min}(t)$ that represents the minimum value of $p(t)$ from which the output of t is worth to add in the cache. Based on Eq. (8), $p_{min}(t)$ can be defined as:

$$p_{min}(t) = n_{min}(t) - 1 \qquad (9)$$

The value $p_{min}(t)$ is a ratio between the cost of adding the output data of the task t into a cache and the possible cost saved if this cached data is used instead of re-executing the task and its parents.

In the case of multiple users, the exact probability $p(t)$ or the number of times the task t will be re-executed is not known when the SWf is executed. We then introduce a threshold p_{tresh} arbitrarily picked by the user. This threshold will be the limit value to decide whether a task output will be added to the cache.

During the execution of each task, the real values of the execution time and data size related to t are known. Thus, the caching decision is made from the Eqs. (6) and (9).

5   Cache Management

This section presents in detail our techniques for cache management. In our solution, cache management is involved during two main steps: *SWf preprocessing* and *cache provisioning*. The preprocessing step transforms the workflow based

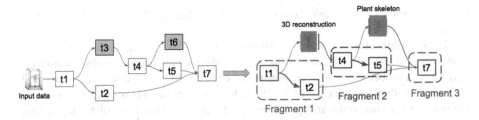

Fig. 4. DAG of tasks before preprocessing (left) and the selected fragments that need to be executed (right).

on the cache by replacing workflow fragments by already computed output data stored in the cache. The preprocessing step occurs just before execution and is done by the SWf manager using the cache index. The SWf manager transform the workflow $W(A, D)$ into an executable workflow $W_{ex}(A, D, T, Input)$, where T is a DAG of tasks corresponding to the activities in A and $Input$ is the input data. The goal of SWf preprocessing is to transform an executable workflow $W_{ex}(A, D, T, Input)$ into an equivalent, simpler subworkflow $W'_{ex}(A', D', T', Input')$, where A' is a subgraph of A with dependencies D', T' is a subgraph of T corresponding to A' and $Input'$ is a subset of $Input$. The preprocessing step uses a recursive algorithm that traverses the DAG T starting from the sink tasks to the source ones. The algorithm marks each task whose output is already in the cache. Then, the subgraphs of T that have each of their sink tasks marked are removed, and replaced by the associated data from the cache. The remaining graph is T'. Finally, the algorithm determines the fragments of T': subgraphs that still need to be executed.

Figure 4 illustrates the preprocessing step on the Phenomenal SWf. The yellow tasks have their output data stored in the cache. They are replaced by the corresponding data as input for the subgraphs of tasks that need to be executed.

The second step, cache provisioning, is performed during workflow execution. Traditional (in memory) caching involves deciding, as data is read from disk into memory, which data to replace to make room, using a cache replacement algorithm, *e.g.*, Least Recently Used (LRU). In our context, using a disk-based cache, the question is different. Unlike memory cache, disk-based cache makes it possible to cache the Terabytes of data generated by the SWf's execution. Caching huge datasets has a cost and the question is to decide which task output data to place in the cache using a cache provisioning algorithm, in order to limit execution costs. This algorithm is implemented by the cache manager and used by the task manager when executing a task.

A simple cache provisioning algorithm, which we will use as baseline in the experimental evaluation, is to use a *greedy* method that simply stores all tasks' output data in the cache. However, since SWf executions produce huge quantities of output data, this approach would incur high storage costs. Worse, for some short duration tasks, accessing cache data from disk may take much more time than re-executing the corresponding task subgraph from the input data in memory.

Thus, we propose a cache provisioning algorithm with an adaptive method that deals with the variations in task execution times and output data complexity and sizes. The principle is to compute, for each task t, the value $p_{min}(t)$ defined in Sect. 4, called cache score of t, which is based on the sizes of the input and output data it consumes and produces, and the execution time of t. Depending on this value, after each task execution, the cache manager decides on whether the output data is added to the cache or not.

The cache score reveals the relevancy of caching the output data of t and takes into account the compression ratio and execution time as well as the caching costs. According to the weights provided by the user, she may prefer to give more importance to the compression ratio or executions time, depending on the storage capacity and available computational resources.

Then, during the execution of each task t, the task manager calls the cache manager to compute $p_{min}(t)$. If the computed value is smaller than the threshold p_{tresh} provided by the user, then t's output data will be cached. This threshold is arbitrarily chosen based on the probability of the SWf being re-executed.

6   Experimental Evaluation

In this section, we first present our experimental setup. Then, we present our experiments and experimental comparisons of different caching methods in terms of speedup and monetary cost in single user and multiuser scenarios. Finally, we give concluding remarks.

6.1   Experimental Setup

Our experimental setup includes the cloud infrastructure, a SWf implementation and an experimental dataset.

The cloud infrastructure is composed of one site with one data node ($N1$) and two identical compute nodes ($N2$, $N3$). The raw data is originally stored in an external server. During computation, raw data is transferred to N1, which contains Terabytes of persistent storage capacities. Each compute node has much computing power, with 80 vCPUs (virtual CPUs, equivalent to one core each of a 2.2 GHz Intel Xeon E7-8860v3) and 3 Terabytes of RAM, but less persistent storage (20 Gigabytes).

We implemented the Phenomenal workflow (see Sect. 2) using OpenAlea and deployed it on the different nodes using the Conda multi-OS package manager. The master node is hosted on one of the compute nodes ($N2$). The metadata repositories are stored on the same node ($N2$) using the Cassandra key-value store. Files for raw and cached data are shared between the different nodes using the Lustre file system. File transfer between nodes is implemented with ssh.

The Phenoarch platform has a capacity of 1,680 plants with 13 images per plant per day. The size of an image is 10 Megabytes and the duration of an experiment is around 50 days. The total size of the raw image dataset represents 11 Terabytes for one experiment. The dataset is structured as 1,680 time series, composed of 50 time points (one per plant and per day).

We use a version of the Phenomenal workflow composed of 9 main activities. We execute it on a subset of the use case dataset, which is $\frac{1}{25}$ of the size of the full dataset, or 440 Gigabytes of raw data, which represents the execution of 30,240 tasks.

The time interval considered for the caching time (see Sect. 4) is 30 days, *i.e.*, the SWf re-executions are done within one month. The user can select longer or shorter time intervals depending on the application.

For the comparison of different cost-based caching methods, we use cost models defined in Sect. 4. To set the price parameters, we use prices from Amazon AWS, *i.e.*, $Cost_{disk}$ is $0.1 per Gigabyte per month for storage and two instances at $5.424 per hour for computation, *i.e.*, $Cost_{cpu}$ is $10.848 per hour. We set the user's parameters ω_t and ω_c at 0.5.

The caching methods we compare, defined in Sect. 5 are noted as:

- *M1* for the execution without cache.
- *M2* for the greedy method where all the created intermediate data produced is cached.
- *M3$_X$* for the adaptive method, with X as the p_{tresh} value. In our experiments, X vary between 10, 40 and 160.

6.2   Experiments

We consider three experiments, based on the use case in order to analyze our caching method under different conditions:

1. This experiment aims at evaluating the scalability and speedup of the caching methods. In this experiment, we assume that the same workflow is computed three times in a month, at different times (one user at a time). This experiment is based on the SWf Phenomenal, *i.e.*, the maize analysis (see Fig. 1.4). The scalability of the SWf execution is studied using different numbers of vCPUs from 10 to 160.
2. This experiment aims at analysing the impact from the variability in execution time and data size of the tasks from each activity, on the components of the proposed cost function.
3. In this experiment, the same workflow is executed with an adaptive cache strategy with different monetary costs. We assume that the same SWf is executed up to six times in a month, starting from an empty cache. This experiment shows the trade-off between better re-execution time and smaller cache size.
4. In this experiment, different users execute different SWfs that reuse sub-parts of the complete Phenomenal SWf. Depending on the caching strategy

and cache size, the result of some tasks may already be present in the cache. We show the impact of the value p_{tresh} (see Sect. 4) on execution time, cache size and overall monetary cost depending on the user executions.

Except for Experiment 1 where the number of vCPUs varies, it is set at 160 for the three other experiments. The execution time corresponds to the time to transfer the raw data files from the remote servers, the time to run the workflow and the time to provision the cache.

Workflow executions of the different users are serial, thus we do not consider concurrency when accessing cached data. Moreover, we assume that there are no execution or data transfer failures.

The raw data is retrieved on the data node as follows: a first file is retrieved from the remote data servers and stored in one cluster's data node. Then, execution starts using this first file while the next files are retrieved in parallel. As executing the SWf on the first file takes longer than transferring one more raw data file, we only count the time of transferring the first chunk in the execution time.

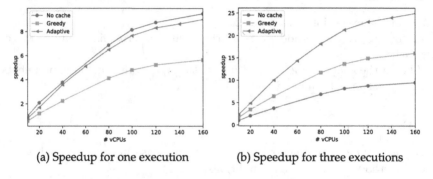

(a) Speedup for one execution   (b) Speedup for three executions

Fig. 5. Speedup versus number of vCPUs: without cache (orange), greedy caching (blue), and adaptive caching (green). (Color figure online)

Speedup. In Experiment 1, we compare the speedup of the three caching methods with a threshold $p_{tresh} = 40$, which is optimal in this case. We define the speedup as $speedup(n) = \frac{T_n}{T_{10}}$, where T_n is the execution time on n vCPUs and T_{10} is the execution time of method $M1$ on 10 vCPUs.

The workflow execution is distributed on nodes $N2$ and $N3$, for different numbers of vCPUs. For one execution, Fig. 5.a shows that the fastest method is $M1$ (orange curve). This is expected as there is no extra time spent to make data persistent and provision the cache. However, the overhead of cache provisioning with method $M3_{40}$ is very small, less than 6% (green curve in Fig. 5.a) compared with method $M2$, up to 40% (blue curve in Fig. 5.a) where all the output data are saved in the cache.

For the first execution, method $M3_{40}$'s overhead is only 5,6% compared to method $M1$, while method $M2$'s overhead goes up to 40.1%. For instance, with 80 vCPUs, the execution time of method $M3_{40}$ (*i.e.*, 3,714 s) is only 5.8% higher than execution time of method $M1$ (*i.e.*, 3,510 s). This is much faster than method $M2$, which adds 2,152 s (1.58 times longer) of computation time in comparison with method $M3_{40}$. In both cases, any re-execution is much faster than the first execution. Method $M2$ re-execution time is the fastest, with a speedup gain of factor that is 102 times (*i.e.*, 34 s) better compared with method $M1$, because all the output data is already cached. Furthermore, while only the master node is working when no computation is done, the re-execution time is independent of the number of vCPUs and can be computed from a personal computer with limited vCPUs. Method $M3_{40}$ re-execution time is 12.6 times (*i.e.*, 258 s) better compared to method $M1$'s re-execution time. With method $M3_{40}$, some computation still needs to be done when the workflow is re-executed, but such re-execution on the whole dataset can be done in a bit more than a day (*i.e.*, 28.7 h) on a 10 vCPUs machine, compared with 7.2 days with method $M1$.

For three executions starting without cache, Fig. 5.b shows that method $M3_{40}$ is much faster than the other methods (about 2.5 and 1.5 times faster of 3 executions compared to methods $M1$ and $M2$ on 80 vCPUs). Method $M2$ is faster than method $M1$ in this case, because the additional time for cache provisioning is compensated by the very short re-execution times of method $M2$. With 80 vCPUs, the speedup of method $M3_{40}$ (*i.e.*, 18.1) is 54.70% better than that the speedup of method $M2$ (*i.e.*, 11.7) and 162.31% better than that of method $M1$ (*i.e.*, 6.9). Method $M3_{40}$ is faster than the other methods on three executions, despite having a re-execution time higher than method $M2$, because the overhead of the cache provisioning is 57% smaller.

Analysis of Tasks Variability. The Phenomenal SWf is composed of nine activities (see Sect. 2), which we denote by A1, A2, ..., A9. During its execution, thousands of tasks are executed that belong to the same activities. In order to assess the behavior of a task with respect to its activity, we analyze the execution time of each task per activity (see Fig. 6) and the cost model through their p_{min} value (see Fig. 7).

In Fig. 6, execution times of tasks that belong to activities A1, A2 and A6 have few variations. The tasks of such activities have predictable execution times and this information can be used to make decisions about static caching. However, the execution times of A3, A4 and A5 have high variability, which makes them unpredictable.

Figure 7 shows that the variability of the p_{min} value is reduced, compared to the variability of the execution times for activities A3 and A7. For activity A9, this is the opposite: the p_{min} values for the tasks of A9 have high variability. Note that the values of p_{min} shown on the figure are limited at 500 for visibility and A9 values are not entirely visible. For activities A2 and A4, the p_{min} value is not computed as it is always more time consuming to get their output data from the cache than recomputing them. This case is explained in Sect. 4 with Eq. 6.

If the variance in the behavior of an activity's tasks is small, then the behavior of the whole SWf execution is predictable, *i.e.*, the tasks' execution times and intermediate data sizes are predictable. In this case, the caching decision can be static, and done prior to execution. However, in our case, there are significant variations in the task behaviors, so we adopt an adaptive approach.

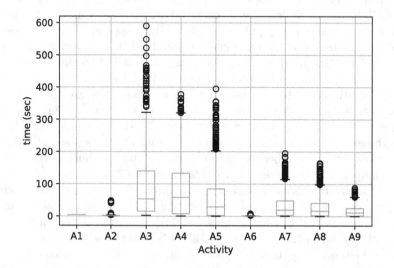

Fig. 6. Execution time of each activity's task.

Monetary Cost Evaluation. The first experiment shows that method $M3_{40}$ scales and reduces re-execution time. However, method $M2$ enables faster re-executions despite a longer first execution time, but it also generates more cached data. In this experiment, we evaluate the monetary costs of the various methods for the executions of SWf (see Fig. 8).

The cost of method $M1$ comes only from the computation, as no data is stored. The whole SWf is completely re-executed so the cost increases linearly with the number of executions and ends at a total of USD 1419 for six executions. Method $M2$ has computation and data storage costs higher than the other two methods for the first execution. The amount of intermediate data added to the cache is huge and the total cost for the first execution is 5.96 times higher than method $M1$ (*i.e.*, 1405$). However, the very small computation cost from re-execution (7.73$) compensates for the data storage cost in comparison with the method $M1$ after the sixth executions.

For the first execution, method $M3_{40}$ adds 6% overhead in regards to method $M1$'s execution cost because it populates the cache with a total of 934 Gigabytes. For any future re-executions, the decrease in computation time for method $M3_{40}$

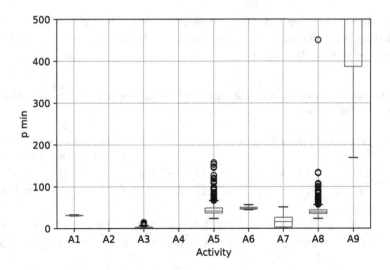

Fig. 7. p_{min} of each activity's task.

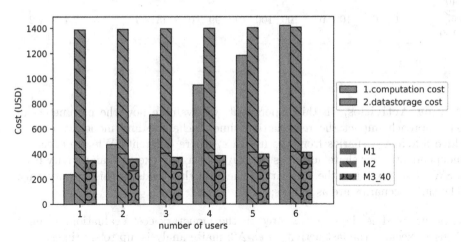

Fig. 8. Monetary cost depending on the number of users that execute the workflow with three different cache strategies with the execution cost (blue) and the storage cost (red). (Color figure online)

makes it less expensive than method $M1$. For six executions, the cost gain is a factor of 3.5 (the total cost of method $M3_{40}$ is 409\$). Method $M3_{40}$ also has a cost gain of a factor of 3.5 compared to $M2$ for six executions. The amount of intermediate data added to the cache is almost 10 times smaller for method $M3_{40}$ than for method $M2$. Thus, the data storage cost of method $M2$ is not worth the decrease in the computation cost compared with method $M3_{40}$.

This shows that method $M3_{40}$ efficiently selects the intermediate data to be added to the cache in order to reduce the cache size significantly while also reducing the re-execution time.

Table 1. Caching decision per task and total cache size and re-execution time for different caching methods.

Caching method	Percentage of tasks cached									Cache size (GB)	Re-execution time (hours)		
	A1	A2	A3	A4	A5	A6	A7	A8	A9		S1	S2	S3
No cache	0	0	0	0	0	0	0	0	0	0	21.8	103.4	69.4
Greedy	100	100	100	100	100	100	100	100	100	9894.9	0.04	0.43	0.13
p_{tresh} 10	0	0	98	0	0	0	41	0	0	49.1	1.6	22.4	9.6
p_{tresh} 40	100	0	100	0	39	0	96	55	0	934.3	0.71	5.5	3.6
p_{tresh} 160	100	0	100	0	100	100	100	99	0	4318.4	0.31	2.4	1.2

Adding Activities. In this experiment, we evaluate how the parameters of our approach impact the re-execution time, cache size and monetary cost in three different scenarios from the use case, where different SWfs are executed independently but share activities. We say that a user executes an activity from a SWf if she executes the sub-part of the SWf that leads to this activity only. The three scenarios are as follows:

1. Scenario S1 is the one presented in the monetary cost evaluation: a single user executes the last activity, *i.e.*, A9: maize analysis, up to six times.
2. Scenario S2 involves nine users, that will each executing a different activity of the SWf up to six times.
3. Scenario S3 involves four users: one executes activity A1, *i.e.*, binarization, the second executes activity A3, *i.e.*, 3D reconstruction, the third executes activity A7, *i.e.*, maize segmentation, and the last one executes activity A9, *i.e.*, maize analysis.

In these scenarios, each user executes a part of the SWf different from the others. Figs. 9, 10 and 11 illustrate the monetary costs for three values of p_{tresh}: 10, 40 and 160. The p_{tresh} values are the threshold set by the user to manage the weight between cache size and re-execution time. With a small p_{tresh}, only a small portion of the output of the tasks is to be added to the cache. A larger p_{tresh} results in more intermediate data added to the cache.

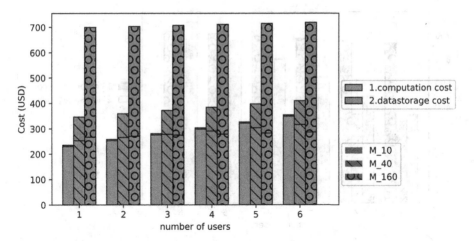

Fig. 9. Monetary cost of scenario S1: Each user executes the last activity of the SWf, for three values of p_{tresh}.

In scenario S1, only one activity, the last one, is re-executed. As this activity is the last, without cache implies the whole SWf to be re-executed. However, as we can see in Fig. 9, re-executions require little computation time even for the smallest $p_{min} = 0.1$. The re-execution times are respectively 1.6, 0.71 and 0.31 hours for methods $M3_{10}$, $M3_{40}$ and $M3_{160}$ (see Table 1) instead of 21.8 hours without cache. In this scenario, the overall monetary cost of method $M3_{160}$ is the highest, 49.1% higher than method $M3_{40}$, which we used as baseline in the previous section. Yet, the monetary cost of method $M3_{160}$ remains 57.1% smaller than that of method $M2$. This shows that adaptive method successfully

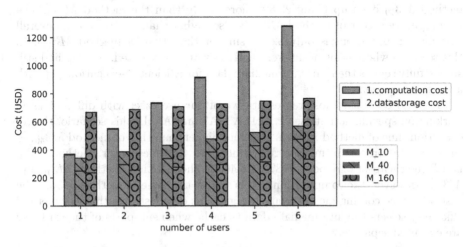

Fig. 10. Monetary cost of scenario S2: Each user executes all the activities of the workflow, for three values of p_{tresh}.

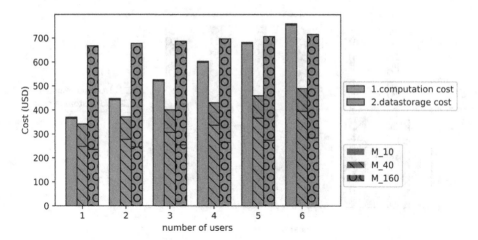

Fig. 11. Monetary cost of scenario S3: Each user executes the activities based on the use case (A1, A3, A7, A9), for three values of p_{tresh}.

selects the intermediate data that is the less costly to store and most worth for re-execution even in the case where a lot of intermediate data is cached.

The computation cost for the re-execution of method $M3_{10}$ is 3.6 and 6.2 times higher than for methods $M3_{40}$ and $M3_{160}$. However, it is the most cost-effective: 324.9\$, $i.e.$, 19.7% less than method $M3_{40}$'s cost. In scenario S1 where a single activity is re-executed, a small cache size is the best option.

In scenario S2, each activity is re-executed, which represents the extreme opposite of scenario S1. In this scenario, the re-execution time for method $M3_{10}$ is much higher: 8.7 hours compared to 3.4 and 1.2 hours. The difference in the cache storage cost is not enough to compensate for the re-computation cost and method $M3_{10}$ ends up being 22.8% more costly than the method $M3_{40}$. The re-computation cost of method $M3_{40}$ is also higher than in S1, and the overall cost for six executions is only 32.4% smaller than that of method $M3_{160}$. In this scenario where a lot of different activities are re-executed, our method still successfully selects the right intermediate data for efficient re-execution, yet with a limited cache size.

Scenario S3 is the most representative of our use case, with different users working on specific activities, $i.e.$, A1, A3, A7 and A9. In this scenario, the re-execution time of method $M3_{10}$ is 4.4 times higher than that of method $M3_{40}$, so the computation cost of method $M3_{10}$ increases 4.4 times faster. Method $M3_{40}$ is still the cheapest one, being 8.8% and 46.4% cheaper than methods $M3_{10}$ and $M3_{160}$. However, the computation cost is almost the same as method $M3_{160}$, the cost difference coming mostly from storage. This demonstrates that our method efficiently selects the intermediate data to cache when sub-parts of the workflow are executed separately.

6.3   Discussion

The proposed adaptive method has better speedup compared to the no cache and greedy methods, with performance gains up to 162.31% and 54.70% respectively for three executions. The execution time gain for each re-execution goes up to a factor of 60 for the adaptive method in comparison to the no cache method (*i.e.*, 0.31 hours instead of 21.8). One requirement from the use case was to make workflow execution time shorter than half a day (12 hours). The adaptive method allows for the user to re-execute the workflow on the total dataset (*i.e.*, 11 Terabytes) in less than one hour in the cloud and still within a day on a 10 CPUs server. In terms of monetary cost, the adaptive method yields very good gains, up to 257.8% with 6 workflow re-executions in comparison to the no cache method and 229.2% in comparison to the greedy method, which represents up to 1000$.

The experiments on several fragments of the SWf as described in the use case, show that the adaptive method succeeds in picking the most worthy intermediate data to cache. The method does work, even though the structure of the SWf is changed across re-executions. Similar to what happens with re-execution of a single SWf, the monetary cost of the greedy method is higher than the no cache method for up to 6 executions with different fragments or different parameters. And the execution time of greedy is always better than no cache. The adaptive method is both faster and cheaper than both no cache and greedy.

The different values of the parameter p_{tresh} allow the user to adjust between a smaller cache size or smaller re-execution time. Table 1 shows the trade-off for three p_{tresh} values. Increasing the amount of intermediate data cached obviously decreases the re-execution time of the workflow in any scenario proposed. But the increase in cache size is not proportional to the decrease of re-execution time. The method first selects the most worthy intermediate data to add in the cache. Then, some intermediate data which is considered not beneficial, will never be added to the cache.

The method proposed in this paper focuses on finding the most cost effective intermediate data to cache during SWf execution, depending on p_{tresh} and on the user's preferences (ω_t and ω_c), assuming the cache size is unlimited. However, in some applications and organizations, data storage may have some limitation. In this case, it could be interesting to get the optimal value of p_{tresh} for each task in order to minimize the re-execution time. As the method is adaptive, the size of the total cached data is unknown until the end of the execution. However, the adaptive method could be coupled with other approaches that would approximate the final cache size. Indeed, even if tasks from the same activity have variations in their caching values and their output data sizes, an approximation could be done by taking the average value or the maximum value of some tasks for each activity, then making a static caching decision on all the rest of the tasks.

The Phenomenal workflow is data-intensive because some activities process/ generate huge datasets. Indeed, some activities are compressing the data by a significant factor, *i.e.*, the binarization is compressing the raw data by a factor

500. Other are expending the data, *i.e.*, the skeletonization is expanding the data by a factor 100 (it generates 2 TB of data while consuming only 30 GB). The Phenomenal workflow is also compute-intensive, as some activities require long computing time, *i.e.*, the 3D reconstruction require 1200 h of total computing time. The Phenomenal workflow is representative of many other data science workflows, that perform long analyses on huge datasets. Thus, the method presented would work on data-intensive workflows where the execution time is significant with regards to the data transfers times However, the method is not suitable for any kind of application. It adds an overhead when the workflow is executed, thus it would be inefficient on workflows that are not data- or compute-intensive.

7   Related Work

Storing and reusing intermediate data in SWf executions can be found in several SWfMSs [7,30]. However, there is no definitive solution for two important problems: 1) how to automatically reuse SWf fragments in multiple SWf's executions. 2) what intermediate data to cache if there is not provenance data available. The related works either focus on an optimized solution for selecting a specific portion of data to cache when all provenance and reuse information are known, or automatic caching for the same SWf.

Different SWfMSs, such as Kepler, VisTrails, OpenAlea, exploit intermediate data for SWf re-execution. Each of these systems has its unique way of addressing data reuse. OpenAlea [30] uses a cache that captures the intermediate results in main memory. When a SWf is executed, it first accesses the cached data. However, the OpenAlea cache is local and main memory-based, while the approach proposed in this paper is distributed and persistent. VisTrails provides visual analysis of SWf results and captures the evolution of SWf provenance, *i.e.*, the steps of the workflow at each execution, as well as the intermediate data from each execution [7]. The intermediate data are then reused when previous tasks are re-executed. This approach allows the user to change parameters or activities in the workflow and efficiently re-execute each workflow activity to analyze the different results. This solution for caching intermediate data has been extended to generate "strong links" between provenance and execution [12,19]. The intermediate data cache is associated with provenance to enhance reproducibility, and the intermediate data that has been cached is always reused. However, VisTrails does not take distribution into account when storing and using the cache, and the selection of the data to be stored becomes manual as the size of the intermediate data increases. Our approach is different as it works in a distributed environment where data transfer costs may be significant.

Storing intermediate data in the cloud may be also beneficial. However, the trade-off between the cost of re-executing tasks and the costs of storing intermediate data is not easy to estimate [2,11]. Yuan et al. [34] propose an algorithm based on the ratio between re-computation cost and storage cost at the task level. The algorithm is based on a graph of dependencies between the intermediate data sets, generated from the provenance data. Then, the cost of storing each intermediate data set is weighted by the number of dependencies in the graph. The algorithm computes the optimized set of intermediate data sets that need to have minimum cost. The algorithm is improved in [35] to take into account workflow fragments. Both algorithms are used before the workflow execution, using the provenance data of the intermediate datasets. They provide near optimal caching intermediate datasets selection. However, this approach requires global knowledge of executions, such as the execution time of each task, the size of each data set and the number of incoming re-executions. This optimization is also based on a single workflow and is not adapted to changing workflows. Our approach is different as it provides efficient caching of intermediate data in evolving workflows.

Kepler [3] provides intermediate data caching for single-site cloud SWf execution. It uses a remote relational database where intermediate data is stored after workflow execution. Two steps are added when executing a workflow. First, the cache database is checked and all intermediate cached data is sent to a specific cloud site before execution. To reduce storage cost, the intermediate data that need to be cached are determined based on how many times the workflow will be re-executed in a given period of time [9]. Finally, reuse is done at the entire workflow level, whereas our solution is finer grain, working at the activity level.

Other approaches propose solutions for caching data in MapReduce workflows. Zhang et al. [37] use the *Memcached* distributed memory caching system to cache the intermediate data between Map and Reduce operations. This approach focuses on a single MapReduce job, and the cached data is not persistent and reused across executions. Elghandour et al. [13] propose a system to manage and cache intermediate data of MapReduce jobs for future reuse. Olston et al. [24] propose two caching strategies on top of the Pig language and propose different methods to manage persistent intermediate data. The problem of this approach is that it is static, *i.e.*, they do not consider automatic caching. Gottin et al. [15] propose an algorithm that finds an optimized cache decision plan for a dataflow execution in Apache Spark. The approach is based on a cost model that uses provenance data, and tries the possible combinations of caching selection in order to select the best one. This approach does not scale with the size of the SWf, and the caching decision still falls in the hands of the user.

8   Conclusion

In this paper, we proposed an adaptive caching solution for efficient execution of data-intensive workflows in the cloud. Our solution automatically manages the storage and reuse of intermediate data, and is adaptive in terms of variations in task execution times and output data size. The adaptive aspect of our solution is to take into account task compression behavior.

We implemented our solution in the OpenAlea SWfMS and performed extensive experiments on real data with the Phenomenal SWf, a real big workflow that consumes and produces around 11 TB of raw data. We compared three methods: no cache, greedy, and adaptive. Our experimental evaluation shows that the adaptive method allows for caching only the relevant output data for subsequent re-executions by other users, without incurring a high storage cost for the cache. The results show that adaptive caching can yield major performance gains, *e.g.*, up to a factor of 3.5 with 6 workflow re-executions.

In this paper, we focused on reducing the monetary cost of running multiple workflows by caching and reusing intermediate data. While our technique show an improvement with respect to greedy approaches, we notice that the scaling up is limited (see Fig. 5). In the case of multiple users, the cloud computing and storage capacities might be a bottleneck to scale up workflow executions. In the use case, multiple cloud sites are available. A next step would be to extend our method to multisite clouds.

The architecture proposed is based on disk storage for data reuse. Writing and reading the cached data on disk adds an significant overhead. A next step to improve our cache architecture would be to add an in memory cache for some of the most used cached data.

This work represents a step forward in experimental science like biology, where scientists extend existing workflows with new methods or new parameters to test their hypotheses on datasets that have been previously analyzed.

Acknowledgments. This work was supported by the #DigitAg French Convergence Lab. on Digital Agriculture (http://www.hdigitag.fr/com), the SciDISC Inria associated team with Brazil, the Phenome-Emphasis project (ANR-11-INBS-0012) and IFB (ANR-11-INBS-0013) from the Agence Nationale de la Recherche and the France Grille Scientific Interest Group.

References

1. Abramova, V., Bernardino, J., Furtado, P.: Testing cloud benchmark scalability with cassandra. In: 2014 IEEE World Congress on Services, pp. 434–441. IEEE (2014)
2. Adams, I.F., Long, D.D., Miller, E.L., Pasupathy, S., Storer, M.W.: Maximizing efficiency by trading storage for computation. In: HotCloud (2009)
3. Altintas, I., Barney, O., Jaeger-Frank, E.: Provenance collection support in the Kepler scientific workflow system. In: Moreau, L., Foster, I. (eds.) IPAW 2006. LNCS, vol. 4145, pp. 118–132. Springer, Heidelberg (2006). https://doi.org/10.1007/11890850_14
4. Artzet, S., Brichet, N., Chopard, J., Mielewczik, M., Fournier, C., Pradal, C.: Openalea. Phenomenal: a workflow for plant phenotyping, September 2018
5. Brichet, N., et al.: A robot-assisted imaging pipeline for tracking the growths of maize ear and silks in a high-throughput phenotyping platform. Plant Methods **13**(1), 96 (2017)
6. Cabrera-Bosquet, L., Fournier, C., Brichet, N., Welcker, C., Suard, B., Tardieu, F.: High-throughput estimation of incident light, light interception and radiation-use efficiency of thousands of plants in a phenotyping platform. New Phytol. **212**(1), 269–281 (2016)
7. Callahan, S.P., Freire, J., Santos, E., Scheidegger, C.E., Silva, C.T., Vo, H.T.: VisTrails: visualization meets data management. In: ACM SIGMOD International Conference on Management of Data (SIGMOD), pp. 745–747 (2006)

8. Chen, T.W., et al.: Genetic and environmental dissection of biomass accumulation in multi-genotype maize canopies. J. Exp. Bot. (2018)

9. Chen, W., Altintas, I., Wang, J., Li, J.: Enhancing smart re-run of Kepler scientific workflows based on near optimum provenance caching in cloud. In: IEEE World Congress on Services (SERVICES), pp. 378–384 (2014)

10. Cohen-Boulakia, S., et al.: Scientific workflows for computational reproducibility in the life sciences: status, challenges and opportunities. Future Gener. Comput. Syst. (FGCS) **75**, 284–298 (2017)

11. Deelman, E., Singh, G., Livny, M., Berriman, B., Good, J.: The cost of doing science on the cloud: the montage example. In: International Conference for High Performance Computing, Networking, Storage and Analysis, pp. 1–12 (2008)

12. Dey, S.C., Belhajjame, K., Koop, D., Song, T., Missier, P., Ludäscher, B.: Up & down: improving provenance precision by combining workflow-and trace-level information. In: USENIX Workshop on the Theory and Practice of Provenance (TAPP) (2014)

13. Elghandour, I., Aboulnaga, A.: ReStore: reusing results of MapReduce jobs. Proc. VLDB Endow. **5**(6), 586–597 (2012)

14. Garijo, D., Alper, P., Belhajjame, K., Corcho, O., Gil, Y., Goble, C.: Common motifs in scientific workflows: an empirical analysis. Future Gener. Comput. Syst. (FGCS) **36**, 338–351 (2014)

15. Gottin, V.M., et al.: Automatic caching decision for scientific dataflow execution in apache spark. In: Proceedings of the 5th ACM SIGMOD Workshop on Algorithms and Systems for MapReduce and Beyond, p. 2. ACM (2018)

16. Heidsieck, G., de Oliveira, D., Pacitti, E., Pradal, C., Tardieu, F., Valduriez, P.: Adaptive caching for data-intensive scientific workflows in the cloud. In: Hartmann, S., Küng, J., Chakravarthy, S., Anderst-Kotsis, G., Tjoa, A.M., Khalil, I. (eds.) DEXA 2019. LNCS, vol. 11707, pp. 452–466. Springer, Cham (2019). https://doi.org/10.1007/978-3-030-27618-8_33

17. Juve, G., Deelman, E.: Scientific workflows in the cloud. In: Cafaro, M., Aloisio, G. (eds.) Grids, Clouds and Virtualization. Computer Communications and Networks, pp. 71–91. Springer, London (2011). https://doi.org/10.1007/978-0-85729-049-6_4

18. Kelling, S., et al.: Data-intensive science: a new paradigm for biodiversity studies. Bioscience **59**(7), 613–620 (2009)

19. Koop, D., Santos, E., Bauer, B., Troyer, M., Freire, J., Silva, C.T.: Bridging workflow and data provenance using strong links. In: Gertz, M., Ludäscher, B. (eds.) SSDBM 2010. LNCS, vol. 6187, pp. 397–415. Springer, Heidelberg (2010). https://doi.org/10.1007/978-3-642-13818-8_28

20. Liu, J., et al.: Efficient scheduling of scientific workflows using hot metadata in a multisite cloud. IEEE Trans. Knowl. Data Eng., 1–20 (2018)

21. Liu, J., Pacitti, E., Valduriez, P., Mattoso, M.: A survey of data-intensive scientific workflow management. J. Grid Comput. **13**(4), 457–493 (2015). https://doi.org/10.1007/s10723-015-9329-8

22. Ogasawara, E., Dias, J., Oliveira, D., Porto, F., Valduriez, P., Mattoso, M.: An algebraic approach for data-centric scientific workflows. Proc. VLDB Endow. (PVLDB) **4**(12), 1328–1339 (2011)

23. de Oliveira, D., Baião, F.A., Mattoso, M.: Towards a taxonomy for cloud computing from an e-science perspective. In: Antonopoulos, N., Gillam, L. (eds.) Cloud Computing. Computer Communications and Networks, pp. 47–62. Springer, London (2010). https://doi.org/10.1007/978-1-84996-241-4_3

24. Olston, C., Reed, B., Silberstein, A., Srivastava, U.: Automatic optimization of parallel dataflow programs. In: USENIX Annual Technical Conference, pp. 267–273 (2008)

25. Özsu, M.T., Valduriez, P.: Principles of Distributed Database Systems, 3rd edn. Springer, New York (2011). https://doi.org/10.1007/978-1-4419-8834-8

26. Perez, R.P., et al.: Changes in the vertical distribution of leaf area enhanced light interception efficiency in maize over generations of maize selection. Plant Cell Environ. **42**, 2105–2119 (2019)

27. Pradal, C., et al.: InfraPhenoGrid: a scientific workflow infrastructure for plant phenomics on the grid. Future Gener. Comput. Syst. (FGCS) **67**, 341–353 (2017)

28. Pradal, C., Cohen-Boulakia, S., Heidsieck, G., Pacitti, E., Tardieu, F., Valduriez, P.: Distributed management of scientific workflows for high-throughput plant phenotyping. ERCIM News **113**, 36–37 (2018)

29. Pradal, C., Dufour-Kowalski, S., Boudon, F., Fournier, C., Godin, C.: OpenAlea: a visual programming and component-based software platform for plant modelling. Funct. Plant Biol. **35**(10), 751–760 (2008)

30. Pradal, C., Fournier, C., Valduriez, P., Cohen-Boulakia, S.: OpenAlea: scientific workflows combining data analysis and simulation. In: International Conference on Scientific and Statistical Database Management (SSDBM), p. 11 (2015)

31. Rajasekar, A., et al.: iRODS primer: integrated rule-oriented data system. Synth. Lect. Inf. Concepts Retrieval Serv. **2**(1), 1–143 (2010)

32. Roitsch, T., et al.: Review: new sensors and data-driven approaches-a path to next generation phenomics. Plant Sci. **282**, 2–10 (2019)

33. Tardieu, F., Cabrera-Bosquet, L., Pridmore, T., Bennett, M.: Plant phenomics, from sensors to knowledge. Curr. Biol. **27**(15), R770–R783 (2017)

34. Yuan, D., Yang, Y., Liu, X., Chen, J.: A cost-effective strategy for intermediate data storage in scientific cloud workflow systems. In: IEEE International Symposium on Parallel & Distributed Processing (IPDPS), pp. 1–12 (2010)

35. Yuan, D., et al.: A highly practical approach toward achieving minimum data sets storage cost in the cloud. IEEE Trans. Parallel Distrib. Syst. **24**(6), 1234–1244 (2013)

36. Zhang, J., et al.: Bridging vistrails scientific workflow management system to high performance computing. In: 2013 IEEE Ninth World Congress on Services, pp. 29–36. IEEE (2013)

37. Zhang, S., Han, J., Liu, Z., Wang, K., Feng, S.: Accelerating MapReduce with distributed memory cache. In: 2009 15th International Conference on Parallel and Distributed Systems, pp. 472–478. IEEE (2009)

From Task Tuning to Task Assignment in Privacy-Preserving Crowdsourcing Platforms

Joris Duguépéroux$^{(\boxtimes)}$ ⓘ and Tristan Allard ⓘ

Univ Rennes, CNRS, IRISA, Rennes, France
{joris.dugueperoux,tristan.allard}@irisa.fr

Abstract. Specialized worker profiles of crowdsourcing platforms may contain a large amount of identifying and possibly sensitive personal information (*e.g.,* personal preferences, skills, available slots, available devices) raising strong privacy concerns. This led to the design of privacy-preserving crowdsourcing platforms, that aim at enabling efficient crowdsourcing processes while providing strong privacy guarantees even when the platform is not fully trusted. In this paper, we propose two contributions. First, we propose the PKD algorithm with the goal of supporting a large variety of aggregate usages of worker profiles within a privacy-preserving crowdsourcing platform. The PKD algorithm combines together homomorphic encryption and differential privacy for computing (perturbed) partitions of the multi-dimensional space of skills of the actual population of workers and a (perturbed) COUNT of workers per partition. Second, we propose to benefit from recent progresses in Private Information Retrieval techniques in order to design a solution to task assignment that is both private and affordable. We perform an in-depth study of the problem of using PIR techniques for proposing tasks to workers, show that it is NP-Hard, and come up with the PKD PIR Packing heuristic that groups tasks together according to the partitioning output by the PKD algorithm. In a nutshell, we design the PKD algorithm and the PKD PIR Packing heuristic, we prove formally their security against *honest-but-curious* workers and/or platform, we analyze their complexities, and we demonstrate their quality and affordability in real-life scenarios through an extensive experimental evaluation performed over both synthetic and realistic datasets.

1 Introduction

Crowdsourcing platforms are online intermediates between *requesters* and *workers*. The former have *tasks* to propose to the latter, while the latter have *profiles* (*e.g.,* skills, devices, experience, availabilities) to propose to the former. Crowdsourcing platforms have grown in diversity, covering application domains ranging

ⓒ Springer-Verlag GmbH Germany, part of Springer Nature 2020
A. Hameurlain et al. (Eds.) TLDKS XLIV, LNCS 12380, pp. 67–107, 2020.
https://doi.org/10.1007/978-3-662-62271-1_3

from micro-tasks[1] or home-cleaning[2] to collaborative engineering[3] or specialized software team design[4].

The efficiency of crowdsourcing platforms especially relies on the wealth of information available in the profiles of registered workers. Depending on the platform, a profile may indeed contain an arbitrary amount of information: professional or personal skills, daily availabilities, minimum wages, diplomas, professional experiences, centers of interest and personal preferences, devices owned and available, *etc.* This holds especially for platforms dedicated to specialized tasks that require strongly qualified workers[5]. But even micro-tasks platforms may maintain detailed worker profiles (see, *e.g.,* the *qualification* system of *Amazon Mechanical Turk* that maintains so-called *premium qualifications*[6] - *e.g.,* sociodemographic information such as *age range, gender, employment, marital status, etc.* - in the profiles of workers willing to participate to surveys). The availability of such detailed worker profiles is of utmost importance to both requesters and platforms because it enables:

Primary usages of worker profiles: to target the specific set of workers relevant for a given task (through *e.g.,* elaborate task assignment algorithms [30]).
Secondary usages of worker profiles: to describe the population of workers available, often through COUNT aggregates, in order *e.g.,* to promote the platform by ensuring requesters that workers relevant for their tasks are registered on the platform[7], or to participate to the task design by letting requesters fine-tune the tasks according to the actual population of workers (*e.g.,* setting wages according to the rarity of the skills required, adapting slightly the requirements according to the skills available).

Both primary and secondary usages are complementary and usually supported by today's crowdsourcing platforms, in particular by platforms dedicated to highly skilled tasks and workers[8].

However, the downside of fine-grained worker profiles is that detailed information related to personal skills can be highly identifying (*e.g.,* typically a unique combination of location/skills/centers of interest) or sensitive (*e.g.,* costly devices

---

[1] https://www.mturk.com/.
[2] https://www.handy.com/.
[3] https://www.kicklox.com/.
[4] https://tara.ai/.
[5] We adopt in this paper a broad definition of *crowdsourcing*, including in particular freelancing platforms (similarly to [29]).
[6] https://requester.mturk.com/pricing.
[7] See for example the Kicklox search form (https://www.kicklox.com/en/) that inputs a list of keywords (typically skills) and displays the corresponding number of workers available.
[8] See for example, Kicklox (https://www.kicklox.com/en/) or Tara (https://tara.ai/). The secondary usage consisting in promoting the platform is sometimes performed through a public access to detailed parts of worker profiles (*e.g.,* Malt (https://www.malt.com/), 404works (https://www.404works.com/en/freelancers)).

or high minimum wages may correspond to a wealthy individual, various personal traits may be inferred from centers of interest[9]). Recent privacy scandals have shown that crowdsourcing platforms are not immune to negligences or misbehaviours. Well-known examples include cases where personally identifiable information of workers is trivially exposed online [27] or where precise geolocations are illegitimately accessed[10,11]. It is noticeable that workers nevertheless expect platforms to secure their data and to protect their privacy in order to lower the privacy threats they face [40]. Moreover, in a legal context where laws firmly require businesses and public organizations to safeguard the privacy of individuals (such as the European GDPR[12] or the California Consumer Privacy Act[13]), legal compliance is also a strong incentive for platforms for designing and implementing sound privacy-preserving crowdsourcing processes. Ethics in general, and privacy in particular, are indeed clearly identified as key issues for next generation *future of work* platforms [15]. Most related privacy-preserving works have focused on the primary usage of worker profiles, such as the task-assignment problem (*e.g.*, based on additively-homomorphic encryption [21] or on local differential privacy [5][14]).

Our goal in this paper is twofold: (1) *consider both primary and secondary usages as first-class citizens* by proposing a privacy-preserving solution for computing multi-dimensional COUNTs over worker profiles and a task assignment algorithm based on recent affordable Private Information Retrieval (PIR) techniques, and (2) *integrate well with other privacy-preserving algorithms possibly executed by a platform* without jeopardizing the privacy guarantees by requiring our privacy model to be composable both with usual computational cryptographic guarantees provided by real-life encryption schemes and with classical differential privacy guarantees as well.

The two problems are not trivial. First, we focus on secondary usages. The problem of computing multi-dimensional COUNTs over distributed worker profiles in a privacy-preserving manner is not trivial. Interactive approaches - that issue a privacy-preserving COUNT query over the set of workers each time needed (*e.g.*, a requester estimates the number of workers qualified for a given task) - are inadequate because the number of queries would be unbounded. This would

---

[9] See, *e.g.*, http://applymagicsauce.com/about-us.

[10] For example, internal emails that were leaked from Deliveroo indicate that the geolocation system of Deliveroo was used internally for identifying the riders that participated to strikes against the platform. https://www.lemonde.fr/culture/article/2019/09/24/television-cash-investigation-a-la-rencontre-des-nouveaux-proletaires-du-web_6012758_3246.html.

[11] In another example, an Uber executive claimed having tracked a journalist using the company geolocation system. https://tinyurl.com/y4cdvw45.

[12] https://eur-lex.europa.eu/eli/reg/2016/679/oj.

[13] https://www.caprivacy.org/.

[14] Note that limiting the information disclosed to the platform (*e.g.*, perturbed information about worker profiles) relieves platforms from the costly task of handling personal data. The European GDPR indeed explicitly excludes anonymized data from its scope (see Article 4, Recital 26 https://gdpr-info.eu/recitals/no-26/).

lead to out-of-control information disclosure through the sequence of COUNTs computed [8,11]. Non-interactive approaches are a promising avenue because they compute, once for all and in a privacy-preserving manner, the static data structure(s) which are then exported and queried by the untrusted parties (*e.g.,* platform, requesters) without any limit on the number of queries. More precisely, on the one hand, hierarchies of histograms are well-known data structures that support COUNT queries and that cope well with the stringent privacy guarantees of differential privacy [34]. However, they do not cope well with more than a few dimensions [34], whereas a worker profile may contain more skills (*e.g.,* a dozen), and they require a trusted centralized platform. On the other hand, privacy-preserving spatial decompositions [9,42] are more tolerant to a higher number of dimensions but require as well a trusted centralized platform. Second, algorithms for assigning tasks to workers while providing sound privacy guarantees have been proposed as alternatives against naive *spamming approaches* - where all tasks are sent to all workers. However they are either based (1) on perturbation only (e.g., [5]) and suffer from a severe drop in quality or (2) on encryption only (e.g., [21]) but they do not reach realistic performances, or (3) they focus on the specific context of spatial crowdsourcing and geolocation data (e.g., [39]).

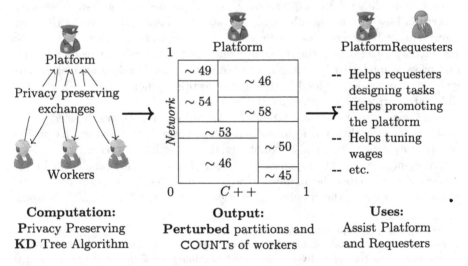

Fig. 1. Overview of the PKD algorithm: supporting secondary usages of worker profiles with privacy guarantees

Our Contribution. First, we propose to benefit from the best of the two non-interactive approaches described above by computing a privacy-preserving space partitioning of the worker profiles (for coping with their dimensionality) based on perturbed 1-dimensional histograms (for their nice tolerance to differentially private perturbations). We propose the Privacy-preserving KD-Tree algorithm

(PKD for short, depicted in Fig. 1), a privacy-preserving algorithm for computing a (perturbed) multi-dimensional distribution of skills of the actual population of workers. The PKD algorithm is distributed between mutually distrustful workers and an untrusted platform. It consists in splitting recursively the space of skills in two around the median (similarly to the *KD-tree* construction algorithm) based on the 1-dimensional histogram of the dimension being split, and it protects workers' profiles all along the computation by combining additively-homomorphic encryption together with differentially private perturbation. No raw worker profile is ever communicated, neither to the platform nor to other workers. The output of the PKD algorithm is a hierarchical partitioning of the space of skills together with the (perturbed) COUNT of workers per partition (see Fig. 1). The PKD algorithm is complementary to privacy-preserving task assignment works and can be used in conjunction with them provided that the privacy models compose well. In particular, since our privacy model is a computational variant of differential privacy, the PKD algorithm composes well with state-of-the-art approaches [5,21] since they are based on usual computational cryptographic model or differential privacy model. Second, we propose to benefit from recent progresses in Private Information Retrieval techniques [2] in order to design a solution to task assignment that is both private and affordable. We perform an in-depth study of the problem of using PIR techniques for proposing tasks to workers, show that it is NP-Hard, and come up with the PKD PIR Packing heuristic that groups tasks together according to the partitioning output by the PKD algorithm. Obviously, the PKD PIR Packing heuristic composes well with the PKD algorithm.

More precisely, we make the following contributions:

1. We design the PKD algorithm, a distributed privacy-preserving algorithm for computing a multi-dimensional hierarchical partitioning of the space of skills within a population of workers.
2. We formally prove the security of the PKD algorithm against *honest-but-curious* attackers. The PKD algorithm is shown to satisfy a computational variant of differential privacy called the ϵ_κ-SIM-CDP model. We provide a theoretical analysis of its complexity.
3. We provide an in-depth study of the problem of using PIR techniques for proposing tasks to workers and design the PKD PIR Packing heuristic that benefits from the partitioning computed by the PKD algorithm for grouping tasks together. We show that the PKD PIR Packing heuristic satisfies our privacy model.
4. We provide an extensive experimental evaluation of the PKD algorithm and of the PKD PIR Packing heuristic over synthetic and realistic data that demonstrates their quality and performance in various scenarios. Our realistic skills dataset is built from data dumps of *StackExchange* online forums.

The paper is organized as follows. Section 2 introduces the participant model, the security and privacy models, and the technical tools necessary in the rest of the paper. Section 3 describes the PKD algorithm in details and formally analyzes its cost and security. Section 4 studies the problem of using PIR techniques for

task assignment, describes the PKD PIR Packing heuristic, and formally ana-
lyzes its security. Section 5 experimentally validates their quality and efficiency.
We discuss updates in the contexts of the PKD algorithm and of the PKD PIR
Packing heuristic in Sect. 6. In Sect. 7, we survey the related work. Finally,
Sect. 8 concludes and discusses interesting future works.

2   Preliminaries

2.1   Participants Model

Three types of participants collaborate together during our crowdsourcing process. *Workers* are interested in solving tasks that are relevant to their profiles;
requesters propose tasks to be solved by relevant workers; and the *platform* is
an intermediary between them.

A worker profile $p_i \in \mathcal{P}$ is represented by an n-dimensional vector of floats,
where each float value $p_i[j] \in [0,1]$ represents the degree of competency of the
worker i with respect to the jth skill. The set of skills available and their indexes
within workers' profiles is static and identical for all profiles.

A task $t_k \in \mathcal{T}$ is made of two parts. First, the *metadata* part is a precise description of the worker profiles that are needed for the task completion.
More precisely it is an n-dimensional subspace of the space of skills. This work
does not put any constraint on the kind of subspace described in the metadata part (*e.g.*, hyper-rectangles, hyper-spheres, arbitrary set operators between
subspaces). However, for the sake of concreteness, we focus below on metadata
expressed as hyper-rectangles. More formally, the metadata $m_k \in \mathcal{M}$ of a task
$t_k \in \mathcal{T}$ is an n-dimensional vector of ranges over skills where the logical connec-
tor between any pair of ranges is the conjunction. We call $m_k[j]$ the range of
float values (between 0 and 1) for task k and skill j. The second part of a task
consists in the necessary information for performing the task and is represented
as an arbitrary bitstring $\{0,1\}^*$. In this work, we essentially focus on the metadata part of tasks. We say that a worker and a task match if the point described
by the worker profile belongs to the subspace described by the task metadata,
i.e., worker p_i and task t_k match if and only if $\forall j \in [0, n-1]$, then $p_i[j] \in m_k[j]$.

We do not make strong assumptions on the resources offered by participants. Workers, requesters, and the platform are equipped with today's commodity hardware (*e.g.*, the typical CPU/bandwidth/storage resources of a personal
computer). However, we expect the platform to be available 24/7 - contrary to
workers or requesters - similarly to a traditional client/server setting.

We assume that all participants follow the *honest-but-curious* attack model
in that they do not deviate from the protocol but make use of the information disclosed, in any computationally-feasible way, for inferring personal data.
Workers may collude together up to a reasonable bound denoted by τ in the
following.

2.2   Privacy Tools

Computational Differential Privacy. Our proposal builds on two families of protection mechanisms: a *differentially private* perturbation scheme and a *semantically secure* encryption scheme. The resulting overall privacy model thus integrates the two families of guarantees together. The original ϵ-differential privacy model [12] (Definition 1) applies to a randomized function $\mathtt{f}$ and aims at hiding the impact of any possible individual value on the possible outputs of $\mathtt{f}$. In our context, the function $\mathtt{f}$ is the PKD algorithm. The ϵ-differential privacy model requires that the probability that any worker profile $p_i \in \mathcal{P}$ participates to the computation of $\mathtt{f}$ be close to the probability that p_i does not participate by an e^ϵ factor, whatever the output of $\mathtt{f}$. ϵ-differential privacy holds against information-theoretic adversaries (unlimited computational power).

Definition 1 (ϵ-differential privacy [12]). *The randomized function $\mathtt{f}$ satisfies ϵ-differential privacy, where $\epsilon > 0$, if:*

$$\Pr[\mathtt{f}(\mathcal{P}_1) = \mathcal{O}] \leq e^\epsilon \cdot \Pr[\mathtt{f}(\mathcal{P}_2) = \mathcal{O}]$$

for any set $\mathcal{O} \in Range(\mathtt{f})$ and any set of worker profiles $\mathcal{P}_1$ and $\mathcal{P}_2$ that differ in at most one profile.

The ϵ_κ-SIM-CDP differential privacy relaxation [31] requires that the function actually computed be *computationally indistinguishable* from a pure (information theoretic) ϵ-differentially private function to adversaries whose size is polynomial in the security parameter $\kappa \in \mathbb{N}$. The ϵ_κ-SIM-CDP model is especially relevant in our context because we combine a differentially private perturbation scheme (information theoretic guarantees) together with an additively-homomorphic encryption scheme that provides computational security guarantees for performance reasons.

Definition 2 (ϵ_κ-SIM-CDP privacy [31] (simplified)). *The randomized function $\mathtt{f}_\kappa$ provides ϵ_κ-SIM-CDP if there exists a function $\mathtt{F}_\kappa$ that satisfies ϵ-differential privacy and a negligible function $negl(\cdot)$, such that for every set of worker profiles $\mathcal{P}$, every probabilistic polynomial time adversary $\mathtt{A}_\kappa$, every auxiliary background knowledge $\zeta_\kappa \in \{0,1\}^*$, it holds that:*

$$|\Pr[\mathtt{A}_k(\mathtt{f}_\kappa(\mathcal{P}, \zeta_\kappa)) = 1] - \Pr[\mathtt{A}_k(\mathtt{F}_\kappa(\mathcal{P}, \zeta_\kappa)) = 1]| \leq negl(\kappa)$$

Achieving Differential Privacy with the Geometric Mechanism. A common mechanism for satisfying ϵ-differential privacy with functions that output floats or integers consists in adding random noise to their outputs. In particular, the Geometric Mechanism (Definition 3) allows functions that output integers to be perturbed and to satisfy ϵ-differential privacy, while maximizing utility for count queries as shown in [16].

Definition 3 (Geometric mechanism [16]). *Let $\mathcal{G}$ denote a random variable following a two-sided geometric distribution, meaning that its probability density* function is $g(z,\alpha) = \frac{1-\alpha}{1+\alpha}\alpha^{|z|}$ for $z \in \mathbb{Z}$. Given any function $\mathbf{f} : \mathbb{N}^{|\mathcal{X}|} \to \mathbb{Z}^k$ the Geometric Mechanism is defined as $M_G(x, f(.), \alpha) = \mathbf{f}(x) + (Y_1, \ldots, Y_k)$ where Y_i are independent identically distributed random variables drawn from $\mathcal{G}(e^{-\epsilon/\Delta\mathbf{f}})$, and $\Delta\mathbf{f}$ is its global sensivity $\Delta\mathbf{f} = \max_{\mathcal{P}_1,\mathcal{P}_2} ||\mathbf{f}(\mathcal{P}_1) - \mathbf{f}(\mathcal{P}_2)||_1$ for all $(\mathcal{P}_1, \mathcal{P}_2)$ pairs of sets of worker profiles s.t. $\mathcal{P}_2$ is $\mathcal{P}_1$ with one profile more.

Intuitively, a distribution is said to be infinitely divisible if it can be decomposed as a sum of an arbitrary number of independent identically distributed random variables. This property allows to distribute the generation of the noise over a set of participants. It is valuable in contexts such as ours where no single trusted party, in charge of generating the noise, exists. Definition 4 below formalizes the infinite divisibility property, and Theorem 1 shows that the two-sided geometric distribution is infinitely divisible.

Definition 4 (Infinite Divisibility [36]). *A random variable Y is infinitely divisible if for every $n \in \mathbb{N}$ there exist independent identically distributed random variables $X_{1,1}, \ldots X_{1,n}$ such that*

$$Y = \sum_{i=1}^{n} X_{i,n}$$

Theorem 1 (Two-sided Geometric Distribution is Infinitely Divisible). *Let Y follow two-sided geometric distribution of probability density function $d(z, \epsilon) = \frac{1-\epsilon}{1+\epsilon}\epsilon^{|z|}$ for any integer z. Then the distribution of Y is infinitely divisible. Furthermore, for every integer $n \geq 1$, the representation of Definition 4 holds. Each $X_{i,n}$ is distributed as $X_n^1 - X_n^2$ where X_n^1 and X_n^2 are independent identically distributed random variable with negative binomial distribution, with probability density function $g(k, n, \alpha) = \binom{k-1+1/n}{k}(1-\alpha)^k\alpha^{1/n}$.*

To prove this result, we will use a similar result for the geometric distribution.

Theorem 2 (Geometric Distribution is Infinitely Divisible [37]). *Let Y follow a geometric distribution of probability density function $f(k, \alpha) = (1-\alpha)\alpha^k$ for $k \in \mathbb{N}$. Then the distribution of Y is infinitely divisible. Furthermore, for every integer $n \geq 1$, the representation of Definition 4 holds. Each $X_{i,n}$ is distributed as X_n where X_n are independent identically distributed random variable with negative binomial distribution, with probability density function $g(k, n, \alpha) = \binom{k-1+1/n}{k}(1-\alpha)^k\alpha^{1/n}$.*

Proof. Using this theorem, proving that a two-sided geometric distribution with density function $d(z, \alpha) = \frac{1-\alpha}{1+\alpha}\alpha^{|z|}$ is equal to the difference between two independent identically distributed geometric distributions with density function $f(k, \alpha) = (1-\alpha)\alpha^k$ is enough to deduce the result. Let X_+ and X_- be two such random variables.

$$P(X_+ - X_- = z) = \begin{cases} \text{if } z \geq 0 \\ \sum_{j=0}^{\infty}((1-\alpha)\alpha^{z+j})((1-\alpha)\alpha^j) \\ \text{if } z < 0 \\ \sum_{j=0}^{\infty}((1-\alpha)\alpha^j)((1-\alpha)\alpha^{-z+j}) \end{cases}$$

$$P(X_+ - X_- = z) = \sum_{j=0}^{\infty}(1-\alpha)^2\alpha^{|z|+2j}$$
$$= (1-\alpha)^2\alpha^{|z|}\sum_{j=0}^{\infty}(\alpha^2)^j$$
$$= (1-\alpha)^2\alpha^{|z|}\frac{1}{1-\alpha^2}$$
$$= \frac{(1-\alpha)^2}{(1-\alpha)(1+\alpha)}\alpha^{|z|}$$
$$= \frac{1-\alpha}{1+\alpha}\alpha^{|z|}$$
$$= P(Y = z)$$

for Y a random variable with a two-sided geometric distribution with parameter α.

Finally, Theorem 3 states that differential privacy composes with itself gracefuly.

Theorem 3 (Sequential and Parallel Composability [13]). *Let f_i be a set of functions such that each provides ϵ_i-differential privacy. First, the* sequential composability *property of differential privacy states that computing all functions on the same dataset results in satisfying $(\sum_i \epsilon_i)$-differential privacy. Second, the* parallel composability *property states that computing each function on disjoint subsets provides $\max(\epsilon_i)$-differential privacy.*

Additively-Homomorphic Encryption. Additively-homomorphic encryption schemes essentially allow to perform addition operations over encrypted data. Any additively-homomorphic encryption scheme fits our approach provided that it satisfies the following properties. First, it must provide *semantic security guarantees*. Stated informally, this property requires that given a ciphertext, the public encryption key, and possible auxiliary information about the plaintext, then no polynomial-time algorithm is able to gain non-negligible knowledge on the plaintext [17]. Second, it must be *additively-homomorphic*. Informally, given a and b two integers, $\mathtt{E}$ the encryption function, X the encryption key, K the decryption key, $\mathtt{D}$ the decryption function, and $+_h$ the homomorphic addition operator, then $\mathtt{D}_K(\mathtt{E}_X(a) +_h \mathtt{E}_X(b)) == a + b$. Third, the scheme must support *non-interactive threshold decryption*. We additionally use this optional property, available in some schemes (*e.g.,* [10,32]). It allows the decryption key to be *split* in n_K *key-shares* K_i such that a complete decryption requires to perform independently $T \leq n_K$ partial decryptions by distinct key-shares. Note that in a typical key generation setting, pairs of keys are generated once and for all by a non-colluding, independent entity. The Paillier cryptosystem [32] and its Damgard-Jurik generalization [10] are instances of encryption schemes that provide the desired properties and are widely available. We refer the interested reader to the original papers for details.

Private Information Retrieval. In a nutshell, Private Information Retrieval (PIR) techniques allow a client to download binary objects (*e.g.,* a record, a movie) stored on a server in a *library* of objects, without revealing to the server which of the binary objects has been downloaded. We call this function the `PIR-get` function. Emerging PIR protocols are now affordable and able to cope with the latency constraints of real-life scenarios (*e.g.,* in media consumption scenarios [2,7,18]). Our approach makes use of the security guarantees of PIR techniques. In this paper, for concreteness, we consider a PIR protocol based on additively-homomorphic encryption called *XPIR* [2]. It is part of the *computational PIR* family of protocols, that provides computational security guarantees. However our approach could use other protocols, that provide different efficiency/security tradeoffs (*e.g.,* an *information-theoretic PIR* protocol such as [7] that uses efficient bitwise XOR operators provides information-theoretic security but assumes no collusion between several supporting servers).

XPIR [2] considers a *library* $\mathcal{L}$ of n binary objects, called *items* in the following. All items are assumed to share the same length in bits, denoted l. The library is stored as a matrix of y-bit integers: $\mathcal{L} \in (\{0,1\}^y)^{n \times (l/y)}$. XPIR uses an additively-homomorphic cryptosystem (see above) and implements the PIR-get function as follows. XPIR assumes that each item has a unique id, and that clients know the list of ids of the existing items in $\mathcal{L}$. Now a client wants to retrieve the item of id i and thus calls PIR-get(i). First, it instanciates a vector of n bits, initializes all bits to 0s, sets to 1 the bit at id i, encrypts each bit separately, and sends the resulting encrypted vector - denoted c - to the server. Second, for all j in $[1, l/y]$, the server computes $r_j = \prod_{i=1}^{n} c[i]^{L_{i,j}}$ (recall that the product between two encrypted integers is the way the additively-homomorphic addition operator $+_h$ is performed by the underlying cryptosystem) and sends it back to the client. Each r_j is thus actually a sum of (1) encrypted 0s (corresponding to the encrypted 0s in c) and (2) an encrypted bit-subsequence of the requested binary object (corresponding to the encrypted 1 in c). Third and finally, the client decrypts each r_j received - obtaining hence the various bit-subsequences of the item requested - and concatenates them to obtain the complete bitstring.

Three main parameters may affect the efficiency of PIR protocols: the size of the library itself, that has to be read for each call to the PIR-get function, the size of items, that impacts the size of downloads (multiplied by an *expansion factor*, the ratio between the size of an encrypted value and the clear value), and the number of items (again, multiplied by the expansion factor), for the size of upload of the request.

2.3   Space Partitionning Based on KD-Trees

A KD-Tree [4] is a well-known data structure designed for partitioning datasets in k-dimensional balanced partitions. It is constructed by recursively dividing the space in two around the median. It is widely used to index data. Moreover, it contains valuable information about the data distribution (it is balanced) without sizing individual data points.

2.4   Quality Measure

We evaluate the quality of the (perturbed) output of the PKD algorithm by measuring the loss of accuracy resulting from its use rather than using non-protected raw profiles. As stated in Definition 5, given a set of tasks T, we compute the average absolute error between (1) the approximate number of workers matching with each task $t \in T$ according to the (perturbed) partitions and counts and (2) the exact non-protected number of matching workers. Note that the error comes from the perturbation used for satisfying differential privacy but also from the inherent approximation due to the use of a coarse grain data structure (partitions and counts) synthesizing raw data.

Definition 5 (Quality). *Given a set of worker profiles P, a set of tasks T, and, for each task $t \in T$, the real number of workers matching with it t_{match} and its approximated value $\widetilde{t_{match}}$ according to the perturbed distribution we provide. We compute the quality of the distribution as*

$$Q = \frac{1}{|T|} \sum_{t \in T} \frac{|t_{match} - \widetilde{t_{match}}|}{t_{match}}$$

We also measure the quality of our assignment by using *precision* (Definition 6), to size the number of tasks that are uselessly downloaded by workers. Note that in our context, all matching tasks will be downloaded, such that a *recall* measure is not relevant as it will always be equal to 1.

Definition 6 (Precision). *For a given assignment, we call precision the fraction of downloaded tasks that match with the worker. This precision is computed as:*

$$precision = \frac{1}{|T|} \sum_{t \in T} (\frac{|\{w : match(w,t) \wedge download(w,t)\}|}{|\{w : download(w,t)\}|})$$

where match(w, t) *(resp.* download(w, t)*) is* True *if worker w matches with (resp. dowloads) task t, and* False *otherwise.*

3   The PKD Algorithm

Our proposal comes from a rethinking of the centralized version of the *KD-Tree* construction algorithm [4], which is essentially a recursive computation of medians. In our setting, each worker holds its own, possibly sensitive, profile and no single centralized party is trusted. Centralizing the profiles of workers in order to compute a KD-Tree over them is therefore not possible. A naive approach could make use of an order-preserving encryption scheme [1] (OPE), but these schemes are well-known for their low security level [6] and especially their inherent weaknesses against frequency analysis attacks. We rather favor sound privacy guarantees - without sacrificing efficiency - by approaching the median through the computation of histograms, with a computation distributed between workers and the platform. Similarly to its centralized counterpart, each iteration of our recursive algorithm divides the space of skills in two around the median (of one dimension at a time) given a perturbed histogram representing the distribution of a single skill in the crowd. For simplicity, the current version of the algorithm terminates after a fixed number of splits, but more elaborate termination criteria can be defined.

3.1 Computing Private Medians

From Private Sum to Private Histogram. We start by explaining how to perform differentially private sums based on noise-shares and additively-homomorphic additions. It allows the platform to get the result of the addition of a single bin over n different workers while satisfying differential privacy. We then show that this function is a sufficient building block for computing perturbed histograms.

Let us consider a fixed $\epsilon > 0$, a maximum size of collusion $\tau \in \mathbb{N}, \tau > 0$, a set of workers $\mathcal{P}$ (of size $|\mathcal{P}|$), and a single bin b_i associated to a range ϕ. Each worker p_i holds a single private local value, *i.e.*, her skill on the dimension that is currently being split. Initially, the bin b_i is set to 0 on all workers. Only the workers whose local values fall within the range of the bin b_i set b_i to 1. Our first goal is to compute the sum of the bins b_i of all workers $p_i \in \mathcal{P}$ such that no set of participant smaller than τ can learn any information that has not been perturbed to satisfy ϵ-differential privacy.

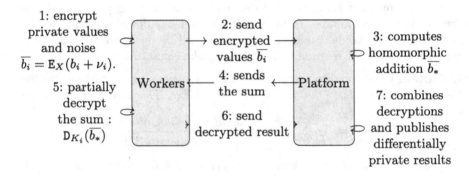

Fig. 2. Computing a private sum

The privacy-preserving sum algorithm, depicted in Fig. 2, considers that keys have been generated and distributed to workers, such that $T > \tau$ key-shares are required for decryption (see Sect. 2.2). The algorithm consists in the following steps:

Step 1 (each worker) - Perturbation and Encryption. First, each worker perturbs its value by adding a noise-share, denoted ν_i, to it. Noise-shares are randomly generated locally such that the sum of $|\mathcal{P}| - \tau$ shares satisfies the two-sided geometric distribution (see Definition 3 for the geometric distribution, and Theorem 1 for its infinite divisibility). Note that noise-shares are overestimated[15] to guarantee that the final result is differentially private even for a group of up to τ workers sharing their partial knowledge of the total noise (their local noise-share). Each worker then encrypts $b_i + \nu_i$ by the additively-homomorphic encryption scheme in order to obtain $\overline{b_i}$: $\overline{b_i} = \mathrm{E}_X(b_i + \nu_i)$.

---

[15] We require that the sum of $|\mathcal{P}| - \tau$ noise-shares be enough to satisfy differential privacy but we effectively sum $|\mathcal{P}|$ noise-shares. Note that summing more noise-shares than necessary does not jeopardize privacy guarantees.

Step 2 (platform) - Encrypted Sum. The platform sums up together the encrypted values received: $\overline{b}_* = \sum_{\forall i} \overline{b}_i$ where the sum is based on the additively-homomorphic addition $+_h$.

Step 3 (subset of workers) - Decryption. The platform finally sends the encrypted sum $\overline{b}_*$ to at least T distinct workers. Upon reception, each worker partially decrypts it based on her own key-share - $\mathrm{D}_{K_i}(\overline{b}_*)$ - and sends it back to the platform. The platform combines the partial decryptions together and obtains $\widetilde{b}_*$, *i.e.*, the differentially private sum of all private bins b_i.

Algorithm 1: `PrivMed` : Privacy-Preserving Estimation of the Median in the `PKD` algorithm

---

Data:
$\mathcal{P}$: Set of workers
$\mathcal{D}_{min}, \mathcal{D}_{max}$: Definition domain of the private local value of workers
l: Number of bins
$(\phi_0, \ldots, \phi_{l-1})$: the l ranges of the bins
X: public encryption key (same for all workers).
$\{K_i\}$: private decryption keys (one per worker).
ϵ_m: differential privacy budget for this iteration
τ: maximum size of a coalition ($\tau < |\mathcal{P}|$)
T: number of key-shares required for decryption ($T > \tau$)
Result: $\widetilde{m}$: estimate of the median of the workers' local private values

1 **for** *all workers $p_i \in \mathcal{P}$* **do**
2   Compute l noise shares $\nu_{i,j} = R_1 - R_2$, where $0 \le j < l$ and R_1 and R_2 are independent identically distributed random variables with probability density function $g(k) = \binom{k-1+\frac{1}{|\mathcal{P}|-\tau}}{k}(e^{-\epsilon_m})^k(1 - e^{-\epsilon_m})^{\frac{1}{|\mathcal{P}|-\tau}}$
3   Set the value of the bin $\overline{b}_{i,k} = \mathrm{E}_X(1 + \nu_{i,k})$, where ϕ_k is the histogram range within which the local value of the worker falls.
4   Set the value of the other bins to: $\overline{b}_{i,j} = \mathrm{E}_X(\nu_{i,j})$, $j \ne k$.
5 **Platform:** sum the encrypted bins at the same index received from different workers in order to obtain the encrypted perturbed histogram :
$(\overline{b}_{*,0} = \sum_{\forall i} \overline{b}_{i,0}, \ldots, \overline{b}_{*,l-1} = \sum_{\forall i} \overline{b}_{i,l-1})$.
6 **Workers (T distinct workers):** Decrypt partially the encrypted perturbed histogram bin per bin and send the resulting partially decrypted histogram to the platform: $(\mathrm{D}_{K_i}(\overline{b}_{*,0}), \ldots, \mathrm{D}_{K_i}(\overline{b}_{*,l-1}))$.
7 **Platform:** Combine the partial decryptions together to obtain the decryption of the histogram and estimate the median $\widetilde{m}$ according to Equation 1.
8 **return** $\widetilde{m}$

Now, assuming that the histogram format is fixed beforehand - *i.e.*, number l of bins and ranges $(\phi_0, \ldots, \phi_{l-1})$ - it is straightforward to apply the private sum algorithm on each bin for obtaining the perturbed histogram based on which the median can then be computed. For example, in order to get a histogram representing the distribution of skill values for, *e.g.*, `Python programming`, and assuming a basic histogram format - *e.g.*, skill values normalized in $[0, 1]$, $l = 10$ bins, ranges ($\phi_0 = [0, 0.1[, \ldots, \phi_9 = [0.9, 1])$ - it is sufficient to launch ten private sums to obtain the resulting perturbed 10-bins histogram.

PrivMed: *Privacy-Preserving Median Computation.* The histogram computed based on the privacy-preserving sum algorithm can be used by the platform to estimate the value of the median around which the split will be performed. When by chance the median falls precisely between two bins (*i.e.*, the sum of the bins on the left is exactly 50% of the total sum, same for the bins on the right) its value is exact. But when the median falls within the range of one bin (*i.e.*, in any other case), an additional hypothesis on the underlying data distribution within the bin must be done in order to be able to estimate the median. For simplicity, we will assume below that the distribution inside each bin is uniform but a more appropriate distribution can be used if known. The resulting `PrivMed` algorithm is detailed in Algorithm 1.

Let's consider the histogram obtained by the private sum algorithm. It is made of l bins denoted $(\widetilde{b_{*,0}}, \ldots, \widetilde{b_{*,l-1}})$, and each bin $\widetilde{b_{*,j}}$ is associated to a range ϕ_j. The ranges partition a totally ordered domain ranging from $\mathcal{D}_{min}$ to $\mathcal{D}_{max}$ (*e.g.*, from $\mathcal{D}_{min} = 0$ to $\mathcal{D}_{max} = 1$ on a normalized dimension that has not been split yet). Let ϕ_k denote the range containing the median, θ denote the sum of all the bins - *i.e.*, $\theta = \sum_{i<l} \widetilde{b_{*,i}}$ - and $\theta_<$ (resp. $\theta_>$) the sum of the bins that are strictly before (resp. after) $\widetilde{b_{*,k}}$ - *i.e.*, $\theta_< = \sum_{i<k} \widetilde{b_{*,i}}$ (resp. $\theta_> = \sum_{i>k} \widetilde{b_{*,i}}$). Then, an estimation $\widetilde{m}$ of the median can be computed as follows[16]:

$$\widetilde{m} = \mathcal{D}_{min} + \frac{\mathcal{D}_{max} - \mathcal{D}_{min}}{l} \cdot (k + \frac{1}{2} + \frac{\theta_> - \theta_<}{2 \cdot \widetilde{b_{*,k}}}) \tag{1}$$

3.2   Global Execution Sequence

Finally, the Privacy-preserving KD-Tree algorithm, `PKD` for short, performs the median estimation described above iteratively until it stops and outputs (1) a partitioning of the space of skills together with (2) the perturbed number of workers within each partition. The perturbed number of workers is computed by using an additional instantiation of the private sum algorithm when computing the private medians[17]. We focus below on the setting up of the parameters of the various iterations, and on the possible use of the resulting partitions and counts by the requesters. An overview is given in Algorithm 2.

Main Input Parameters. Intuitively, the privacy budget ϵ input of the `PKD` algorithm sets an upper bound on the information disclosed along the complete execution of the algorithm - it must be *shared* among the various data structures

---

[16] Note that in the specific case where the median falls within a bin equal to 0 (*i.e.*, $\widetilde{b_{*,k}} = 0$), then any value within ϕ_k is equivalent.

[17] Note that the perturbed histograms could have been used for computing these counts but using a dedicated count has been shown to result in an increased precision.

disclosed. Thus, each iteration inputs a portion of the initial privacy budget such that the sum of all portions remains lower than or equal to ϵ - see the composability property in Theorem 3. Computing a good budget al.location in a tree of histograms is a well-known problem tackled by several related works [9,33]. In this work, we simply rely on existing privacy budget distribution methods. For example, based on [9], ϵ is divided as follows. First, ϵ is divided in two parts: one part, denoted ϵ^m, is dedicated to the perturbations of the medians computations (*i.e.*, the bins of the histograms), and the other part, denoted ϵ^c, is dedicated to the perturbation of the number of workers inside each partition. Second, a portion of each of these parts is allocated to each iteration i as follows. For each iteration i such that $0 \leq i \leq h$, where h is the total number of iterations (*i.e.*, the height of the tree in the KD-Tree analogy), the first iteration is h (*i.e.*, the root of the tree) and the last one is 0 (*i.e.*, the leaves of the tree) :

$$\epsilon_i^c = 2^{(h-i)/3} \epsilon^c \frac{\sqrt[3]{2} - 1}{2^{(h+1)/3} - 1} \tag{2}$$

$$\epsilon_i^m = \frac{\epsilon^m}{h} \tag{3}$$

Note that similarly to [9], we set the distribution of ϵ between ϵ^c and ϵ^m as follows: $\epsilon^c = 0.7 \cdot \epsilon$ and $\epsilon^m = 0.3 \cdot \epsilon$. Other distributions could be used.

The PKD algorithm stops after a fixed number of iterations known beforehand. Note that more elaborate termination criteria can be defined (*e.g.*, a threshold on the volume of the subspace or on the count of worker profiles contained). The termination criteria must be chosen carefully because they limit the number of splits of the space of skills and consequently the number of dimensions of worker profiles that appear in the final subspaces. Ideally, the termination criteria should allow at least one split of all dimensions. However, this may not be possible or suitable in practice because of the limited privacy budget. In this case, similarly to a composite index, a sequence of priority dimensions must be chosen so that the algorithm splits them following the order of the sequence. The dimensions that are not part of the sequence will simply be ignored. Note that the number of dimensions in worker profiles, and their respective priorities, is closely related to the application domain (*e.g.*, How specific does the crowdsourcing process need to be?). In this paper, we make no assumption on the relative importance of dimensions.

Post-processing the Output. Considering the successive splits of partitions, we can enhance the quality of the counts of workers by exploiting the natural constraints among the resulting tree of partitions: we know that the number of workers in a parent partition must be equal to the number of workers in the union of its children. *Constrained inference techniques* have already been studied as a post-processing step to improve the quality of trees of perturbed histograms, first in [20] and then improved in [9] which adapts the method to non-uniform distribution of budget. These constrained inference techniques can be used in our context in a straightforward manner in order to improve on the quality of the resulting partitioning. We refer the interested reader to [9,20] for details.

Algorithm 2: The PKD Algorithm

    Data:
    $\mathcal{P}$: Set of workers
    E the current space of skills of d dimensions
    h: height of the KD-Tree
    Result: T: A Privacy-preserving KD-tree with approximate counts of workers
                for each leaf

1   We create T as a single leaf, containing the whole space E and a count of all workers.

2   **while** *current height is smaller than final height* **do**

3   Choose a dimension d (for exemple, next dimension).

4   **for** *all leaves of the current tree T* **do**

5   Compute m the private median of the space of the leaf, as explained in Section 3.1.

6   For both subspaces separated by the median, compute a private count as explained in Section 3.1.

7   Create two leaves, containing the two subspaces and associated counts.

8   Replace the current leaf by a node, containing the current space and count, and linking to the two newly created leaves.

9   Increment the current height.

10   Apply post-processing techniques explained in Section 3.2.

11   **return** *Tree T*

3.3 Complexity Analysis

We evaluate here the complexity of the PKD algorithm with respect to the number of encrypted messages computed and sent both to and by the platform. The results are summed up in Table 1.

The first step to consider is the number of partitions created in the KD-tree. Seen as an index (with one leaf for each point), the construction of a KD-tree requires $2^{h+1} - 1$ nodes, including $2^h - 1$ internal nodes, where h is the maximum height of the KD-Tree. For each node, an encrypted sum is performed, and for each internal node, a histogram is additionally computed, which require l sums, for a total of $(2^{h+1} - 1) + (l \cdot (2^h - 1))$ sums. These counts all require the participation of every worker: for each count, $|\mathcal{P}|$ encrypted messages are computed and sent.

The platform also sends back encrypted messages for each sum, for decryptions to be performed. For each sum, it sends at least T times the homomorphically computed sum, where T is the threshold number of key-shares required for decryption. For simplicity, we assume that the platform sends the cyphertexts to T workers (these are the only encrypted messages that have to be sent to workers during this protocol). Each contacted worker then answers by an encrypted value (the partial decryption). As a conclusion, the total number of encrypted values sent by the workers to the platform $\mathcal{M}_{\Sigma w}$ is:

$$\mathcal{M}_{\Sigma w} = (|\mathcal{P}| + T) \cdot (l \cdot (2^h - 1) + (2^{h+1} - 1)) \tag{4}$$

However, as our computation is distributed among all workers, each worker only sends fewer encrypted messages on average $\overline{\mathcal{M}_w}$.

$$\overline{\mathcal{M}_w} = (1 + \frac{T}{|\mathcal{P}|}) \cdot (l \cdot (2^h - 1) + (2^{h+1} - 1)) \qquad (5)$$

Finally, the platform sends $\mathcal{M}_{pf}$ encrypted messages.

$$\mathcal{M}_{pf} = T \cdot (l \cdot (2^h - 1) + (2^{h+1} - 1)) \qquad (6)$$

Table 1. Number of encrypted messages sent. $\mathcal{P}$ is the set of workers, T the number of partial keys required for decryption, h the depth of the KD-tree, and l the number of bins per median

To the platform	$(\|\mathcal{P}\| + T) \cdot (l \cdot (2^h - 1) + (2^{h+1} - 1))$
By worker (avg)	$(1 + \frac{T}{\|\mathcal{P}\|}) \cdot (l \cdot (2^h - 1) + (2^{h+1} - 1))$
By the platform	$T \cdot (l \cdot (2^h - 1) + (2^{h+1} - 1))$

3.4 Security Analysis

The only part of the PKD algorithm that depends on raw data is the private sum. The security analysis thus focuses on proving that a single private sum is secure, and then uses the composability properties (see Theorem 3). Theorem 4 proves that the privacy-preserving sum algorithm is secure. We use this intermediate result in Theorem 5 to prove the security of the complete PKD algorithm.

Theorem 4 (Security of the privacy-preserving sum algorithm). *The privacy-preserving sum algorithm satisfies* ϵ_κ*-SIM-CDP privacy against coalitions of up to* τ *participants.*

Proof (sketch). First, any skill in a profile of a participating worker is first summed up locally with a noise-share, and then encrypted before being sent to the platform. We require the encryption scheme to satisfy semantic security, which means that no computationally-bounded adversary can gain significant knowledge about the data that is encrypted. In other words, the leak due to communicating an encrypted data is negligible. Second, the homomorphically-encrypted additions performed by the platform do not disclose any additional information. Third, the result of the encrypted addition is decrypted by combining $T > \tau$ partial decryptions, where each partial decryption is performed by a distinct worker. The threshold decryption property of the encryption scheme guarantees that no coalition of participants smaller than τ can decrypt an encrypted value, and the honest-but-curious behaviour of participants guarantees that no other result but the final one will be decrypted (*e.g.*, the platform does not ask for a decryption of a value that would not have been sufficiently perturbed). The final sum consists in the sum of all private values, to which are added $|\mathcal{P}|$ noise-shares. These shares are computed such that the addition of $|\mathcal{P}| - \tau$ shares is enough to satisfy ϵ-differential privacy. Thanks to the post-processing property of differential privacy, adding noise to a value generated by a differentially-private function does not impact the privacy level. The addition of τ additional noise-shares consequently allows to resist against coalitions of at most τ participants without thwarting privacy. As a result, since the privacy-preserving sum algorithm is the composition of a semantically secure encryption scheme with an ϵ-differentially private function, it is computationally indistinguishable from a pure differentially private function, and consequently satisfies ϵ_κ-SIM-CDP privacy against coalitions of up to τ participants.

Theorem 5 (Security of the PKD algorithm). *The PKD algorithm satisfies ϵ_κ-SIM-CDP privacy against coalitions of up to τ participants.*

Proof (sketch). In the PKD algorithm, any collected information is collected through the PrivMed algorithm based on the privacy-preserving sum algorithm. Since (1) the privacy-preserving sum algorithm satisfies ϵ_κ-SIM-CDP (see Theorem 4) against coalitions of up to τ participants, (2) ϵ_κ-SIM-CDP is composable (see Theorem 3), and (3) the privacy budget distribution is such that the total consumption does not exceed ϵ (see Sect. 3.2), it follows directly that the PKD algorithm satisfies ϵ_κ-SIM-CDP against coalitions of up to τ participants.

4   Privacy-Preserving Task Assignement

Once the design of a task is over, it must be assigned to relevant workers and delivered. Performing that while satisfying differential privacy and at the same time minimizing the number of downloads of the task's content is surprisingly challenging. We already discarded in Sect. 1, for efficiency reasons, the *spamming* approach in which each task is delivered to all workers. More elaborate approaches could try to let the platform filter out irrelevant workers based on the partitioned space output by the PKD algorithm (see the Sect. 3). The partitioned space would be used as an index over workers in addition to its primary task design usage. For example, workers could subscribe to their areas of interest (*e.g.,* by sending an email address to the platform together with the area of interest) and each task would be delivered to a small subset of workers only according to its metadata and to the workers' subscriptions. However, despite their appealing simplicity, these *platform-filtering* approaches disclose unperturbed information about the number of workers per area, which breaks differential privacy, and fixing the leak seems hard (*e.g.,* random additions/deletions of subscriptions, by distributed workers, such that differential privacy is satisfied and the overhead remains low).

We propose an alternative approach, based on Private Information Retrieval (PIR) techniques, to reduce the cost of download on the workers side, while preserving our privacy guarantees.

4.1   PIR for Crowdsourcing: Challenges and Naive Approaches

The main challenge in applying PIR in our context consists in designing a PIR-library such that no information is disclosed during the retrieval of information, and performance is affordable in real-life scenarios. To help apprehending these two issues, we present two naive methods that break these conditions and show two extreme uses of PIR: the first one is efficient but unsecure, the second one is secure but unefficient.

A first PIR-based approach could consist in performing straightforwardly a PIR protocol between the workers and the platform, while considering the PIR-library as the set of tasks itself. The platform maintains a key-value map that stores the complete set of tasks (the values, bitstrings required to perform the tasks) together with a unique identifier per task (the keys). The workers download the complete list of tasks identifiers and metadata, select locally the identifiers associated to the metadata that match with their profiles, and launch one PIR-get function on each of the selected identifiers. However, this naive approach leads to blatant security issues through the number of calls to the PIR-get function. Indeed, the platform could deduce the precise number of workers within a specific subspace of the space of skills: with the number of downloads per worker[18], it is possible to deduce, for each k, the number of workers downloading k tasks, which is the number of workers located in subspaces where k tasks intersect. This information, protected by the PKD algorithm, breaks differential privacy guarantees.

A secure but still naive approach could be to consider the power set of the set of tasks as the PIR-library, with padding to all tasks such that they are all the same size (in bits). A worker would choose the PIR-object corresponding to the set of tasks she intersects with, and would call PIR-get on it. Although this method prevents the previously observed breach (all behaviours are identical to the platform since each worker downloads exactly one PIR-object, and all PIR-objects are of the same size), this method would lead to extremely poor results: as every object of the library is padded to the biggest one, and the biggest set of the super set of tasks is the set of tasks itself, this algorithm is even worse than the spamming approach (everyone downloads at least as much as the sum of all tasks, with computation overheads).

These two naive uses of PIR illustrate two extreme cases: the first one shows that using PIR is not sufficient to ensure privacy, and the second one illustrates that a naive secure use can lead to higher computation costs than the spamming approach. In the following, we introduce a method to regroup tasks together, such that each worker downloads the same number of PIR items (to achieve security), while mitigating performance issues by making these groups of tasks as small as possible.

---

[18] Even if the identity of workers is not directly revealed, it is possible to match downloads together to break *unlinkability* and deduce that these downloads come from the same individual, for example by using the time of downloads, cookies or other identification techniques.

4.2   PIR Partitioned Packing

The security issue highlighted above comes from the fact that the number of downloads directly depends on the profiles of workers. In order to break this link, we propose to ensure that each worker downloads the same number of items, whatever their profile. For simplicity, we fix this number to 1^{19}, and call *packing* a PIR library that allows each worker to retrieve all their tasks with only one item, and *bucket* an item of such a library, as seen in Definition 7. We prove in Theorem 6 that any packing fulfills our security model.

We can now formalize the conditions that a PIR library must fulfill in order to both satisfy privacy and allow any worker to download all the tasks she matches with.

Definition 7 (Packing, Bucket).
A packing L is a PIR library which fulfills the following conditions:

1. **Security condition.** *Each worker downloads the same number of buckets. This number is set to 1.*
2. **PIR requirement.** *Each PIR item has the same size in bits (padding is allowed):*
$$\forall b_1, b_2 \in L, ||b_1|| = ||b_2||$$
   This condition comes from the use of PIR.
3. **Availability condition.** *For all points in the space of skills, there has to be at least one item containing all tasks matching with this point. In other words, no matter their skills (position in the space), each worker can find a bucket that provides every task they match with.*

A **bucket** $b \in L$ *is an item of a packing. We note $|b|$ for the number of tasks contained in the bucket b, and $t \in b$ the fact that a task t is included in bucket b. The size in bits of a bucket b is denoted as $||b||$.*

Theorem 6. *The use of PIR with libraries which fulfill the packing conditions satisfy ϵ_κ-**SIM-CDP** privacy against coalitions of up to τ participants.*

Proof (sketch). In order to prove the security of packing, we observe that (1) the XPIR protocol has been proven computationally secure in [2], such that it satisfies ϵ_κ-SIM-CDP, and (2) the use of packing prevents any sensitive information on workers to leak through the number of downloads. Indeed, Condition 7.1 (security) makes each worker call the PIR-get function only once, such that the behaviours of any two workers are indistinguishable. Therefore, the number of PIR-get calls does not depend on profiles. More precisely, the number of PIR-get calls can only leak information on the number of workers (which is bigger than or equal to the number of PIR-get calls), which does not depend on their profiles, and is already known by the platform.

---

[19] In general, more files can be downloaded at each worker session, but this does not impact significantly the overall amount of computation and does not impact at all the minimum download size for workers.

Before considering how to design an efficient packing scheme, we highlight a few noticeable implications of these conditions. First, due to Condition 7.3 (availability), any worker is matched with at least one bucket. To simplify this model, we propose to focus on a specific kind of packing, that can be seen as a partitioning of the space, where each bucket can be linked to a specific subspace, and where all points are included in at least one subspace. We call *partitioned packing* such a packing (Definition 8).

Definition 8 (Partitioned Packing). *A partitioned packing is a packing that fulfills the following conditions:*

1. *Each bucket is associated with a subspace of the space of skills.*
2. *A bucket contains exactly the tasks that intersect with the subspace it is associated with (this means that all workers in this subspace will find at least the task they match with in the bucket)*
3. *Subspaces associated with the buckets cover the whole space (from Condition 7.3 (availability)).*
4. *Subspaces associated with the buckets do not intersect each other*

In the following, we will focus on partitioned packing. However, in order not to lose generality, we first prove that these packings do not impact efficiency. Indeed, efficiency can be affected by two main issues: the number of items and the size of the largest item (in our case, bucket) impact the communication costs, while the size of the overall library impacts the computation time on the platform. Note that the size of the overall library is equal to the product of the size of items by their number. We show in Theorem 7 that with any packing, we can build a partitioned packing that is equivalent or better.

To prove this theorem, we introduce a specific kind of packing that we call *consistent packing*, defined in Definition 9. Essentially, a consistent packing is a packing where no useless task is added to any bucket: in all buckets b, all tasks match with at least one point (a possible worker profile) which has all her tasks in the bucket b. As a result, a consistent packing avoids cases where tasks are in a bucket, but no worker would download it as the bucket does not match with all their needs.

Definition 9 (Consistent packing). *A packing P is called consistent if and only if, for all buckets $b \in P$, for all tasks $t \in b$, there exists at least one point w in the subspace of t such that all tasks matching with w are in b. We also define match such that* match(w, t) *is* True *if the point w is in the subspace t and* False *otherwise.*

$$\forall b \in P, \forall t \in b, \exists w, (match(w,t) \wedge \forall t' \in T, match(w,t') \Rightarrow t' \in b)$$

Theorem 7. *For any packing P of tasks, there exists a partitioned packing that either has the same size of buckets, number of buckets, or smaller ones.*

Proof (sketch). Let P be a packing of tasks that is not partitioned. To prove that a partitioned packing can be created that is more efficient than P, we distinguish two cases. First, we consider that each bucket of P can cover a subspace, containing exactly the tasks that intersect with that subspace (thus fulfilling Conditions 8.1 and 8.2). Then, we prove that any consistent packing (as in Definition 9) fulfills Condition 8.2. After that, we consider the case where P does not fulfill this condition, and create a new, smaller packing P_f from P that is consistent, and therefore fulfills Condition 8.2, and use previous results.

We first consider the case where all buckets of P can cover a subspace while fulfilling Condition 8.2, meaning that each bucket contains exactly the tasks that intersect with the subspace it covers. In that case, Condition 8.1 is trivially fulfilled. If Condition 8.3 is not fulfilled, this means that there is at least a subspace that is not covered by the packing P. Let w be a point in such a subspace. Since P is a packing, the Condition 7.3 (availability) makes it possible to match with any point of the space with at least one bucket. In particular, w can be matched with a bucket b. It is enough to extend the subspace associated with b such that it includes w (note that this extension does not break Condition 8.2. We can proceed that way for any point (or more likely any subspace) that is not covered by a subspace, to associate subspaces to a bucket of P, such that this matching fulfills Conditions 8.1, 8.2 and 8.3. If, in this matching, two subspaces associated with buckets of P intersect, it is trivial to reduce one of them to fulfill Condition 8.4 too. Therefore, if all buckets of P can be matched with a subspace while fulfilling Condition 8.2, the theorem holds, since P is equivalent to a partitioned packing.

It can be noticed that if a packing is consistent (Definition 9), Condition 8.2 is fulfilled. Indeed, if $\forall b \in P, \forall t \in b, \exists w, (match(w,t) \land \forall t' \in T, match(w,t') \Rightarrow t' \in b)$ (Definition 9), then, for all b in P, we can take V as the union of the $|b|$ points w described in the equation, one for each task t in b. In that case, Condition 8.2 is fulfilled: for each bucket b and its associated subspace V, all tasks in b intersect with V (by definition, as we took V as the union of one point in each task in b), and b contains all tasks that intersect with V (again, by definition, as each task t' that match with a point of V are in b).

In other words, and using the above case, making a packing consistent is sufficient to create a partitioned packing.

We now consider the case where at least one bucket b of P does not cover a subspace such that Condition 8.2 does not stand. In particular, P is not consistent. This means that there is at least one task $t \in b$ such that for all points w in the subspace of t, there is at least one task t' with which w matches and that is not contained by the bucket b. In other words, no points in t can be matched with the bucket b, as b lacks at least one task for each point of t. As a consequence of the Condition 7.3 (availability), this means that all points in t are matched with another bucket. Therefore, the task t can be removed from bucket b, without breaking the properties of a packing, and without increasing the number of buckets, the minimal size of buckets. We proceed so, by removing all such tasks in all buckets recursively: this trivially ends thanks to the finite number of tasks and buckets. By construction, the final packing P_f is consistent.

Therefore, packing P_f is smaller than P, and fulfills Condition 8.2, and we proved in the first case that a packing that fulfills this condition is equivalent to a partitioned packing, so P_f is equivalent to a partitioned packing.

4.3   Optimizing the Packing

With this secure partitioned packing approach, we can discuss how to optimize the overall complexity. First, it can be noticed that Conditions 7.2 and 7.3 (PIR requirement and availability) set a minimal size of bucket: according to Condition 7.3 (availability), there has to be a bucket containing the largest (in bits) intersection of tasks, and Condition 7.2 (PIR requirement) prevents any bucket from being smaller. Furthermore, this minimum is reachable if we consider a packing that creates a partition for each different intersection of tasks and pad to the largest one. However, by building a different bucket for all the possible intersections of tasks, this packing strategy is likely to lead to a very large number of buckets (*e.g.*, if a task's subspace is included in another, this packing leads to two buckets instead of one: one containing both tasks, and the other containing only the largest one as it is a different intersection), while we would like to minimize it (and not only the size of buckets). Therefore, although this packing scheme reaches the minimal size of buckets, we cannot consider it as optimal. However, it illustrates what we call an *acceptable* packing (Definition 10), which will be used to define optimality: a packing in which the size of buckets is minimal.

Definition 10 (Acceptable partitioned packing).   *Let E be a multidimensional space, T a set of tasks, i.e. a set of positively weighted volume (the volume is the one of the task, and the weight is the size in bits, denoted w_t for $t \in T$) in the space E and P a packing of these tasks. We call weight of a packing w_P the size in bits of a bucket in P (due to Condition 7.2 (PIR requirement), this size is unique). We call weight of a point w_p in E the sum of the weights of all tasks in T which match with p.*

We call minimal weight m_T of the set of tasks T the maximum weight of a point in E: it is the maximum size a worker could require to download. A partitioning P is called acceptable for T if the size of P is equal to m_T: $m_T = w_P$.

NP-Hardness of Optimal Packing.   To define optimality, we take this minimum size of buckets, but also try to minimize the number of buckets (or in an equivalent way, the size of the PIR library), as expressed in Definition 11.

Definition 11 (Optimal partitioned packing).   *For a set of tasks T, we call optimal packing an acceptable packing that minimizes the number of buckets.*

However, we prove in Theorem 8 that determining whether there exists an acceptable packing of size n is NP-hard, and therefore, finding the optimal partitioned packing is also NP-hard.

Theorem 8. *Given a set of tasks T, it is NP-hard in $|T|$ to determine whether there exists an acceptable partitioning of n buckets. We call $\mathcal{P}(T, n)$ this problem.*

Proof (sketch). To prove that this problem is NP-hard, it is enough to demonstrate that a certain problem $\mathcal{P}^+$ known to be NP-complete can be polynomially reduced to $\mathcal{P}$.

We recall that the Partition Problem is NP-complete (see [22]): $\mathcal{P}^+(S)$: given a multiset S of N positive integers $n_i, i \in [0, N-1]$, decide whether this multiset can be divided into two submultisets S_1 and S_2 such that the sum of the numbers in S_1 equals the sum of the numbers in S_2, and the union of S_1 and S_2 is included in S.

Let us consider a multiset S and the problem $\mathcal{P}^+(S)$. We assume the existence of a deterministic algorithm A that solves $\mathcal{P}(T, n)$ in a polynomial time in $|T|$. We first distinguish a trivial case where the problem $\mathcal{P}^+(S)$ can be solved in polynomial time. Then, we build an algorithm that uses $\mathcal{P}(T, 3)$ to solve $\mathcal{P}^+(S)$ in polynomial time similarly to the remaining cases, which leads to a contradiction.

We first consider a trivial case: if there exists n_k in S such that $n_k > \sum_{i \in [0, N-1], i \neq k} n_i$, then we return *False*. Deciding whether S falls in that specific case is linear in $|S|$, and so is the computation of the answer. If not, let E be a one dimensional space, with bounds $[0, |S|+1[$. We build T as a set of $|S|+1$ tasks ($T = \{t_i, i \in [0, N]\}$), such that no task intersects with each other: therefore, the minimum size m_T of T (from Definition 10) will be the same as the size of the biggest task t in T. The $|S|$ first tasks are all associated with an element of S, while the last one will be used to fix m_T. More precisely, we build T as follows:

-- the range of t_i is $[i, i+1[$
-- for $i \neq N$, the weight of t_i is equal to the value of n_i; $w_{t_N} = \frac{\sum_{i \in [0, N-1]} n_i}{2}$.

Building T and t_{max} is subpolynomial.

By hypothesis, $\forall k, n_k \leq \sum_{i \in [0, N-1], i \neq k} n_i$ (as we dealt with this case previously), and by construction, no volume intersects any other, so the minimal weight is the size of the biggest task, which is the last one: $m_T = max_{t_i}(w_{t_i}) = w_{t_{max}}$. Therefore, if S can be divided into two submultisets S_1 and S_2 of the same size, this size is $\frac{\sum_{i \in [0, N-1]} n_i}{2}$, and $\mathcal{P}(T, 3)$ answers *True*.

Reciprocally, if $\mathcal{P}(T, 3)$ answers *True*, this means that there exists a packing of size 3 such that no packing is bigger than $m_T = \frac{\sum_{i \in [0, N-1]} n_i}{2}$. In particular, as $w_{t_N} = m_T$, this means that no task is added to the bucket containing it, and that the two remaining buckets contain all tasks $t_i, i \neq N$. If one of these buckets where smaller than m_T, the other would be bigger than m_T (as $m_T = \frac{\sum_{i \in [0, N-1]} n_i}{2}$), and therefore, both buckets weight exactly m_T. Therefore, it is possible to separate S in S_1 and S_2 such that the sum of the numbers in S_1 equals the sum of the S_2 by taking all the elements corresponding to the tasks in the first bucket for S_1, and the elements corresponding to the second bucket for S_2.

Therefore, if we are not in the trivial case treated above, $\mathcal{P}(T,3)$ answers *True* if and only if $\mathcal{P}^+(S)$ is true in polynomial time. As both deciding whether we are in that trivial case and computing the answer in that trivial case can be computed in polynomial time, an algorithm deciding $\mathcal{P}^+(S)$ in polynomial time can be built. The assumption of $\mathcal{P}(T,n)$ not being NP-hard leads to a polynomial algorithm solving $\mathcal{P}^+$, which is absurd, so $\mathcal{P}(T,n)$ is NP-hard.

Static Packings. Another point can be highlighted: the difference between what we call *static* packing and *dynamic* partitioning. Indeed, when trying to optimize the use of partitioned buckets, two main approaches can be used: adapt buckets to tasks, or adapt tasks to buckets. In the first case, we consider a fixed set of tasks, and try to build partitions in order to minimize the cost of PIR. On the one hand, this optimization makes it possible to perform the best with any set of tasks. On the other hand, as we consider a fixed set of tasks, we may have to compute a new partitioning when this set evolves (when a task is added or removed, at least when it affects the largest bucket). In the second case however, we consider a fixed partitioning, that is independent from the set of tasks. This method is more likely to be suboptimal, but it avoids heavy computation of optimal packing and allows a greater flexibility in the context of crowdsourcing, by allowing a large variety of choices and policies from the platform, which can even lead to other kinds of optimization. For instance, it allows the platform to manage prices policies (*e.g.* making tasks pay for each targeted subspace, higher prices for tasks willing to target highly demanded subspaces, etc.), in order to even the load within the whole space, and to reduce the redundancy of tasks within the PIR library (tasks that target more than one partition).

As finding the optimal is NP-hard, we prefer to set aside dynamic packings, as its main asset is the theoretical possibility to reach optimality while remaining unrealistic in a real-life scenario, and focus instead on static packings.

Static packing means that the design of partitions is independent of tasks: the tasks contained within the bucket may change, but not the subspace delimited by the partition. These heuristic packing schemes are not optimal in general but may be affordable in real-life scenarios. We propose to use a simple heuristic static packing scheme, the PKD PIR Packing, consisting in using the partitioned space of workers profiles computed primarily for task design purposes: to each leaf partition corresponds a bucket containing all the tasks that have metadata intersecting with it (possibly with padding). The resulting algorithm is presented in Algorithm 3. The accordance of this scheme with the distribution of workers can lead to both useful and efficient buckets (as assessed experimentally, see Sect. 5), and the stability over time of the space partitioning (static approach) makes it easier to design policies to approach optimality through incentives on the task design (rather than through the bucket design).

Algorithm 3: PKD PIR Packing

 Data:
 T a Tree computed with the PKD algorithm
 $\mathcal{T}$ a list of tasks
 Result: P: A static partitioned packing depending on workers distribution
 1 Create an empty packing P
 2 **for** *all leaves l of the tree T* **do**
 3   Create a new empty bucket b, assigned to the subvolume of l
 4   **for** *all tasks t in $\mathcal{T}$* **do**
 5   **if** *t and l intersect* **then**
 6   Add t to the bucket b
 7   Add b to P

 8 **return** *Packing P*

---

5 Experimental Validation

We performed a thorough experimental evaluation of the quality and performances of both the PKD algorithm and our PKD PIR Packing heuristic (that we abbreviate as *PIR* in the experiments).

5.1 Datasets

In this section, we introduce the datasets and data generators that are used in our experiments.

Realistic Dataset. To the best of our knowledge there does not exist any reference dataset of worker profiles that we could use for our experiments. This led us to building our own dataset from public open data. The *StackExchange*[20] data dumps are well-known in works related to experts finding. We decided to use them as well in order to perform experiments on realistic skills profiles. We computed profiles by extracting skills from users' posts and votes. In *StackExchange*, users submit posts (questions or answers) that are tagged with descriptive keywords (*e.g.,* "python programming") and vote positively (resp. negatively) for the good (resp. bad) answers. We consider then that each user is a worker, that each tag is a skill, and that the level of expertise of a given user on a given skill is reflected on the votes. We favored a simple approach for computing the expertise of users. First, for each post, we compute a *popularity ratio* as follows: $r = \texttt{upvotes}/(\texttt{upvotes} + \texttt{downvotes})$, where $\texttt{upvotes}$ is the number of positive votes of the post and $\texttt{downvotes}$ is the number of negative votes. Second, for each user p_i, for each tag j, the aggregate level of expertise $p_i[j]$ is simply the average popularity ratio of

---

[20] *StackExchange* is a set of online forums where users post questions and answers, and vote for good answers https://archive.org/download/stackexchange.

the posts from p tagged by j. Note that more elaborate approaches can be used (see the survey [35]). Finally, we removed the workers that do not have any skill level higher than 0. We applied this method on three *StackExchange* datasets: `stackoverflow.com-Posts.7z`, `stackoverflow.com-Tags.7z`, and `stackoverflow.com-Votes.7z` which resulted in 1.3M worker profiles[21]. Figure 3(a) shows for ten common skills[22] and for the possible levels divided in ten ranges (*i.e.*, $[0.0, 0.1[, [0.1, 0.2[, \ldots, [0.9, 1])$ their corresponding frequencies. It shows essentially that whatever the skill considered, most workers have a skill level at 0. The rest of the distribution is not visible on this graph so we show in Fig. 3(b) the same graph but *excluding*, for each tag, the workers having a skill level at 0.

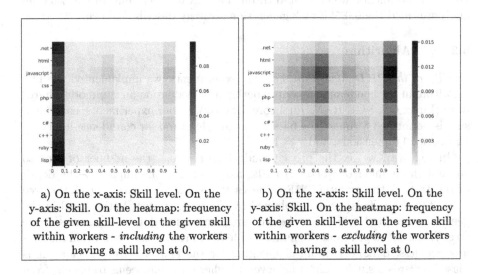

a) On the x-axis: Skill level. On the y-axis: Skill. On the heatmap: frequency of the given skill-level on the given skill within workers - *including* the workers having a skill level at 0.

b) On the x-axis: Skill level. On the y-axis: Skill. On the heatmap: frequency of the given skill-level on the given skill within workers - *excluding* the workers having a skill level at 0.

Fig. 3. Frequencies of ten common skills within the STACK dataset.

Data Generators. We performed our experiments over both synthetic and realistic data. Our two synthetic generators are specifically dedicated to evaluating the PKD algorithm with two different kinds of assumptions. First, our UNIF synthetic data generator draws skills uniformly at random between 0 and 1 (included) (1) for each dimension of a worker's profile and (2) for each dimension of a task (more precisely, a min value and a max value per dimension). Second, our ONESPE generator considers that workers are skilled over a single dimension and that tasks look for workers over a single dimension. The specialty of each worker is chosen uniformly at random, and its value is drawn uniformly at random

---

[21] The scripts for generating our dataset are available online: https://gitlab.inria.fr/crowdguard-public/data/workers-stackoverflow.

[22] The ten common skills considered are the following: .net, html, javascript, css, php, c, c#, c++, ruby, lisp.

between 0.5 and 1. The other skills are drawn uniformly at random between 0 and 0.5. Similarly to workers, the specialty looked for by a task is chosen uniformly at random as well, its min value is chosen uniformly at random between 0.5 and 1 and its max value is set to 1. The min values of the other dimensions of a task are 0, and their max values are chosen uniformly at random between 0 and 0.5. Although this second heuristic is obviously not perfect, it seems far more realistic than the previous one. For the two task generation heuristics, we require that all tasks must contain at least one worker so that the mean error can be correctly computed.

Finally, our realistic data generator, called STACK, consists in sampling randomly workers (by default with a uniform probability) from the STACK dataset. For our experiments, we generated through STACK workers uniformly at random and performed the ONESPE task generation strategy described above.

5.2 PKD **Algorithm**

*Quality of the **PKD** Algorithm.* For our experiments, we implemented the PKD algorithm in Python 3 and run our experimental evaluation on commodity hardware (Linux OS, 8 GB RAM, dual core 2.4 GHz). In our experiments, each measure is performed 5 times (the bars in our graphs stand for confidence interval), $1k$ tasks, 10 dimensions, and $\tau = 1$.

In Fig. 4(a), we fix the privacy budget to $\epsilon = 0.1$, the number of bins to 10, and the number of workers to $10k$, and we study the impact of the depth of the tree on the quality. UNIF achieves the lowest error, as long as the tree is not too deep. This can be explained by the uniform distribution used in the generation method, which matches the uniform assumption within leaves in the tree. When the depth (and the number of leaves) grows, this assumption matters less and less. ONESPE is more challenging for the PKD algorithm because it is biased towards a single skill. It achieves a higher error but seems to benefit from deeper trees. Indeed, deep trees may be helpful in spotting more accurately the specialized worker targeted. The results for STACK are very similar. For all of these distributions, we can see that having a tree deeper than the number of dimensions leads to a significant loss in quality.

In Fig. 4(b), we analyze the variations of quality according to the value of ϵ, with 10 bins, a depth of 10, and $10k$ workers. In this case, the relative error seems to converge to a non-zero minimum when ϵ grows, probably due to inherent limits of KD-Tree's precision for tasks.

In Fig. 4(c), we fix the privacy budget to $\epsilon = 0.1$, the depth of the tree to 10 and $10k$ workers. We can see the impact of the number of bins for each histogram used to compute a secure median. This value does not greatly impact the relative error for the UNIF and STACK models, although we can see that performing with 1 bin seems to give slightly less interesting results, as it looses its adaptability toward distributions. For the ONESPE model, having only 1 bin gives better results: indeed, the uniformity assumption within the bin implies that all dimensions are cut at 0.5, which is also by construction the most important value to classify workers generated with this procedure.

In Fig. 4(d), we compare the quality according to the number of workers with $\epsilon = 0.1$, 10 bins and a depths of 10. As the ϵ budget is the same, the noise is independent from this number, and thus, the quality increases with the number of workers.

We can notice that our results for the relative error are quite close to the state of the art results, such as the experiments from [9], which are performed on 2-dimensional spaces only, with strong restrictions on the shapes of queries (tasks in our context) and in a centralized context.

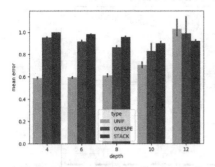

a) Variations according to the depth of the tree.
10 dimensions, $10k$ workers, $1k$ tasks, $\tau = 1$, $\epsilon = 0.1$, 10 bins

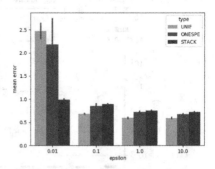

b) Variations according to ϵ privacy budget.
10 dimensions, $10k$ workers, $1k$ tasks, $\tau = 1$, 10 bins, $depth = 10$

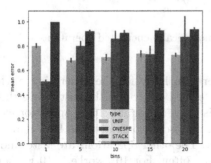

c) Variations according to the number of bins.
10 dimensions, $10k$ workers, $1k$ tasks, $\tau = 1$, $\epsilon = 0.1$, $depth = 10$

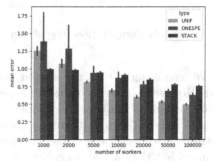

d) Variations according to the number of workers.
10 dimensions, $1k$ tasks, $\tau = 1$, $\epsilon = 0.1$, 10 bins, $depth = 10$

Fig. 4. Mean relative error (see Definition 5, the lower the better)

*Computation Time of the **PKD** Algorithm.* Our performance experiments were performed on a laptop running Linux OS, equipped with 16 GB of RAM and an

Intel Core $i7 - 7600U$ processor. We measured the average computation time across 100 experiments of each of the atomic operations used in the PKD algorithm: encryption, partial decryption, and encrypted addition. The results are summed up in Fig. 5, with keys of size 2048 bits, using the University of Texas at Dallas implementation for its accessibility[23]. We use our cost analysis together with these atomic measures for estimating the global cost of the PKD algorithm over large populations of workers (see Eq. 4, Eq. 5, and Eq. 6 in Sect. 3.3).

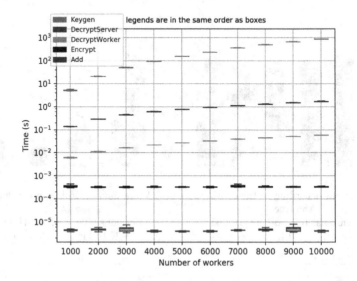

Fig. 5. Computation time of homomorphically encrypted operations

We can observe that the slowest operation is by far the generation of the keys. However, since this operation is performed only once, the cost of less than 1000 s (about 17 min) for 10k workers is very reasonable: this operation can be performed as soon as there are enough subscriptions, and the keys may be distributed whenever the workers connect. The other operations are faster individually, but they are also performed more often. For 10k workers, 10 workers required for decryption, a depth of the KD-Tree of 10 and 10 bins, we can observe that: each worker will spend less than 10 s performing encryptions, the platform will spend less than 1000 s performing encrypted additions, the average worker will spend less than 1 s performing decryptions, and the platform will spend less than 3000 s performing decryptions.

Overall, these costs are quite light on the worker side: less than 20 s with commodity hardware. On the server side, the computation is more expensive (about one hour), but we could expect a server to run on a machine more powerful than the one we used in our experiments. Additionally, it is worth to note that: (1) the perturbed skills distribution is computed only once for a given a

---

[23] http://cs.utdallas.edu/dspl/cgi-bin/pailliertoolbox/index.php?go=download.

population of workers and then used repeatedly, and (2) we do not have any real time constraints so that the PKD algorithm can run in background in an opportunistic manner.

5.3 Assignment Using Packing

Quality of our packing. We here propose to evaluate the quality of our partitioned packing approach. Our experiments are performed with the same settings as those used to measure the quality of the PKD algorithm (see Sect. 5.2). To do so, we propose two main metrics. First, me measure the mean precision for tasks, as defined in Definition 6. Although this measure is useful to understand the overall improvement of our approach, it does not take into account the fact that downloads caused by PIR scale with the largest item. Therefore, we introduce a second measure, the mean number of tasks that a worker would download. This value, that we call *maximum tasks*, is computed as the maximum number of tasks that a leaf of the KD-tree intersects with: indeed, due to Condition 7.2 (PIR requirement), all workers will download as many data as contained in the biggest bucket.

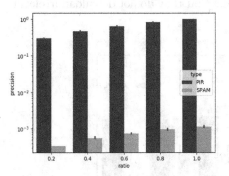 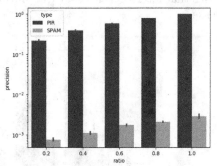

a) Precision in log scale, according to the task ratio for the UNIF model. 10 dimensions, $10k$ workers, $1k$ tasks, $\tau = 1$, $\epsilon = 0.1$, 10 bins, *depth* = 10

b) Precision in log scale, according to the task ratio for the ONESPE model. 10 dimensions, $10k$ workers, $1k$ tasks, $\tau = 1$, $\epsilon = 0.1$, 10 bins, *depth* = 10

Fig. 6. Precision (the higher the better)

In the task generation methods introduced previously, tasks are built independently from the KD-tree itself. This independence was logical to measure the quality of the PKD algorithm. However, this leads to poor results when it comes to building efficient packing on top of a KD-tree: as tasks are independent from the KD-tree, they have little restriction on how small they are (meaning that few workers will match, although all workers in leaf that intersect with it will download it), or on how many leaves they intersect with, leading to low precision, and high size of buckets.

Therefore, we introduce a new method to build tasks: SUBVOLUME. With this method, we build tasks as *subleaves*, meaning that all tasks are strictly included within *one* leaf of the KD-tree. Furthermore, we also enforce the size of the task as a parameter, such that the volume of the task is equal to a given ratio of the task. More precisely, for a ratio $r \in [0, 1]$, a space E of d dimensions and a picked leaf l, the interval of a task in a given dimension d_i is $l_{d_i} \times r^{1/d}$, where l_{d_i} is the interval of the leaf in dimension d_i. The SUBVOLUME model of tasks can easily be introduced by economic incentives from the platform, such as having requesters pay for each targeted leaf, which is likely to induce a maximization of the volume taken, and a reduction of the tasks that intersect with more than one leaf. Note that we do not perform experiments with this generation of tasks on the Stack dataset, as most workers have their skills set to either 0 or 1, which leads to very unreliable results as tasks almost never encompass either of these values.

The comparison between the PKD PIR Packing heuristic and the spamming approach using this new method to generate tasks, presented in Fig. 6, shows that our approach improves precision by at least two orders of magnitude. Also, note that for $r = 1$, the precision is equal to 1 in the PIR approach. This result comes from the fact that, with $r = 1$, all workers within a leaf are targeted by all tasks that intersect with that leaf, meaning that they do not download irrelevant tasks.

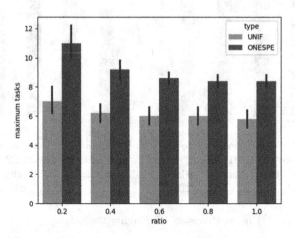

Fig. 7. Number of tasks downloaded according to the task ratio for the packing approach. 10 dimensions, $10k$ workers, $1k$ tasks, $\tau = 1$, $\epsilon = 0.1$, 10 bins, *depth* = 10

The maximum number of tasks connected to a leaf, showed in Fig. 7, show that the cost of download is also significantly improved (these values are to be compared to 1000, the total number of tasks that are downloaded with the spamming approach). It also shows great improvement (around 2 orders of magnitude) as tasks are more evenly spread within the leaves (there are $2^{10} =$ 1024 leaves for a depth 10 of the tree, which can explain this improvement).

Cost of the PIR Protocol. We here study the impact of the number of files and of the size of files on the computation time. In the experiments, we used a computer with 8 GB of RAM, and a Ryzen 5 1700 processor, using the implementation of [2][24].

As we can see in Fig. 8 with keys of size 1024 bits, computation time is proportional to the overall size of the PIR library (the coefficient of determination gives $r^2 = 0.9963$), and that it grows at $0.14\,\text{s/MB}$ for a given request, as long as the library can be stored in RAM[25].

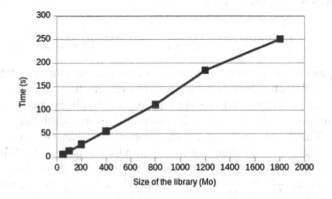

Fig. 8. Computation time of the retrieval of a file according to the PIR library's size

We now evaluate the maximum number of tasks n_{max} that our system can take into account, according to two parameters: first, the time t that workers accept to wait before the download begins, and second, the size s that workers accept to download. As n_{max} does not solely depend on t and s, we introduce a few other notations:

-- f is the expansion factor of the encryption scheme.
-- $|task|$ the mean size of a task.
-- k the proportion of tasks that are in the biggest leaf of the KD-tree (for instance, $k = 0.1$ means that the biggest leaf contains one tenth of all tasks)
-- *depth*, the depth of the KD-tree (that is linked with the number of buckets)

In the spamming approach, the maximum number of tasks that can be managed by our system is independent from t and can be simply computed as:

$$n_{max,SPAM} = \frac{s}{|task|}$$

---

[24] https://github.com/XPIR-team/XPIR.
[25] If it cannot, accesses to the secondary storage device are necessary. This would increase the runtime accordingly. However, since the library is scanned once per query, sequentially, the cost would remain linear in the size of the library.

For the `PKD PIR Packing` heuristic, both s and t lead to a limitation on $n_{max,PIR}$. We first consider the limit on the computation time t: according to our results in Fig. 8, the PIR library cannot be bigger than $\frac{t}{0.14}$, and the size of a bucket, can be computed as $k \times |task| \times n_{max,PIR}$ (by definition of k, as all buckets weight as much as the biggest one). As the library can be computed as the product of the number of buckets and their size, this leads us to $2^{depth} \times k \times |task| \times n_{max,PIR} \leq \frac{t}{0.14}$, or equivalently $n_{max,PIR} \leq \frac{t}{0.14 \times 2^{depth} \times k \times |task|}$. We now consider the limit s on the size of download. For each worker, the size of a download will be the same, computed as the product of the expansion factor and the size of a bucket: $f \times k \times n_{max,PIR} \times |task| \leq s$. This inequality leads to $n_{max,PIR} \leq \frac{s}{f \times |task| \times k}$. By combining these two inequalities, $n_{max,PIR}$ takes its maximum value when

$$n_{max,PIR} = min(\frac{s}{f \times |task| \times k}, \frac{t}{2^{depth} \times 0.14 \times |task| \times k})$$

In Fig. 9, we compare the number of tasks that a crowdsourcing platform can manage with different values of t and s, using either the spamming approach or our `PKD PIR Packing` heuristic. For the sake of simplicity, we consider that the expansion factor f is 10, although smaller values are reachable with XPIR protocol [2]. This factor will impact the amount of tasks that a worker can download. We take $d = 10$ similarly to our previous experiments. We consider a mean size of task $|task| = 1\,MB$. It can be noticed that $|task|$ has no impact on the comparison ($\frac{max_{n,PIR}}{max_{n,SPAM}}$ does not depend on $|task|$). For k, we consider two possible values: $k = 0.01$, as suggested by the experiments in Fig. 7, and $k = \frac{1}{2^{10}}$, which represents the optimal case, where tasks are perfectly spread among buckets (for instance, due to strong incentives from the platform).

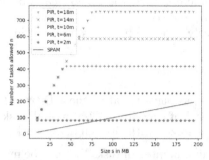
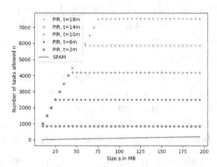

a) Number of tasks n manageable by our system according to the size s a worker accepts to download.
$k = 0.01$, $|task| = 1MB$, $f = 10$, $depth = 10$

b) Number of tasks n manageable by our system according to the size s a worker accepts to download.
$k = 0.001$, $|task| = 1MB$, $f = 10$, $depth = 10$

Fig. 9. Precision (the higher the better); curves are in the same order as the captions

In these experiments, we can notice that our approach depends on both the computation time allowed and the size of the number of task in the largest bucket. In a real-life scenario, platforms would benefit from enforcing incentives to even the load between buckets. However, if workers are willing to limit their download to less than 100 MB, the PKD PIR Packing heuristic outperforms the spamming approach as long as users are willing to limit their download even with relatively short computation times (less than 10 min) by up to several orders of magnitude. Our method is especially interesting in settings where the bandwidth is low (*e.g.*, with mobile devices), with low values of s. On the opposite, it is interesting to highlight that high computation times are not necessarily prohibitive: as the computation is performed by the platform, a worker could very well ask for a bucket of tasks and download it later on when it is ready.

6   Discussion

In this section, we propose a discussion on questions raised by our work that are not our primary focus. More precisely, we elaborate our views on updates that our system may or may not allow (both for the PKD algorithm and the PKD PIR Packing heuristic), with some advantages and drawbacks.

6.1   Updating Tasks and PIR Libraries

In this work, we dealt with the download of tasks as a *one-shot* download, meaning that a worker will download tasks once and for all. However, in a real-life scenario tasks are likely to evolve (*e.g.*, new tasks will be added and old tasks will be outdated), and workers are equally likely to update their tasks. Without further improvement, our design would require each worker to download a whole packing for each update of the available tasks. However, more elaborate approaches are possible. Although it is not our focus to develop them exhaustively, we propose a few tracks that are likely to diminish the costs greatly.

For that purpose, we propose to divide time into fixed duration *periods* (*e.g.*, a day, a week, etc.) and to additionally take into account the period at which a task is issued in order to pack it. We give below two options for allowing updates. Although their improvement have not been quantified nor validated experimentally, These schemes aim at increasing the memory cost on the server in order to alleviate the overall computation required.

Packing by Period. A simple scheme that allows easier updates while reducing the size of single PIR request consists in designing packing not only according to a specific partitioning but also according to time periods. The platform builds one PIR library per period, *i.e.*, considering only the tasks received during that period.[26]. Workers simply need to perform PIR requests over the missing period(s) (one request per missing period). As a result, the `PIR-get` function is executed on the library of the requested period, which is smaller than or equal to the initial library.

However, this scheme may result in high costs if the distribution of tasks is skewed. For instance, let's consider two time periods p_1 and p_2, two subspaces of the space of skills s_1 and s_2, and three tasks t_1, t_2 and t_3 such that t_1 and t_2 appear only in p_1 and s_1, while t_3 appears only in p_2 and s_2. In that case, all workers will download first the PIR item for period p_1, which is the same size as $w_{t_1} + w_{t_2}$ (due to padding for workers not in p_1) and then a second PIR item for p_2, of size w_{t_3}. Without that period strategy, a worker who performs regular updates would have downloaded tasks t_1 and t_2 (or equivalent size) twice due to the update, and t_3 once, but a worker who would not have performed the intermediary download would have downloaded $max(w_{t_3}, w_{t_1} + w_{t_2})$. Therefore workers who update frequently would benefit from this strategy, while workers who do not would have worse results.

Personalized Packing by Period. In order to tackle the previously mentioned issue caused by skewed distribution of tasks, and to optimize the size of the downloaded bucket for any frequency of downloads, we propose to adapt the packing to the workers frequency of downloads.

Indeed, we observe that it is enough to perform as many packings as there are possible time-lapses for workers, *e.g.,* one packing for the last period, one packing for the last two periods, one packing for the last three periods, *etc.* As a result, each `PIR-get` request is associated with a time-lapse in order to let the PIR server compute the buckets to be downloaded (or use pre-computed buckets). With this method, we can get the best of both worlds with the previous example: someone who downloads frequently will only have small updates, while someone who does not will not suffer from overcosts.

The main (and limited) drawback of this method is that the platform will have to store multiple PIR-libraries, which increases the storage required.

Security of Packing by Period. In both of the above schemes, we consider multiple downloads from workers. Even worse, in the second case the number of downloads may vary depending on workers habits. If the above proposition were to be used, more accurate proofs of security would have to be done. Although it is not our focus to propose them in this article, we provide here some intuitions on their requirements. In the first case, the number of downloads is the same for all workers, and would therefore not lead to great modifications of our proof. In the second case however, the number of downloads depends on the frequency of

---

[26] In this kind of methods, a task can be either maintained into its starting period up till it's lifespan, or one can consider keeping up a limited number of periods (*e.g.* all daily periods for the current month) and re-adding tasks on new periods packing each time they are deleted (*e.g.* for tasks that are meant to be longer than a month). More elaborate or intermediate methods are also possible, but we will not explore this compromise in this paper.

downloads of workers. In order not to reveal information about worker's profiles, a new hypothesis is likely to be required, that states or implies that the frequency of downloads of workers is independent from their profiles.

6.2 Updating PKD

The PKD algorithm is not meant to allow users to update their profiles, as they would have to communicate information to do it, and this would either break our security policy, or exceed the ϵ privacy budget. However, departures or arrivals are not inherently forbidden by our security policy. A simple and naive way to upgrade the PKD algorithm to take new arrivals into account is to create multiple KD-trees, and to combine them. For instance, one could imagine using the PKD algorithm on every new k arrivals (e.g. $k = 1000$ or $k = 10000$). The estimation of workers within a subspace would be the sum of the estimations for each KD-tree, and a new PIR library could be built for each of these KD-trees. For retrieval of workers, as it is impossible to know where the worker was, the most naive way to proceed is to retrieve a given value to each leaf of the approximated KD-tree, for instance $\frac{n_{leaf}}{n_{tree}}$, where n_{leaf} is the approximated number of workers in the leaf, and n_{tree} the total number of workers. Once again, more elaborate methods are possible, but stand out of the focus of this paper.

7 Related Work

Privacy-Preserving Task Assignment. Recent works have focused on the privacy-preserving task assignment problem in general crowdsourcing. In [5], each worker profile - a vector of bits - is perturbed locally by the corresponding worker, based on a local differentially private bit flipping scheme. A classical task-assignment algorithm can then be launched on the perturbed profiles and the tasks. An alternative approach to privacy-preserving task-assignment has been proposed in [21]. It is based on the extensive use of additively-homomorphic encryption, so it does not suffer from any information loss, but this has a prohibitive cost in terms of performance. Other works have focused on the specific context of spatial crowdsourcing [38, 39, 41]. They essentially differ from the former in that spatial crowdsourcing focuses on a small number of dimensions (typically, the two dimensions of a geolocation) and is often incompatible with static worker profiles. All these works explore solutions to ensure an assignment between tasks and workers in a private way, and are complementary to our approach.

Decentralized Privacy-Preserving Crowdsourcing Platform. ZebraLancer [29] is a decentralized crowdsourcing platform based on blockchains, zero-knowledge proofs, and smart contracts and focuses on the integrity of the reward policies and the privacy of the submissions of workers against malicious workers or requesters (e.g., spammers, free-riders). Zebralancer does not consider using worker profiles (neither primary nor secondary usages).

Privacy-Preserving KD-Trees. The creation and the publication of private KD-Trees has been studied in depth in [9], but in our context, this work suffers from two main deficiencies. First, it considers a trusted third party in charge of performing all the computations while in our work we do not assume any trusted third party. Second, it restricts the number of dimensions to two, which is unrealistic in our high-skills crowdsourcing context. Enhancements to the technique have been proposed, for example [33], but without tackling the trusted third party assumption.

Privacy-Preserving COUNTs. Other differentially private count algorithms exist and use histograms. With the use of constrained inference, the approaches proposed *e.g.,* in [20,34] outperform standard methods. But they are limited to centralized contexts with a trusted third party, and only consider datasets with at most three dimensions. The `PrivTree` approach [42] eliminates the need of fixing the height of trees beforehand, but their security model also considers a trusted third party, and their experiments are limited to four dimensions, which is lower than the number of skills that we consider. `DPBench` [19] benchmarks these methods in a centralized context and considers one or two dimensions. Finally, the authors of [23] tackle the efficiency issues of privacy-preserving hierarchies of histograms. It suffers from the same dimension and privacy limitations as the above works.

Task Design. To the best of our knowledge, the problem of designing a task according to the actual crowd while providing sound privacy guarantees has not been studied by related works. Most works focus on the complexity of the task [14], on the interface with the worker [14,24,28], on the design of workflows [25,26], or on the filters that may be embedded within tasks and based on which relevant workers should be selected [3]. However, these approaches ignore the relevance of tasks with respect to the actual crowd, and thus ignore the related privacy issues.

8   Conclusion

We have presented a privacy-preserving approach dedicated to enabling various usages of worker profiles by the platform or by requesters, including in particular the design of tasks according to the actual distribution of skills of a population of workers. We have proposed the `PKD` algorithm, an algorithm resulting from rethinking the *KD-tree* construction algorithm and combining additively-homomorphic encryption with differentially-private perturbation. No trusted centralized platform is needed: the `PKD` algorithm is distributed between workers and the platform. We have provided formal security proofs and complexity analysis, and an extensive experimental evaluation over synthetic and realistic data that shows that the `PKD` algorithm can be used even with a low privacy budget and with a reasonable number of skills. Exciting future works especially include considering stronger attack models (*e.g.,* covert or malicious adversaries), evaluating more precisely our propositions for updates, protecting the tasks in addition to worker profiles, and guaranteeing the integrity of worker profiles.

References

1. Agrawal, R., Kiernan, J., Srikant, R., Xu, Y.: Order-preserving encryption for numeric data. In: Proceedings of SIGMOD 2004, pp. 563–574 (2004)
2. Aguilar-Melchor, C., Barrier, J., Fousse, L., Killijian, M.O.: XPIR: private information retrieval for everyone. In: Proceedings of PET 2016, vol. 2016, no. 2, pp. 155–174 (2016)
3. Allahbakhsh, M., Benatallah, B., Ignjatovic, A., Motahari-Nezhad, H.R., Bertino, E., Dustdar, S.: Quality control in crowdsourcing systems: issues and directions. IEEE Internet Comput. **17**(2), 76–81 (2013)
4. Bentley, J.L.: Multidimensional binary search trees used for associative searching. Commun. ACM **18**(9), 509–517 (1975)
5. Béziaud, L., Allard, T., Gross-Amblard, D.: Lightweight privacy-preserving task assignment in skill-aware crowdsourcing. In: Benslimane, D., Damiani, E., Grosky, W.I., Hameurlain, A., Sheth, A., Wagner, R.R. (eds.) DEXA 2017. LNCS, vol. 10439, pp. 18–26. Springer, Cham (2017). https://doi.org/10.1007/978-3-319-64471-4_2
6. Boldyreva, A., Chenette, N., O'Neill, A.: Order-preserving encryption revisited: improved security analysis and alternative solutions. In: Rogaway, P. (ed.) CRYPTO 2011. LNCS, vol. 6841, pp. 578–595. Springer, Heidelberg (2011). https://doi.org/10.1007/978-3-642-22792-9_33
7. Chor, B., Goldreich, O., Kushilevitz, E., Sudan, M.: Private information retrieval. In: Proceedings of FOCS 1995, pp. 41–50 (1995)
8. Cohen, A., Nissim, K.: Linear program reconstruction in practice. CoRR (2018)
9. Cormode, G., Procopiuc, C., Srivastava, D., Shen, E., Yu, T.: Differentially private spatial decompositions. In: Proceedings of ICDE 2012, pp. 20–31 (2012)
10. Damgård, I., Jurik, M.: A generalisation, a simplification and some applications of Paillier's probabilistic public-key system. In: Kim, K. (ed.) PKC 2001. LNCS, vol. 1992, pp. 119–136. Springer, Heidelberg (2001). https://doi.org/10.1007/3-540-44586-2_9
11. Dinur, I., Nissim, K.: Revealing information while preserving privacy. In: Proceedings of SIGACT-SIGMOD-SIGART 2003, pp. 202–210 (2003)
12. Dwork, C.: Differential privacy. In: Proceedings of ICALP 2006, pp. 1–12 (2006)
13. Dwork, C., Roth, A.: The algorithmic foundations of differential privacy. Found. Trends Theor. Comput. Sci. **9**(3–4), 211–407 (2014)
14. Finnerty, A., Kucherbaev, P., Tranquillini, S., Convertino, G.: Keep it simple: reward and task design in crowdsourcing. In: Proceedings of SIGCHI 2013, pp. 14:1–14:4 (2013)
15. Future of work participants: imagine all the people and AI in the future of work. ACM SIGMOD Blog Post (2019)
16. Ghosh, A., Roughgarden, T., Sundararajan, M.: Universally utility-maximizing privacy mechanisms. SIAM J. Comput. **41**(6), 1673–1693 (2012)
17. Goldreich, O.: Foundations of cryptography-a primer. Found. Trends® Theor. Comput. Sci. **1**(1), 1–116 (2005)

18. Gupta, T., Crooks, N., Mulhern, W., Setty, S.T., Alvisi, L., Walfish, M.: Scalable and private media consumption with popcorn. In: Proceedings of NSDI 2016, pp. 91–107 (2016)
19. Hay, M., Machanavajjhala, A., Miklau, G., Chen, Y., Zhang, D.: Principled evaluation of differentially private algorithms using DPBench. In: Proceedings of SIGMOD 2016, pp. 139–154. ACM (2016)
20. Hay, M., Rastogi, V., Miklau, G., Suciu, D.: Boosting the accuracy of differentially private histograms through consistency. Proc. VLDB Endow. **3**(1–2), 1021–1032 (2010)
21. Kajino, H.: Privacy-preserving crowdsourcing. Ph.D. thesis, University of Tokyo (2015)
22. Karmarkar, N., Karp, R.M.: The differencing method of set partitioning. Computer Science Division (EECS), University of California Berkeley (1982)
23. Kellaris, G., Papadopoulos, S., Papadias, D.: Engineering methods for differentially private histograms: efficiency beyond utility. IEEE TKDE **31**(2), 315–328 (2018)
24. Kucherbaev, P., Daniel, F., Tranquillini, S., Marchese, M.: Crowdsourcing processes: a survey of approaches and opportunities. IEEE Internet Comput. **20**(2), 50–56 (2015)
25. Kulkarni, A., Can, M., Hartmann, B.: Collaboratively crowdsourcing workflows with turkomatic. In: Proceedings of CSCW 2012, pp. 1003–1012 (2012)
26. Kulkarni, A.P., Can, M., Hartmann, B.: Turkomatic: automatic, recursive task and workflow design for mechanical turk. In: Proceedings of HCOMP 2011 (2011)
27. Lease, M., et al.: Mechanical turk is not anonymous. SSRN Electron. J. (2013). https://papers.ssrn.com/sol3/papers.cfm?abstract_id=2228728
28. Li, G., Wang, J., Zheng, Y., Franklin, M.J.: Crowdsourced data management: a survey. IEEE TKDE **28**(9), 2296–2319 (2016)
29. Lu, Y., Tang, Q., Wang, G.: Zebralancer: Private and anonymous crowdsourcing system atop open blockchain. In: Proceedings of ICDCS 2018, pp. 853–865. IEEE (2018)
30. Mavridis, P., Gross-Amblard, D., Miklós, Z.: Using hierarchical skills for optimized task assignment in knowledge-intensive crowdsourcing. In: Proceedings of WWW 2016, pp. 843–853 (2016)
31. Mironov, I., Pandey, O., Reingold, O., Vadhan, S.: Computational differential privacy. In: Halevi, S. (ed.) CRYPTO 2009. LNCS, vol. 5677, pp. 126–142. Springer, Heidelberg (2009). https://doi.org/10.1007/978-3-642-03356-8_8
32. Paillier, P.: Public-key cryptosystems based on composite degree residuosity classes. In: Stern, J. (ed.) EUROCRYPT 1999. LNCS, vol. 1592, pp. 223–238. Springer, Heidelberg (1999). https://doi.org/10.1007/3-540-48910-X_16
33. Qardaji, W., Yang, W., Li, N.: Differentially private grids for geospatial data. In: Proceedings of ICDE 2013, pp. 757–768 (2013)
34. Qardaji, W., Yang, W., Li, N.: Understanding hierarchical methods for differentially private histograms. Proc. VLDB Endow. **6**(14), 1954–1965 (2013)
35. Srba, I., Bielikova, M.: A comprehensive survey and classification of approaches for community question answering. ACM TWEB **10**(3), 1–63 (2016). Article no. 18. https://dl.acm.org/toc/tweb/2016/10/3
36. Steutel, F.W., Kent, J.T., Bondesson, L., Barndorff-Nielsen, O.: Infinite divisibility in theory and practice [with discussion and reply]. Scand. J. Stat. **6**(2), 57–64 (1979)
37. Steutel, F.W., Van Harn, K.: Infinite divisibility of probability distributions on the real line (2003)

38. To, H., Ghinita, G., Shahabi, C.: A framework for protecting worker location privacy in spatial crowdsourcing. Proc. VLDB Endow. **7**(10), 919–930 (2014)
39. To, H., Shahabi, C., Xiong, L.: Privacy-preserving online task assignment in spatial crowdsourcing with untrusted server. In: Proceedings of ICDE 2018, pp. 833–844 (2018)
40. Xia, H., Wang, Y., Huang, Y., Shah, A.: Our privacy needs to be protected at all costs: crowd workers' privacy experiences on amazon mechanical turk. In: Proceedings of HCI 2017, vol. 1 (2017). Article no. 113
41. Zhai, D., et al.: Towards secure and truthful task assignment in spatial crowdsourcing. World Wide Web **22**, 2017–2040 (2019). https://doi.org/10.1007/s11280-018-0638-2
42. Zhang, J., Xiao, X., Xie, X.: PrivTree: a differentially private algorithm for hierarchical decompositions. In: Proceedings of SIGMOD 2016, pp. 155–170 (2016)

Secure Distributed Queries over Large Sets of Personal Home Boxes

Riad Ladjel[1,2](✉), Nicolas Anciaux[1,2], Philippe Pucheral[1,2], and Guillaume Scerri[1,2]

[1] Inria Saclay, 91120 Palaiseau, France
{riad.ladjel,nicolas.anciaux,philippe.pucheral,
guillaume.scerri}@inria.fr
[2] University of Versailles, 78000 Versailles, France
{riad.ladjel,nicolas.anciaux,philippe.pucheral,
guillaume.scerri}@uvsq.fr

Abstract. Smart disclosure initiatives and new regulations such as GDPR allow individuals to get the control back on their data by gathering their entire digital life in a Personal Data Management Systems (PDMS). Multiple PDMS architectures exist and differ on their ability to preserve data privacy and to perform collective computations crossing data of multiple individuals (e.g., epidemiological or social studies) but none of them satisfy both objectives. The emergence of Trusted Execution Environments (TEE) changes the game. We propose a solution called Trusted PDMS, combining the TEE and PDMS properties to manage the data of each individual, and a complete framework to execute collective computation on top of them, with strong privacy and fault tolerance guarantees. We demonstrate the practicality of the solution through a real case-study being conducted over 10.000 patients in the healthcare field.

Keywords: Trusted execution environment · Secure distributed computing · Data privacy

1 Introduction

As Tim Berners Lee advocates, "time has come to restore the power of individuals on the web" [38]. Smart disclosure initiatives (e.g., Blue and Green Button in the US, MiData in UK, MesInfos in France) and new privacy-protection regulations (e.g., GDPR in Europe [18]) are a first step in this direction, allowing individuals to retrieve their personal data from the companies and administrations hosting them. Hence, they can gather their complete digital environment in a single place, called Personal Cloud or Personal Data Management Systems (PDMS) [4] and manage it under their control.

Several companies are now riding this wave with highly diverse architectural solutions, ranging from *centralized web hosting PDMSs* (e.g., CozyCloud or Meeco and governmental programs like MyData.org in Finland or MesInfos.fing.org in France), to *Zero-knowledge personal clouds* (e.g., SpiderOak or Sync), up to fully *decentralized PDMS hosted at home* (e.g., CloudLocker or MyCloudHome).

The architectural dimension of the PDMS concept raises two important and potentially conflicting challenges: (1) gathering personal data previously scattered

A. Hameurlain et al. (Eds.) TLDKS XLIV, LNCS 12380, pp. 108–131, 2020.
https://doi.org/10.1007/978-3-662-62271-1_4

across distinct data silos generates new opportunities but incurs new privacy threats depending on where and how these data are hosted and (2) giving the power back to each individual on his data could impede the development of new collective services of high societal interest (e.g., computing statistics or clustering data for an epidemiological study).

Decentralized PDMS architectures have recognized privacy protection virtues wrt. challenge (1) by decreasing the Benefit/Cost ratio of an attack compared to their centralized web hosting counterparts. However, they make challenge (2) harder to tackle. How can we convince individuals who selected a decentralized PMDS setting to engage their personal data in a distributed process they do not control? Conversely, how could a service provider trust a processing performed by a myriad of untrusted participants? No existing work, including Multi-Party Computation (MPC) [9, 13], gossip-based [2], homomorphic encryption-based [11, 19] or differential privacy-based [14] protocols fully answer this dual question in a practical way. Existing solutions are able either to compute a limited set of operations (e.g., count, sum) in a scalable way or to compute arbitrary functions on a limited number of participants.

In this paper, we argue that the emergence of Trusted Execution Environments (TEE) [32] at the edge of the network - Intel SGX, ARM's TrustZone or TPM components are becoming omnipresent on every PC, tablets, smartphones and even smart objects - drastically changes the game. TEEs are able to efficiently compute arbitrary functions over sensitive data while providing data confidentiality and code integrity. However, TEEs have been designed to protect individual device/server rather than large scale distributed edge computing processes. Moreover, while TEE tamper-resistance makes attacks difficult and costly, side-channel attacks have been shown feasible [37]. Without appropriate counter-measures, a minority of corrupted participants in a distributed processing could endanger data from the majority.

In a previous paper [25], we have introduced a generic Manifest-based framework which answers the preceding requirements by establishing a mutual trust between participants and service provider that a data processing task distributed among a large set of TEEs will deliver a correct result in a privacy-preserving way, even in the presence of corrupted participants. In a second paper [24], we have instantiated this generic framework in the medical context and demonstrated the practicality of the approach through an ongoing deployment of the technology over 10.000 patients. Capitalizing on the manifest-based framework background [25], the current journal paper extends the work initiated in [24] in two main directions:

- First, we make the manifest-based framework fault-tolerant to handle any form of participants' failures (i.e., unexpected participant disconnections, shuts down, too slow communication throughput, etc.) without aborting the complete protocol. Fault-tolerance is paramount in a fully decentralized context as the one considered in [24].
- Second, we improve the communication protocol considered in [24] by obfuscating the communication patterns that could leak critical personal data. Anonymizing the communications is mandatory in the medical field where highly sensitive data can be easily inferred by observing the information flow between computation nodes.

The rest of the paper is organized as follows. Section 2 recalls background material from [25] mandatory to understand the philosophy and principles of the manifest-based framework. Section 3 details the concrete instantiation of this framework in the medical field. Section 4 presents our new fault-tolerance protocol while Sect. 5 is devoted to our new anonymized communication protocol. Section 6 evaluates the solution, both in terms of lessons learned and performance. Finally, Sect. 7 summarizes relevant state of the art solutions and Sect. 8 concludes.

2   Background Material

2.1   TEE as Game-Changer

The emergence of *Trusted Execution Environments* (TEE) [32] drastically changes the game regarding management of personal data. A TEE combines tamper-resistant hardware and software components to guarantee: (1) *data confidentiality*, meaning that private data residing in a TEE cannot be observed from the outside and (2) *code integrity*, meaning that an attacker controlling a corrupted user environment (or OS) cannot influence the behavior of a program executing within a TEE. TEE are now omnipresent in end-user devices like PCs (e.g., Intel's Software Guard eXtention (SGX) in Intel CPUs since Skylake version in 2015), mobile devices (e.g., ARM's TrustZone in ARM processors equipping smartphones and set-top boxes) and dedicated platforms (e.g., TPM combined with CPU or MCU). All these solutions provide the two properties mentioned above with different levels of performance and resilience to side-channel attacks which could compromise data confidentiality [37]. Anyway, side-channel attacks remain complex to perform and require physically instrumenting the TEE, which prevents large scale attacks. Code integrity is more difficult to compromise and not challenged today in most environments [35].

In this paper, and as in [24], we assume that each individual is equipped with a trusted PDMS (TPDMS), that is the combination of a TEE and a PDMS in a same dedicated hardware device. This device embeds a Trusted Computing Base, i.e. a certified software composed of: (1) a PDMS managing and protecting the individual's data (storing, updating, querying data and enforcing access control rules) and (2) a code loader ensuring the confidentiality and integrity of the code (in the TEE sense) executed in the box. Thus, only the trusted PDMS, the code loader, and additional external code certified and verified by the code loader (through a signature of that code) can run in the box. Persistent personal data are stored outside the security sphere, in a stable memory attached to the box (e.g., a SD card or a disk), but encrypted by the TPDMS to protect them in confidentiality and integrity. Considering the omnipresence of TEE in most end-user devices today, various concrete instantiations of TPDMS can be devised (e.g., combination of a TPM - Trusted Platform Module - with a microcontroller, a Raspberry-Pi with ARM Trustzone or a personal cloud server with Intel SGX).

2.2   Related Trust Model

We derive the following trust model from the previous section:

Large Set of Trusted TPDMS, Small Set of Corrupted TPDMS. We assume that each individual is equipped with a TPDMS managing his personal data. As mentioned above, despite the TEE tamper-resistance and the cost of such attacks, side-channel attacks have been shown feasible. Hence, in a large scale setting, we cannot totally exclude the fact that a small subset of TPDMS could have been instrumented by malicious participants opening the door to side-channel attacks compromising the confidentiality property.

Trusted Computation Code. We consider that the code distributed to the participants to contribute to a distributed computation has been carefully reviewed and approved beforehand by a regulatory body (e.g., an association or national privacy regulatory agency) which signed this code. But the fact that the downloaded code is trusted does not imply that a whole distributed execution is trusted.

Untrusted Infrastructure. Besides the presence of TPDMS, no security assumptions can be made about the user's environment or the communication infrastructure.

2.3 Expected Properties

The problem to be solved can be formulated as follows: how to translate the trust put in the computation code declaration, as certified by the regulatory body, into a mutual trust from all parties in the concrete distributed execution of that code under the trust model above? Solving this problem leads to satisfying the following properties:

– *Mutual trust:* assuming that the declared code is executed within TPDMSs, mutual trust guarantees that: (1) only the data strictly specified for the computation is collected at each participants' PDMS, (2) only the final result of the computation can be disclosed, i.e., none of the collected raw data of any participant is leaked, (3) this final result is honestly computed as declared and (4) the computation code has the ability to check that any collected data is genuine.
– *Deterrence of side-channel attacks:* assuming a small fraction of malicious participants are involved in the computation with instrumented TPDMS, the deterrence property must (1) guarantee that the leakage remains circumscribed to the data manipulated by the sole corrupted TPDMS and (2) prevent the attackers from targeting a specific intermediate result (e.g., sensitive data or some targeted participants).

To have a practical interest, the solution must finally: (1) be generic enough to support any distributed computations (e.g., from simple aggregate queries to advanced machine learning computations) and (2) scale to a large population (e.g., tens of thousands) of individuals.

2.4 Manifest-Based Framework for Trusted PDMS

To ensure a collective computation that scrupulously respects the properties described above, we propose a framework based on a Manifest describing the computation on which all the actors agree and a distributed protocol based on TPDMSs performing the computation in compliance with that Manifest. The solution is described in Fig. 1. It is conducted in three main steps:

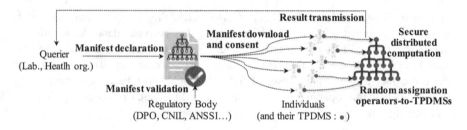

Fig. 1. Manifest-based distributed computation framework.

Manifest Declaration. The entity wishing to execute a distributed computation over personal data (e.g., a statistic agency, association of patients), called the *Querier*, acts as a data controller in the GDPR sense and produces a Manifest describing the computation. Individual contributors give their consent on the basis of the purpose of that manifest, and rely on regulatory bodies (e.g., WP29 members, CNIL) which validate the entire Manifest with regard to good confidentiality practices. To this end, the manifest indicates the identity of the *Querier*, which must be authorized for the purpose. It also provides the collection queries expressed in any easily interpretable declarative language (e.g., SQL), so that the regulatory body can verify that they reflect the principle of limited collection established by the legislation for the intended use. The code of the implemented operators and the organization of the data flow between them are also provided, and must correspond to the declared purpose. The number of participants plays a dual role: it represents both a threshold to be achieved for a sufficiently relevant result for the stated purpose and a privacy threshold preventing the risk of re-identification of individual data in the final result, which the regulator must also check. Once certified, the Manifest is published in a Public store where it can be downloaded by individuals wishing to participate. Example 1 shows the manifest of a distributed *group-by* query in the social-health context.

Random Assignment of Operators to Participants. Participants download the manifest, and when a sufficient number consent to contribute with their data, each participant is assigned an operator of the Manifest. Ensuring a random assignment is critical to deter side-channel attacks on participants, by prohibiting corrupted participants from selecting specific operators in the execution process for malicious purpose (operators manipulating a large amount of data or receiving outputs from participants targeted by the attacker).

Secure Distributed Evaluation. Each participant's TPDMS downloads the code of the operator assigned to it and checks its signature, authenticates the TPDMS of participants supposed to exchange data with it (as specified in the random assignment) and establishes communication channels with them. The participant then executes his operator, potentially contributes personal data, and allows the computation to proceed by sending its output to its successor. Once all participants have executed their operator, the end-result is published on the public store encrypted with the public key of the *Querier*.

```
Purpose:
  Compute the avg number days of hospitalization prescribed
  group by patient's age and dependency-level (Iso-Resource
Group, GIR)
Operators code:
  mapper source code
  reducer source code
Dataflow between the operators:
  Number of mappers: 10000
  Number of reducers: 10
Collection queries:
  SELECT GIR, to_year(sysdate-birthdate) FROM Patient;
  SELECT avg(qty)FROM Prescription WHERE prescType = 'hospital-
ization';
Number of participants: 10000
Querier: ARS-Health-Agency, Public key: Rex2%ÃźHj6k7åÃę
```

Example 1. 'Group-by' Manifest expressed by health organization.

2.5   Random Assignment Protocol

Obtaining a random assignment of operators to participants is key to prevent any potential attackers (Querier or any participants) colluding with corrupted TPDMS from being assigned a targeted operator or position in the dataflow at execution. While existing solutions have been proposed to ensure that a random number is chosen and attested in distributed settings, e.g., [7], none can be applied to reach this specific goal as they assume the list of participants is known in advance, as opposed to our case where the participant list is chosen based on collected users' consents. We propose a solution to produce a provably random assignment, detailed in Fig. 2. As we consider TPDMS as trusted, the random assignment can be delegated to any TPDMS. However, the challenge is avoiding any malicious Participant or Querier aborting and replaying the assignment process a large number of times, picking the best one for a potential attack.

To avoid such attacks, we make sure, in a first step of our protocol, that the Querier commits to an assigning participant among the consenting participants. More precisely, each consenting participant first declares itself by publishing its identity and the hash of a random number used later to prove reception of the list of participants. Second, the protocol ensures that once the list of participants has been fixed, the assignment is actually performed randomly, and that this randomness can be checked by every participant. Hence, once the Querier has gathered enough participants willing to participate, it broadcasts the full list of participants together with the designated assigning participant, which is acknowledged by each participant by disclosing the random number chosen in the initial step. Following this, the designated assigning participant is sent the full list of participants together with all the acknowledgements. He then checks that all acknowledgements are valid, and performs a random assignment of operators to participants. Finally, he signs this assignment and sends it back to the Querier.

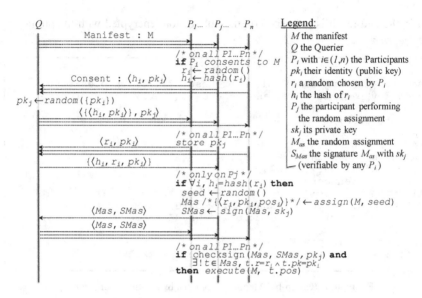

Fig. 2. Random assignment of operators to participants.

Thus, the protocol ensures that when an individual consents to a manifest, the assignment can only be made once, at random (any attempt to replay the assignment would be visible to the participants and a restart require to obtain their consents again).

2.6 Global Assessment of the Manifest-Based Framework

We sum up by showing how the framework satisfies the properties identified in Sect. 2.3.

Deterrence of Attacks. This property first states that *the data leakage due to an attack must be circumscribed to the sole data manipulated by the corrupted TPDMS*. This is intrinsically achieved by never sharing any cryptographic information among different TPDMS. Hence, any persistent data residing in a TPDMS is encrypted with secret keys known only by that TPDMS and intermediate results in transit between a predecessor and a successor TPDMS is encrypted with a session key (see below) and managed in clear-text in that successor (inheriting the confidentiality property from the TEE processing it). The second requirement is to prevent *any attacker from targeting specific personal data*, which is the precise goal of the *Random Assignment Protocol* introduced in Sect. 2.5.

These requirements satisfy deterrence of attacks by drastically increasing the Cost/Benefit ratio of an attack. Indeed, even if a fraction of TPDMSS is instrumented with side-channel attacks compromising data confidentiality, such attack incurs a high cost of tampering with secure hardware (with physical intervention of the PDMS owner) with a benefit limited to obtaining the data manipulated by the sole corrupted TPDMSS, and negligible probability for gaining any personal data of interest. Indeed, in a computation manifest, we distinguish between participants assigned to a collection operator (which only extracts personal raw data from the participant) and participants assigned to a computation operator (which process personal data collected from others). Then, attacking any TPDMS running a collection operator is of no interest since the attacker only gains access to his own data. Moreover, the probability of a corrupted node being assigned a computation operator is negligible in practice (see security analysis in Sect. 6). Thus, although more elaborate strategies could be adopted to further maximize the Cost/Benefit ratio (e.g., blurring data), they are considered unnecessary in our context.

Mutual Trust. The *mutual trust* property is guaranteed if two hypotheses hold: (H1) all data exchanged between the participants' TPDMSs are encrypted with session keys and (H2) each TPDMS involved in the computation authenticates its neighboring participants as legitimate TPDMSs complying with the random assignment for that manifest. The first condition for *mutual trust* (see Sect. 2.3) stems from the fact that (1) the collection queries are part of the manifest certified by the Regulatory body, (2) its authenticity is cryptographically checked by each TPDMS and (3) the TPDMS evaluating these queries is part of the Trusted Computing Base thereby guaranteeing the integrity of this collection phase. The second condition is satisfied by construction since each TPDMS guarantees the confidentiality of local data and H1 guarantees the confidentiality of intermediate data in transit. The final result is itself encrypted with the public key of the Querier so that no other data is ever leaked outside the TPDMS ecosystem. The third condition is again satisfied by construction by H2 guaranteeing that only genuine operators are computed and conform to the dataflow specified in the manifest. The last condition stems from the fact that (1) local data can be manipulated in clear-text inside each TPDMS, allowing any form of verification (e.g., check signature of data produced by a smart meter or quantified-self device, or issued by an employer or a bank) and (2) H2 guarantees the integrity of the data collection operator at each participant. Note that this guarantee holds even in the presence of corrupted TPDMSs which could compromise the *confidentiality* property.

In conclusion, the proposed solution is generic enough to capture any distributed execution plan where any node can be an operator of any complexity and edges are secure communication channels between the TPDMS of participants executing the operators. Compared to the state of the art, our manifest-based approach has the ability to reconcile security with genericity and scalability. First, the TEE *confidentiality* property can be leveraged to execute each operation over clear-text genuine data. Second, the number of messages exchanged among participants only results from the distributed computation to be performed, but not from the underlying security mechanism. Hence, unlike secure Multiparty computations (MPC), homomorphic encryption, Gossip or Differential privacy approaches, no computational constraint hurting genericity nor scalability need to be introduced in the processing for security reasons.

3   A Trusted PDMS in the Medical-Social Field

This section presents an on-going deployment of a TPDMS in the medical-social field and assesses the practicality of the Manifest framework.

Overview. End of 2017, the Yvelines district in France launched a public call for tender to deploy an Electronic Healthcare Record (EHR) infrastructure facilitating the medical and social care at home for elderly people. 10.000 patients are primarily targeted by this initiative, with the objective to use it as a testbed for a larger medium-term national/international deployment. The question raised by this initiative is threefold:

– How to make patients, caregivers and professionals trust the EHR security despite the recent and massive privacy leakages due to piracy, scrutinization and opaque business practices inherent to any data centralization process?
– How to combine privacy expectations with the collective benefits of data analysis tools to rationalize care, improve business practices and predict disease evolution?
– How to make patient's healthcare folder available even in a disconnected mode considering the low adoption of internet by elderly people?

The Hippocad company, in partnership with the Inria research institute and the University of Versailles (UVSQ), won this call for tender with a solution called hereafter THPC (Trusted Health Personal Cloud). THPC is based on a home box, pictured in Fig. 3, combining 3 usages: (1) effectiveness control and vigilance, (2) home care coordination and (3) supervision (forthcoming). The hardware incorporates a number of sensors and communication modules (in particular SigFox) managed by a first microcontroller (called MCU1) devoted to the communication and sensing tasks. The data delivered by the box are used by the Yvelines district to cover usage (1), that is adjusting the care payment to their duration and performing a remote vigilance of the patient home. A second microcontroller (MCU2: STM32F417, 168 MHz, 192 KB RAM, 1 MB of NOR storage) is devoted to the PDMS managing the patient folder, a μ-SD card hosting the raw patient data (encrypted by the PDMS) and a tamper-resistant TPM (Trusted Platform Module) securing the cryptographic keys and the boot phase of the PDMS in MCU2. As detailed next, the combination of a TPM with MCU2 forms a TPDMS. Care professionals interact with the PDMS (i.e., query and update the patient's folder) through Bluetooth connected smartphone apps, covering usage (2). Finally, volunteer patients accepting to contribute to distributed computations (usage (3)), will be equipped with a box variant where the SigFox module is replaced by a GPRS module.

The PDMS engine itself has been specifically designed by Inria/UVSQ to accommodate the constraints of MCU2. This embedded PDMS is a full-fledged personal database server capable of storing data in tables, querying them in SQL, and provides access control policies. Hence, care professionals can each interact with the patient's folder according to the privileges associated to their role (e.g., a physician and a nurse will not get access to the same data). Finally, the patient's data is replicated in an encrypted archive on a remote server to be able to recover it in case of crash. A specific master key recovery process (based on Shamir's secret sharing) has been designed to guarantee that no one but the patient can recover this master key.

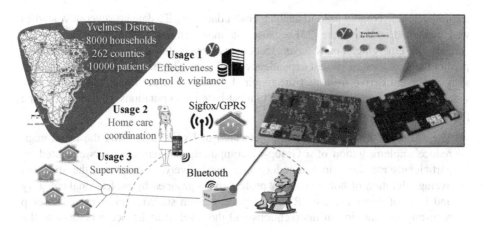

Fig. 3. Architecture of the THPC solution.

THPC as an Instance of Trusted PDMS. The THPC platform described above is an illustrative example of TPDMS. As introduced in Sect. 2.1, a TPDMS is a combination of a TEE and a PDMS software embedded in a same dedicated hardware device, providing confidentiality and integrity guarantees for the code running in this device. The presence of two separate MCUs answers security concerns, indeed the Trusted Computing Base (TCB) is limited to the code located in MCU2 and does not include drivers and sensors (managed by MCU1) and is thus minimalistic. Additionally, the TCB is cryptographically signed. The TPM protecting the box is used at boot time (and NOR flash time) to check the genuineness of the PDMS code by checking the signature. The PDMS code in turn can download external pieces of code corresponding to the operators extracted from a Manifest, check their integrity thanks to the code signature provided by the Regulatory body, and run it. Hence, no code other than the TCB and signed operators can run in the box. The TPM also protects the cryptographic certificate that securely identifies the box and the master key protecting the personal database footprint on the μ-SD card. Note however that, while the TPM is tamper-resistant, the MCU2 is not. Hence, a motivated attacker could physically instrument his box to spy the content of the RAM at run time.

Distributed Computations of Interest. The next critical step of the project is to integrate usage (3) (supervision). GPRS variant of the boxes are under development to establish a communication network via a central server settled by the Hippocad company, which plays the role of a communication gateway between the THPC boxes (it relays encrypted data bunches between THPC boxes but cannot access to the underlying data). Two essential distributed computations are considered, namely the *Group-by* and *K-means* computations. *Group-by* allows computing simple statistics by evaluating aggregate functions (sum, average, min, max, etc.) on population subsets grouped by various dimensions (the level of dependence or GIR, age, gender, income, etc.). Such statistics are of general interest in their own and are also often used to calibrate more sophisticated data analysis techniques (e.g., accurately calibrate the k parameter of a *K-means* computation). *K-means* is one of the most popular clustering technique and is broadly used to analyze health data [26]. To date however, few studies was conducted on home care [23] because data management techniques for this type of care are still emerging. Yet, *K-means* techniques already delivered significant results to predict the evolution of patient dependency level after a hip fracture [16] or Alzheimer symptoms, and derive from that the required evolution of the home cares to be provided and their cost. The first two Manifest-based computations considered in the project cover these use cases as follows:

– The *Group-by* manifest is the one presented in Example 1, using the usual map-reduce implementation of a Group-by computation, where operators executed by participants are the map and reduce task respectively. It computes the sum and average duration of home visits by professionals grouped by professional category and level of dependence (GIR) of the patient. Such statistics are expected to help adjusting the duration of interventions and the level of assistance according to the patients' situation.

– The *K-means* manifest is inspired by a previous study conducted in Canada with elderly people in home care. This study analyses 37 variables, and provides 7 centroids [6] that finely characterize the people cared for. On a similar map-reduce basis, we define K-means manifests computed over distributed PDMSs in three steps: (1) k initial means representing the centroid of k clusters are randomly generated by the Querier and sent to all participants to initialize the processing, (2) each participant playing a mapper role computes its distance with these k means and sends back its data to the reducer node managing the closest cluster, (3) each reducer recomputes the new centroid of the cluster it manages based on the data received from the mappers and sends it back to all participants. Steps 2 and 3 are repeated a given number of times or until convergence.

In Sect. 6, we give preliminary measures obtained by a combination of real measures and simulations for these two manifests since they are not yet deployed. Running manifests in the THPC context has required an adaptation of the random assignation protocol to cope with the intrinsic communication bandwidth's limitation of GPRS.

Adaptation of the Random Assignment Protocol to the THPC Context. Given the low bandwidth of the THPC boxes (GPRS communications), a critical problem is limiting the amount of data transmitted to all participants, as hundreds of KBs broadcasted to all thousands of participants would not be compatible with acceptable performance. In order to reach this goal, we optimize the two main parts of the random assignation protocol (Sect. 2.5) that lead to transmission of large amounts of data. The main optimization is making sure that we do not need to transmit neither the whole assignment nor the whole manifest to all participants as they only need their part of the assignment and the manifest related to their part of the computation. However, we need to make sure that the integrity of the whole manifest and assignment is ensured. In order to achieve these two seemingly antagonistic goals, we make use of Merkle hash trees [27] over the corresponding data structures. The properties of the Merkle hash tree ensures that given the root of the hash tree, it is possible to provide a small checksum proving (in the cryptographic sense) that an element belongs to the corresponding hash tree, and it is computationally infeasible to forge such a proof. Note that the checksum is a logarithmic (in the number of values in the tree) number of hashed values and thus stays manageable (small size). Additionally, we avoid broadcasting the whole list of participants as only the assigning participant needs to perform checks on this list. We only broadcast a cryptographic hash of this list, and only send it in full to the assigning participant who actually needs to check it. The assigning participant however does not need to send back the full assignment, only a Merkle hash tree signed with its private key, and the random seed used to generate the assignment (so that the Querier can reconstruct it) is sent back. Finally, in order to perform its task in the manifest, any participant only needs its position together with the corresponding operator, collection queries and data flow and proof of membership to the logical manifest. Additionally, the participant needs to receive proof that the assignment is correct.

Summing up, we reduce the communication load during assignment building phase from a few broadcasts of a few hundreds of KB (for tens of thousands of participants) to only one large download for the assigning participant (again a few hundreds of KB), and small downloads/uploads (a few tens of Bytes) for all other participants, drastically reducing the overall communication load, and making it manageable in constrained setting.

4   Fault Tolerance Protocol

Any distributed solution involving end-users computing resources must consider the case of participants' failures, i.e., becoming unreachable due to unexpected disconnections, shuts down, low communication throughput, etc. This statement is particularly true in our medical-social context involving battery-powered devices connected to the network by a GPRS module.

With the Manifest-based framework presented in Sect. 2.4, any participant failure conducts to stop the execution (fortunately without exposing any result), forcing the querier to restart processing from its beginning. The objective is thus to support a ratio of participant failures while enabling the execution to be completed. However, failures may impact the security of the solution: a malicious participant may deliberately attempt to weaken other participants' connectivity (e.g., denial of service attack) to harm the confidentiality or integrity of the computation. We consider here both the security and the performance aspects of handling failures.

Participants failures in our context may occur either during step 2 (random assignment of operators) or step 3 (secure distributed evaluation). Failures at step 2 are easily tackled by removing faulty participants from the protocol. Failures at step 3 are more difficult to address. Traditional fault-tolerant solutions rely either on redundant execution methods (e.g., perform k independent executions of a same operator and select a result) or on check-pointing mechanisms (e.g., store intermediate results of operators and restart computation from these points). Both solutions unfortunately increase data exposure, either increasing the number of participants processing the same data or introducing additional persistent copies of such data. We select the first solution anyway (redundant execution) because its negative effects are largely alleviated by the randomness measure integrated in our protocol, proscribing attackers targeting specific nodes.

We explain below how to integrate redundant execution in a manifest, for the case of a n-ary tree-based execution plan. Let assume a redundancy factor of k (with k = 2 or 3 in practice), a failure-resilient solution can be formed as follows:

1. For a manifest M requesting N participants, $k.N$ participants are actually selected.
2. When assigning operators to participants, k participants are assigned the same operator in M. They inherit the same position in the execution plan and the same operator to run, to form a so-called bundle of redundant participants. Hence, participants p_i, p_j, ..., $p_k \in$ bundle$_l$ all execute the same operator op_l.
3. The assignment function from participant to role is de facto no longer injective. However, the position of each participant in the execution plan is still determined at random. Consequently, bundles are also populated randomly.
4. Each participant in a successor bundle is connected to all participants in an antecedent bundle by edges in the execution plan (antecedent/successor refer to the position of participants/bundles in the execution plan/tree).
5. Instead of iterating for each antecedent, a participant iterates for each bundle, and the participants in this bundle are considered one after the other at random. If one does not answer after a certain delay, it is considered as 'failed' and a next participant in the same bundle is contacted. If all participants of the same bundle fails, the whole processing is abandoned.

Correctness. Any participant consuming an input data (resp. sending an output data) checks beforehand the integrity and identity of its antecedents (resp. successor) in the execution plan, as in a standard (i.e., non-fault-tolerant) execution. If a complete bundle fails, the error is propagated along the execution plan such that the execution ends with an error and no result is published. Finally, what if participants of a bundle play the role of data collectors, each being connected to its local PDMS? The local data are not the same at each participant and the output delivered by the bundle hence depends on which active participant is finally selected in the bundle. This randomness in the result of the computation is actually not different from the one incurred by selecting N among potentially P consenting participants in the protocol and does not hurt the consistency of the execution.

In terms of performance, this strategy does not impact the response time since participants in the same bundle work in parallel (it can even be better considering that the input of an antecedent bundle may arrive faster than the one of a single antecedent). However, the overall computation cost (sum of all computation costs) is increased by a factor of k and the number of communications by a factor of k*k. While this grows extremely rapidly, note that we only need to consider very small values of k (typically 2) as we allow for one failure per bundle, and the probability of a whole bundle failing is extremely small even if bundles are small.

5   Anonymous Communication Protocol

Anonymizing the communications is mandatory in the medical field. In our distributed computation framework, sensitive data can be inferred by observing the information flow between computation nodes. Typically, in canonical map-reduce computations encoded with our manifest-based framework, as shown in Example 1, each participant acting as a mapper node sends its <*GIR*, [*age*, *#days-of-hospitalization*]> to the given reducer in charge of aggregating the information for that *GIR*. Observing the communications would reveal the recipient reducer for any participant and hence disclose its *GIR* value (i.e., its level of dependence).

Distributed execution plans often exhibit such data dependent data flows, as directing tuples to be processed together to a same computation node is necessary to evaluate certain statistics (e.g., computing a median) and/or improve performance. In the general case, two main strategies can be adopted to hide data dependent communications: (1) use anonymous communication networks (e.g., use TOR) to hide any link between data recipient nodes and source nodes, or (2) "cover" data dependent communications within fixed, data independent patterns. Resorting to the first approach requires tackling the issue of adapting onion routing protocols to our resource constrained THPC platform. This is still considered an open issue in the general case of constrained IoT devices (see, e.g. [20]), making such approach infeasible in practice in the short term.

Using the second approach would simply mean replacing sensitive communication patterns with data independent ones (e.g., broadcasts) at the price of extra communications. In the previous example, this could be achieved by enforcing (as part of the manifest) that any message sent from a mapper node to a reducer node also triggers sending one extra 'empty' messages of same size to all other reducers, thus forming a 'broadcast-like' communication pattern (and hence hiding the value of GIR). The expected performance penalty is high, especially in the context of our THPC solution, considering the limitation of GPRS in terms of communication bandwidth.

We present below a simple way to adopt data independent communication patterns in a manifest, while limiting the communication overhead to a minimum acceptable in our context.

Adopting Data Independent Communication Patterns. Let consider for simplicity a n-ary tree-based execution plan in the manifest, where at a given level l in the tree, the data exchanges issued from the child nodes to the parent nodes (at level $l + 1$) reveal information on data values processed at the child nodes. For the sake of simplicity, we consider that each child node transmits a unique message to a given parent node, selected on the basis of a sensitive information hold at the child node. The naive solution to avoid exposing sensitive information is to cover such child-to-parent message by broadcasting an empty message of same size to all other potential parent nodes at level $l + 1$. In terms of extra communications, with n_l nodes at level l each with a single message of size $|t|$ bytes to be transmitted to a parent node at level $l + 1$, this causes $n_l \times (n_{l+1} - 1)$ additional messages, with extra size $|t| \times n_l \times (n_{l+1} - 1)$ bytes in total. In practice, considering, e.g. *10.000* mappers and *10* reducers as in Example 1 and a tuple size of *100* bytes, this leads to *9.000* extra communications with

900 KB data exchanged (mostly composed of 'empty' tuples), with unacceptable performance in the THPC setting.

Minimizing Communication Overhead. To reduce the communication overhead, we modify the distributed execution plan in the manifest as follows (see Fig. 4): for each level l in the tree where data exchanges issued from child nodes to parent nodes (at level $l + 1$) reveal information on data values (1) we form a k-equipartition[1] of the set of child nodes, we allocate one *scrambler* node per k-partition (with n_l/k scrambler nodes allocated in total) and connect each child node to the scrambler node responsible for its k-partition; and (2) we connect each scrambler node to all the parent nodes and fix at exactly $k' \leq k$ the number of messages each scrambler sends to each parent node.

Each scrambler node acts in two phases. First, it collects one tuple $<P_i, E_{K_{P_i}}(M_{C_j})>$ per child node C_j of the k-partition it takes in charge, with P_i the parent node the message has to be transmitted and $E_{K_{P_i}}(M_{C_j})$ the message M produced by C_j encrypted with the public key[2] K of P_i. Second, the scrambler prepares k' messages packages (each of same size) destined to each parent node, it places the encrypted messages collected from the child nodes in the appropriate package for the expected parent nodes and fills in the remaining packages with '*empty*' messages (indistinguishable from others, as being same size and encrypted). In terms of extra communications, this causes $n_{l+1} \times n_l/k$ additional messages, each of size $k' \times |t|$ bytes.

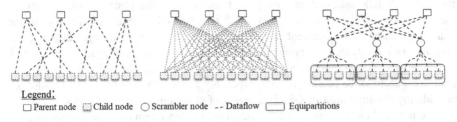

Legend:
☐ Parent node ⬚ Child node ○ Scrambler node -- Dataflow ▭ Equipartitions

Fig. 4. Covering sensitive data exchanges with data independent communication patterns (Left: data dependent; Middle: naive, Right: scrambler-based with $k = 4$).

Resilience to Attacks. The communication pattern introduced by scrambler nodes is fully deterministic and prevents from disclosing sensitive information (the only information disclosed is the size $k' \times |t|$ of data exchanged from scramblers to parent nodes). The *deterrence of side-channel attacks* property must (1) guarantee that the leakage remains circumscribed to the data manipulated by the sole corrupted TPDMS and (2) prevent the attackers from targeting a specific intermediate result (e.g., sensitive data or data of some targeted participants). If a given scrambler is corrupted, it only reveals information regarding the data flow of the partition it has in charge, which

---

[1] A k-equipartition of a set is the partitioning of this set in partitions of cardinality k.

[2] We assume that each node is endowed with a public/private key pair.

ensures that the leakage remains circumscribed (first part of the property). Remark also that only the local communication pattern is exposed to corrupted scramblers, but not the content (payload) of the routed messages (as being encrypted with the recipient node's public key). Hence, lower k leads thus to more k-partitions and more scramblers, with a better resilience to side channel attacks. In addition, the random assignment of the (scrambler) operators to participants prevents potential attackers from targeting specific scramblers (enforcing the second part of the property). Note also that the impact on *mutual trust* is null, as the addition of scramblers does not change the deterministic nature of the query execution plan (nodes can check the integrity of predecessors, enforcing the global integrity of the query tree).

Performance Analysis. In terms of performance, the value of k determines the size of the k-partitions and the number of scramblers $\lceil n_l/k \rceil$, but has no effect on the total volume of data exchanged. Indeed, the addition of scramblers let unchanged the number of messages issued from child nodes (in our setting, n_l messages, one per child node, transmitted to the scrambler responsible for its partition), but it introduces $\lceil n_l/k \rceil \times n_{l+1} \times k'$ (with $1 \leq k' \leq k$) additional messages from scramblers to parent nodes, each of size $|t|$ bytes. Hence, the lower k' leads to the better efficiency. The worst case in terms of communications is $k = k'$. At one extreme, with $k = k' = n_l$ a single scrambler is introduced which transmits n_{l+1} groups of $k' = n_l$ messages with in total the same overhead as that of the naïve solution in number of transmitted bytes. At the other extreme, $k = k' = 1$ leads to introduce n_l scramblers each sending n_{l+1} messages (one message per parent node) with the same global overhead. The performance with scramblers hence becomes better than the naïve solution when $k'/k < (n_{l+1} - 1)/n_{l+1}$.

Calibration of the Parameters k and k'. Reducing the value of k increases the resilience to attacks (with lower k, more scramblers, and a better resilience to side channel attacks). It also improves the degree of parallelism (more scramblers run in parallel) and plays on the overall resource/energy consumption (due to less messages processed at each scrambler, with less memory consumed and less energy). This is of importance in the THPC context where the memory, processing and lifetime of each node is limited. Assuming k has been reduced appropriately to match (privacy and) resource constraints, the second step is to minimize the value of k' to reduce the communication overhead. At the same time, a too small value k' increases the risk of execution failure, if more than k' messages have to be transmitted at execution from a given scrambler to a given parent node. To enable fine tuning the value of k' at runtime, the strategy we adopt is to ask each scrambler, once all input tuples have been collected from the k-partition they have in charge, to first transmit to all parent nodes the maximum number of tuples each has to transmit to this parent nodes, and ask the parent nodes to send back to scramblers the maximal received value, such that k' is fixed in all as the maximal value received from all parent nodes[3]. Note that during this phase, the only additional data transmitted from scrambler to parent is the number of intended

---

[3] Note that this formally makes the communication flow data dependent as the chosen k' depends on the data sent to each scrambler. This, however, only leaks information on the distribution of data, not on any individual data. We do not view this as a significant threat.

messages for this specific parent node. As this data is known to the parent node regardless of the protocol used to fix k, it does not negatively impact security. In practice, well calibrated query execution tree lead to process in all parent nodes a roughly similar amount of tuples (for good load balancing and efficiency), leading to select k' bigger but close to $\lceil n_l/k \rceil$ to minimize the number of empty tuples to be send. Typically, considering Example 1, where $n_{l+1} = 10$ and $n_l = 10.000$, with 10 scramblers (i.e., $k = 1000$), most executions end up with $k' \leq 200$, which means 5 times less data transmitted than using the naïve strategy (equivalent to $k' = 900$).

In conclusion, the principle described here can be implemented to protect sensitive (data dependent) communication patterns with acceptable overhead in many practical examples of distributed PDMS calculations, ranging from simple statistical queries to big-data (map-reduce style) processing, as illustrated in the section on validation. The process of adding scramblers can be performed automatically by a precompiler taking as input a logical manifest and producing a transformed logical manifest covering the communications identified as sensitive. The appropriate value of the k' parameter does not need to be established at pre-compilation, but can be adjusted at runtime (as described above). The selection of the value of k to form the k-equipartitions is dictated by resource constraints in our context and must be provided for at pre-compilation. Tuning of the value of k and study of optimal strategies, as well as their integration in a precompiler are left for future work.

6   Validation

While the THPC platform is still under deployment over the 10.000 targeted patients, we can already draw interesting lessons learned and present preliminary performance and security results of the Manifest framework applied to the *Group-by* and *K-means* cases.

6.1   Lessons Learned for the Deployment of THPC Solution

An important criterion for the Yvelines District when selecting the THPC solution was its compliance with the new GDPR regulations and its ability to foster its adoption by patients and professionals.

Adoption by Patients. From the patients' perspective, a crucial point was to provide differentiated views of their medical-social folder (e.g., a nurse is not supposed to see the income of the elderly person). To this end, a RBAC matrix (role-based access control) has been defined so that a professional owning a badge with a certificate attesting role R can play this role with the appropriate privileges on all patients' boxes. Each patient can explicitly - and physically - express his consent (or not) to the access of a given professional by allowing access to his box during the consultation, as he would do with a paper folder. The patient can also express his consent, with the help of his referent, for each manifest. A notable effect of our proposal is to consent to a specific use of the data and to disclose only the computed result rather than all raw data as usual (e.g., consenting to an Android application manifest provides an unconditional access to the raw data).

Adoption by Professionals. Professionals are reluctant to use an EHR solution which could disclose their contact details, planning and statistical information that may reveal their professional practice (e.g., quantity of drugs prescribed or duration and frequency of home visits). A decentralized and secured solution is a great vector of adoption compared to any central server solution. Similarly, professionals are usually reluctant to see the data related to their practice involved in statistical studies unless strict anonymization guarantees can be provided. While the consent of the professionals is not requested for distributed computations, a desirable effect of our proposal is to never disclose individual data referring to a given professional, and submit all computation to regulatory approval.

6.2 Performance and Security Evaluation of the Manifest-Based Framework

We validate the effectiveness of our approach on the Group-by and K-means use-cases.

Experimental Setting. We implemented the corresponding mappers and reducers code in the THPC box with a server used to route (encrypted) messages between participants, as described in Sect. 4. We computed the execution time while considering different numbers of participants and amount of data transferred during the computations. We used a simulation to derive execution times with large numbers of participants. The results are shown in Fig. 4 (the curves are in log. scale). For the Group-by case we consider an implementation with 10 reducers and 50 different group keys, while for the K-means we consider 7 different clusters with 1 cluster per reducer as in [5] using a traditional distance metric [21]. We used synthetic datasets, as the objective is not to choose the most efficient implementation of a given computation, but rather to assess the efficiency of the manifest-based protocol on real use-cases. As cryptographic tools we used ECC 256 bits for asymmetric encryption, ECDSA signature scheme, AES 128 bits for symmetric encryption and SHA-2 as a hash function, leveraging the hardware acceleration provided by MCU2.

Performance Evaluation. Figures 5.a-b-d-e plot the various costs associated with our protocol. First, the optimization of our random assignment protocol has a strong impact on its execution time, from 75 s without optimization down to 22 s with 10000 participants (this cost depends on the number of participants, but not on the query performed), as well as on the volume of data exchanges, from 800 KB per participant without optimization down to 13 KB (with in total, 7 GB exchanged data down to 130 MB). Once the assignation is performed, the query computation time remains reasonable, with 18 s (resp. 40 s) for a Group-by (resp. K-means) over 10000 participants. Finally, the overhead incurred by the random assignation is limited (e.g., between 20 and 30% of overall time), and the main part of the cost is due to communications (see Fig. 5.c).

Figure 5.f shows the tremendous impact of the random assignment protocol in terms of security. It plots the probability for a set of colluding malicious participants, acting with corrupted TPDMSs in Group-by and K-means computations, to be assigned a reducer operator (hence gaining access to data produced by other participants) or to the data of a given participant of interest (targeted attack). This probability remains very low (few percent) even if several participants successfully corrupt their TPDMS and collude.

The main lessons drawn from these experiments are: First, even with the hardware limitations of the box in terms of computing power and communication throughput, the global time is rather low and acceptable for this kind of study (less than a minute for 10000 participants in comparison with manual epidemiological surveys which may last weeks). Second, the optimization of the assignment protocol has a decisive impact on both execution times and data volumes exchanged, with a significant financial benefit in the context of pay-per-use communication services (such as GPRS network).

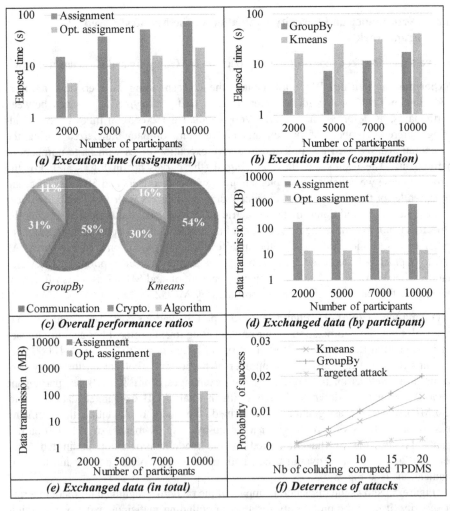

Fig. 5. Performance and security evaluation.

7 Related Works

The first part of this section analyses the pros and cons of existing alternatives in terms of PDMS architectures and positions the TPDMS solution in this landscape. The second part of this state of the art is devoted to the solutions proposed to perform secure database computations and it positions our manifest-based contribution relatively to these works.

7.1 Analysis of PDMS Architecture Alternatives

The *Personal Data Management Systems* (PDMS) [4] concept, also called Personal Cloud, PIMS [1], Personal Data Server [3] or Personal Data Store [28], attracts significant attention from the research and industrial communities. We briefly review the main families of solutions and compare their ability to tackle the two challenges identified in the introduction, namely privacy preservation and distributed collective computations.

Centralized Web Hosting Solutions. CozyCloud, Digi.me, Meeco, or Perkeep and governmental programs like MyData.org (Finland), MesInfos.fing.org (France) or MyDex.org (UK) are representative of this family. Individuals centralize their personal data in a server managed by the PDMS provider and can access them through the internet. These approaches rely on strong security hypotheses: (i) the PDMS provider and its employees are assumed to be fully-honest, and (ii) the PDMS code as well as all applications running on top of it must be trusted. This is critical in a centralized context exacerbating the Benefit/Cost ratio of an attack. On the other hand, collective computations are simplified by the centralization but the security of such processing remains an issue.

Zero-knowledge personal clouds such as SpiderOak or Sync and to a certain extent Digi.me mentioned above, propose a variation of the centralized web hosting solutions where data is stored encrypted in the cloud and the user inherits the responsibility to store and manage the encryption keys elsewhere. The price to pay for this increase of security is the difficulty to develop advanced (local or distributed) services on top of zero-knowledge personal clouds, reducing their use to a robust personal data safe.

Home cloud software solutions (e.g., OpenPDS [28], DataBox [12]) manage personal data at the extremities of the network (e.g., within the user's equipment) to circumvent the security risks of data centralization. Hence, queries on user's data can be computed locally and only the result is sent back to the querier. However, these solutions implicitly assume that the computing platform at the user side is trusted and cannot be tampered with.

Home cloud box (e.g., CloudLocker, MyCloudHome and many personal NAS solutions) go further in this direction by offering a dedicated box that can store TBs of data and run a server plugged on an individual's home internet gateway. This solution alleviates the burden of administrating a server on the individual's device and logically isolates the user's computing environment from the box, they, however do not focus on security. Home cloud software nor home cloud box consider secure distributed processing as a primary target.

The first conclusion that can be drawn from this analysis is that online personal cloud solutions have the technical ability to perform distributed computations but suffer from very strong hypotheses in terms of security. Conversely, decentralized approaches are more likely to gain acceptance from the individuals but do not provide any - privacy preserving - solution to perform distributed computation (exporting their data on a central server to perform the computation would obviously hurt the decentralization principle).

Decentralizing the processing implies to temporarily transfer personal data among participants, transforming each into a vulnerability point. Two guarantees must then be provided: (i) data confidentiality, i.e., any PDMS owner cannot access the data in transit of other participants, and (ii) distributed computation integrity, i.e., any participant's PDMS can attest that any result it supplies corresponds to the assigned computation.

Our proposed TPDMS solution falls in the Home cloud box family, with the salient difference that the box now provides tamper-resistant defenses against attacks. Indeed, compared to a regular Home cloud box, a TPDMS provides means to securely execute external code in the box, opening the door to the design of secure distributed computation protocols, in the line of the Manifest-based framework.

7.2 Secure Database Computations Alternatives

A large majority of works on secure database computations address the case of outsourced databases where honest-but-curious cloud services manage large sets of sensitive data. We position our contribution relatively to these works, and then analyze the main approaches to address secure distributed databases computations, including works relying on TEEs.

Secure Database Outsourcing. Several works focus on protecting outsourced databases with encryption, either by using onion encryption [30] or by exploiting homomorphic encryption [11, 19]. However, most of the existing encryption schemes applied to databases have been shown vulnerable to inference attacks [10]. Going further induce fully homomorphic encryption with intractable performance issues. In any case, these solutions hurt the decentralized assumption of our work. Data can also be protected thanks to differentially private principles [14], again usually performed by an honest-but-curious central server. These principles apply only to specific problems and deliver imprecise results, hurting our genericity objective.

Multi-party Computations (MPC). MPC allows n users to perform computations involving their inputs without learning anything more than the final result. However, MPC assumes honest-but-curious users while the participants in our context can be active attackers (e.g., may attempt corrupting processing, replay messages, execute alternative code, etc.). Second, the cryptographic techniques involved in MPC either do not scale in the number of participants for performance reasons or can solve only specific problems. Typically, MPC adaptations to distributed databases contexts, like

SMCQL [9, 13], either support only few tens of participants or are limited to specific database operations.

Secure Distributed Database Computations Schemes. Several works suggest distributed computation schemes providing anonymous data exchanges and confidential processing mixing gossip-style protocols, encryption and differential privacy. Gossip-based protocols, such as [2], allow to work on fragmented clear-text data exchanged among nodes and, when communication may reveal data content, noise is added to provide differentially private communication patterns. Gossip protocols scale well but are not generic in terms of possible computations. Moreover, they consider an honest-but-curious threat model.

Hardware-Based Database Computing. Some works [5, 8] deploy secure hardware at database server side. They basically split the query processing in one part executed directly on the encrypted data and the other executed inside the secure hardware on clear-text data and make the processing oblivious to prevent adversary learning anything from the data access pattern. These solutions are centralized by nature and do not match our context. Decentralized processing solutions based on secure hardware have also been proposed for aggregate queries [36] or participatory sensing [34] but do not match our genericity objective.

SGX-Based Data Computing. To the best of our knowledge, all works regarding executing data oriented task using SGX have a unique controller (e.g., [15, 29, 33]), as opposed to our setting where no unique individual is supposed to be in control of the computation. Additionally, most of the time this controller also provides the data to be computed on. This greatly simplifies the problem as a same controller verifies all enclaves and organizes the computation. Additionally, various works [17, 31] focus on performing data operations, from indexing to a whole DBMS, within SGX. These works are not directly related to ours as they are all in a centralized setting. The work closest to ours is Ryoan [22] but the techniques for organizing the computation are fundamentally distinct from ours.

8 Conclusion

The concept of TPDMS combined with a Manifest-based framework leverages the security properties provided by TEE to build a comprehensive personal data management solution. This solution reconciles the privacy preservation expected by individuals with the ability to perform collective computations of prime societal interest. We expect that such solution could pave the way to new research works and industrial initiatives tackling the privacy-preserving distributed computing challenge with a new vision.

References

1. Abiteboul, S., André, B., Kaplan, D.: Managing your digital life. CACM **58**(5), 32–35 (2015)
2. Allard, T., Hébrail, G., Pacitti, E., Masseglia, F.: Chiaroscuro: transparency and privacy for massive personal time-series clustering. In: ACM SIGMOD (2015)
3. Allard, T., et al.: Secure personal data servers: a vision paper. In: VLDB (2010)
4. Anciaux, N., Bonnet, P., Bouganim, L., Nguyen, B., et al.: Personal data management systems: the security and functionality standpoint. Inf. Syst. **80**, 13–35 (2019)
5. Arasu, A., Kaushik, R.: Oblivious query processing. arXiv:1312.4012 (2013)
6. Armstrong, J., Zhu, M., Hirdes, J., Stolee, P.: K-means cluster analysis of rehabilitation service users in the home health care system of Ontario: examining the heterogeneity of a complex geriatric population. Arch. Phys. Med. Rehab. **93**(12), 2198–2205 (2012)
7. Backes, M., Druschel, P., Haeberlen, A., Unruh, D.: A practical and provable technique to make randomized systems accountable. In: NDSS, vol. 9 (2009)
8. Bajaj, S., Sion, R.: Trusteddb: a trusted hardware-based database with privacy and data confidentiality. IEEE Trans. Knowl. Data Eng. **26**(3), 752–765 (2013)
9. Bater, J., Elliott, G., Eggen, C., Rogers, J.: SMCQL: secure query processing for private data networks. PVLDB **10**(6), 673–684 (2017)
10. Bindschaedler, V., Grubbs, P., Cash, D., Ristenpart, T., Shmatikov, V.: The tao of inference in privacy-protected databases. Proc. VLDB Endow. **11**(11), 1715–1728 (2018)
11. Boneh, D., Gentry, C., Halevi, S., Wang, F., Wu, D.J.: Private database queries using somewhat homomorphic encryption. In: Jacobson, M., Locasto, M., Mohassel, P., Safavi-Naini, R. (eds.) ACNS 2013. LNCS, vol. 7954, pp. 102–118. Springer, Heidelberg (2013). https://doi.org/10.1007/978-3-642-38980-1_7
12. Chaudhry, A., et al.: Personal data: thinking inside the box. In: Critical Alternatives (2015)
13. Damgård, I., Keller, M., Larraia, E., Pastro, V., Scholl, P., Smart, N.P.: Practical covertly secure MPC for dishonest majority – or: breaking the SPDZ limits. In: Crampton, J., Jajodia, S., Mayes, K. (eds.) ESORICS 2013. LNCS, vol. 8134, pp. 1–18. Springer, Heidelberg (2013). https://doi.org/10.1007/978-3-642-40203-6_1
14. Dwork, C.: Differential privacy. In: ICALP (2006)
15. Dinh, T.T.A., Saxena, P., Chang, E.C., Ooi, B.C., Zhang, C.: M2R: enabling stronger privacy in MapReduce computation. In: 24th USENIX Security Symposium (USENIX Security 2015), pp. 447–462 (2015)
16. Elbattah, M., Molloy, O.: Clustering-aided approach for predicting patient outcomes with application to elderly healthcare in Ireland. In: Workshops at AAAI (2017)
17. Fuhry, B., Bahmani, R., Brasser, F., Hahn, F., Kerschbaum, F., Sadeghi, A.R.: Hardidx: practical and secure index with SGX in a malicious environment. J. Comput. Secur. **26**(5), 677–706 (2018)
18. General Data Protection Regulation (2016). https://gdpr-info.eu/. Accessed May 2020
19. Ge, T., Zdonik, S.: Answering aggregation queries in a secure model. In: VLDB (2007)
20. Hiller, J., Pennekamp, J., Dahlmanns, M., Henze, M., Panchenko, A., Wehrle, K.: Tailoring onion routing to the Internet of Things: security and privacy in untrusted environments. In: IEEE 27th International Conference on Network Protocols ICNP (2019)
21. Huang, Z.: Extensions to the k-means algorithm for clustering large data sets with categorical values. Data Min. Knowl. Discov. **2**, 283–304 (1998)
22. Hunt, T., Zhu, Z., Xu, Y., Peter, S., Witchel, E.: Ryoan: a distributed sandbox for untrusted computation on secret data. TOCS **35**(4), 1–32 (2018)

23. Johnson, S., Bacsu, T., Jeffery, B., Novik, N.: No place like home: a systematic review of home care for older adults. Can. J. Aging **37**(4), 400–419 (2018)
24. Ladjel, R., Anciaux, N., Pucheral, P., Scerri, G.: A manifest-based framework for organizing the management of personal data at the edge of the network. In: ISD (2019)
25. Ladjel, R., Anciaux, N., Pucheral, P., Scerri, G.: Trustworthy distributed computations on personal data using trusted execution environments. In: TrustCom (2019)
26. Liao, M., Li, Y., Kianifard, F., Obi, Z., Arcona, S.: Cluster analysis and its application to healthcare claims data: a study of end-stage renal disease patients who initiated hemodialysis. BMC Nephrol. **17**, 25 (2016)
27. Merkle, C.: Protocols for public key cryptosystems. In: S&P (1980)
28. De Montjoye, Y., Shmueli, E., Wang, S., Pentland, A.: OpenPDS: protecting the privacy of metadata through SafeAnswers. PloS One **9**(7), e98790 (2014)
29. Pires, R., Gavril, D., Felber, P., Onica, E., Pasin, M.: A lightweight MapReduce framework for secure processing with SGX. In: 2017 17th IEEE/ACM International Symposium on Cluster, Cloud and Grid Computing (CCGRID), pp. 1100–1107. IEEE (2017)
30. Popa, R.A., Redfield, C.M., Zeldovich, N., Balakrishnan, H.: CryptDB: processing queries on an encrypted database. Commun. ACM **55**(9), 103–111 (2012)
31. Priebe, C., Vaswani, K., Costa, M.: EnclaveDB: a secure database using SGX. In: 2018 IEEE Symposium on Security and Privacy (SP), pp. 264–278. IEEE (2018)
32. Sabt, M., Achemlal, M., Bouabdallah, A.: Trusted execution environment: what it is, and what it is not. In: TrustCom/BigDataSE/ISPA, vol. 1 (2015)
33. Schuster, F., et al.: VC3: trustworthy data analytics in the cloud using SGX. In: 2015 IEEE Symposium on Security and Privacy, pp. 38–54. IEEE (2015)
34. That, D.H.T., Popa, I.S., Zeitouni, K., Borcea, C.: PAMPAS: privacy-aware mobile participatory sensing using secure probes. In: Proceedings of the 28th International Conference on Scientific and Statistical Database Management, pp. 1–12 (2016)
35. Tramèr, F., Zhang, F., Lin, H., Hubaux, J., Juels, A., Shi, E.: Sealed-glass proofs: using transparent enclaves to prove and sell knowledge. In: EuroS&P (2017)
36. To, Q.C., Nguyen, B., Pucheral, P.: Privacy-preserving query execution using a decentralized architecture and tamper resistant hardware. In: EDBT, pp. 487–498 (2014)
37. Wang, W., et al.: Leaky cauldron on the dark land: understanding memory side-channel hazards in SGX. In: CCS (2017)
38. September 2018. www.inrupt.com/blog/one-small-step-for-the-web. Accessed May 2020

Evaluating Classification Feasibility Using Functional Dependencies

Marie Le Guilly[✉], Jean-Marc Petit, and Vasile-Marian Scuturici

Univ Lyon, INSA Lyon, LIRIS, UMR 5205 CNRS, Villeurbanne, France
marie.le-guilly@insa-lyon.fr

Abstract. With the vast amount of available tools and libraries for data science, it has never been easier to make use of classification algorithms: a few lines of code are enough to apply dozens of algorithms on any dataset. It is therefore "super easy" for data scientists to produce machine learning (ML) models in a very limited time. On the counterpart, domain experts may have the impression that such ML models are just a black box, almost magic, that would work on any dataset without really understanding why. For this reason, related to interpretability of machine learning, there is an urgent need to reconcile domain experts with ML models and to identify at the right level of abstraction, techniques to get them implied in the ML model construction.

In this paper, we address this notion of trusting ML models by using data dependencies. We argue that functional dependencies characterize the existence of a function that a classification algorithm seeks to define. From this simple yet crucial remark, we have made several contributions. First, we show how functional dependencies can give a tight upper bound for the classification's accuracy, leading to impressive experimental results on UCI datasets with state-of-the art ML methods. Second, we point out how to generate very difficult synthetic datasets for classification, showing evidence about the fact that for some datasets, it does not make any sense to use ML methods. Third, we propose a practical and scalable solution to assess the existence of a function before applying ML techniques, allowing to take into account real life data and to keep domain experts in the loop.

Keywords: Functional dependencies · Classification · Feasibility

1 Introduction

As the number of machine learning libraries keeps increasing, with more and more tools and technologies, it is getting easier to apply classification models on any dataset, with a very limited number of steps. Indeed, for a data scientist, it only takes a few lines of code to train and test a model in her data, and to get first results in a few minutes. If this is very practical, it can also be dangerous: it is possible to try and classify on data for which it might not make any sense, or for which much more cleaning and preprocessing is necessary. Of course, in such

© Springer-Verlag GmbH Germany, part of Springer Nature 2020
A. Hameurlain et al. (Eds.) TLDKS XLIV, LNCS 12380, pp. 132–159, 2020.
https://doi.org/10.1007/978-3-662-62271-1_5

cases, the scores used to evaluate the model will likely be pretty low, indicating to the data scientist that there is room for improvement, regarding either the data or the algorithm's parameters.

Another problem of classification algorithm is its black box aspect: when applied on a dataset, the domain expert will not necessarily trust them, as it is not always possible to explain simply why it works or the prediction it produces. For this reason's models interpretability is an extremely important topic [8, 16]. Some models are interpretable by nature, such as decision tree, and there are many ongoing work to propose models that can be easily explicable [46, 48]. Having domain experts understanding why the model is adapted to their data, and then trust it, is crucial to build new artificial intelligence applications.

In this paper, we address this notion of trusting ML models by using data dependencies. We argue that *functional dependencies characterize the existence of a function that a classification algorithm seeks to define.* Rather than focusing on the model itself, we propose to explain the limitation of the main input of a classification problem, i.e. the classification dataset, to show why the accuracy of any classifier is limited by the available data, while keeping domain experts in the loop. Indeed, the existence of a function is much easier to understand than the function itself and turns out to be a very convenient concept for data scientists to get closer to domain experts.

On the one hand, functional dependencies are a key concept, at the foundation of the theory for relational database design (see [2]), data cleaning [5] or for query optimization, to mention a few. Supervised classification, on the other hand, is a traditional problem in machine learning: it seeks to find a model that can predict the class of a sample described by its value over some given attributes. Many algorithms have been developed to build such models (see [21] for an overview), from simple decision trees to the trendy deep neural networks. These algorithms have gained in popularity this last few years, especially thanks to the volume of data that is now available to data scientists. Classification problems arise in very different areas, and models are being produced for an even wider range of applications, from cancer prediction to targeted advertising.

Functional dependencies on one side, and supervised classification on the other, therefore appear as two problems that do not seem to have much in common. For instance, they do not look at data in the same way: for functional dependencies, the values themselves are not important, only their comparabilities matter, while values are crucial for learning algorithms. Nevertheless, these approaches turn out to be complementary, as shown in the following general observation:

Given a dataset r over $\{A_1, \ldots, A_n, C\}$ where C C values represent the class to be predicted, classification algorithms seek to find out a function to predict an output (C value) based on a given input ($A_1, \ldots, A_n$ values) whereas the satisfaction of the functional dependency $A_1, \ldots, A_n \to C$ in r expresses nothing else than the existence of that function.

Between these two notions, one is clearly easier than the other. This observation raises a simple question: *Does it make sense to look for a function when the data themselves show that no function exists?*

Indeed, there exist many machine learning libraries and tools that allow to build dozens of models, and therefore look for a function... that does not even exist.

As a result, in a classification setting, studying the existence of a functional dependency between the attributes and the class of the dataset could produce meaningful information regarding the possible performances of the classifier. No matter how complicated the function to find out is, looking at the data dependencies allow to simply validate its existence. It can also identify relevant counterexamples, i.e. tuples in the dataset that will cause a classifier to fail when predicting an output for it, because several outputs are possible for the exact same input. More precisely, we propose to qualify the existence of the functional dependency using well-known metrics, such that an upper bound for the classifier accuracy can be given. This can then be used for data analysts to better explain to domain experts what is going on with their data, before building a model on top of it. Using the score, they can make an informed decision, by being aware of some limitations of the model they are trying to build. Moreover, it can assist them in deciding whether or not they should jump into the learning phase, or if they should spend more time to do more data cleaning, add other attributes, etc.

Example 1. Let's take a small dataset from Table 1 as an example. This is the dataset about passengers of the famous Titanic, with their ticket class (first or second), their age range (child or adult), their gender, and whether or not they survived. The purpose of this problem is to predict if a passenger has survived or not. Such an analysis can then be used to determine if some passengers were more likely to survive than the other.

Table 1. Toy dataset: Titanic relation

id	Ticket	Age	Gender	Survived
t_1	1st	Child	Female	No
t_2	2nd	Child	Male	Yes
t_3	1st	Adult	Male	No
t_4	2nd	Adult	Female	Yes
t_5	2nd	Child	Male	No
t_6	2nd	Child	Male	Yes
t_7	1st	Adult	Male	No
t_8	1st	Adult	Male	Yes
t_9	2nd	Child	Male	Yes
t_{10}	1st	Child	Female	Yes

In this dataset, the available attributes are not enough to determine the class. For example, tuples t_2 and t_5 both concern male children in second class, however one survived while the other did not. Similarly, the two adult males in first class from tuples t_7 and t_8 had two different outcomes. Whatever the classifier, it will irremediably misclassify at least one of them.

This very simple example shows how the satisfaction of the functional dependency between the attributes (Ticket, Age, Gender) and the class (Survived) in a classification dataset highlights the limits a classifier reaches on a dataset: according to the measure G_3 [23] (see Sect. 3), the accuracy of classifiers on this dataset can not be more than 70%. In addition, the counterexamples do not only highlight why the classification performance will not be above a certain value, but also what are the tuples that cause problems.

To summarize, this paper is based on a dramatically simple but powerful observation, making a clear relationship between supervised classification and functional dependencies, especially on the interest of first studying the existence of a function before applying machine learning techniques. Thus, we propose the following contributions:

1. We give a tight upper bound of classifier's accuracy based on the G_3 measure [24] for functional dependencies. An algorithm is given to compute the upper bound, and experimentations are provided on datasets from the UCI repository. This is a practical solution to give understandability to the learning process, by quantifying whether or not it makes sense to use machine learning techniques on the considered dataset.
2. An algorithm to generate difficult synthetic classification datasets with a predictable upper bound for accuracy, whatever the classification algorithms. As far as we know, this is the first contribution to generate synthetic datasets so that their classification accuracy can be as hard as desired.
3. A practical and scalable solution to deal with real life datasets, and assess the existence of a function. The solution relies on a dataset reduction technique and crisp functional dependencies, delivering complex and meaningful counterexamples, crucial to keep domain experts in the loop. Experiments conducted on real-life datasets point out the scalability of our technique.

This work contributes to bridge the gap between data dependencies and machine learning, a timely and active research trend, see for example [1,35,38].

Section 2 introduces the necessary preliminary notions on functional dependencies and supervised classification. Section 3 explains the thought process that goes from the existence of a function using functional dependencies to finding the function with a classification algorithm. Section 4 exposes the generation of difficult datasets and the corresponding tests. Section 5 explains how to use counterexamples in practical settings, with our practical and scalable solution for real life datasets. Finally Sect. 6 describes the related work, before concluding in Sect. 7.

2   Preliminaries

We first recall basic notations and definitions that will be used throughout the paper. It is assumed that the reader is familiar with databases notations (see [28]).

Let U be a set of attributes. A relation schema R is a name associated with attributes of U, i.e. $R \subseteq U$.

Let D be a set of constants, $A \in U$ and R a relation schema. The domain of A is denoted by $dom(A) \subseteq D$. The definition of a tuple t over R t over R is a function from R to D. A relation r over R is a set of tuples over R. In the sequel, we will use interchangeably the term relation or dataset. If $X \subseteq U$, and if t is a tuple over U, then we denote the restriction of t to X by $t[X]$. If r is a relation over U, then $r[X] = \{t[X], t \in R\}$. The active domain of A in r, denoted by $adom(A, r)$, is the set of values taken by A in r.

2.1   Functional Dependencies

We now define the syntax and the semantics of a Functional Dependency (FD).

Definition 1. *Let R be a relation schema, and $X, Y \subseteq R$. A FD on R is an expression of the form $R : X \to Y$ (or simply $X \to Y$ when R is clear from context)*

Definition 2. *Let r be a relation over R and $X \to Y$ a functional dependency on R. $X \to Y$ is satisfied in r, denoted by $r \models X \to Y$, if and only if for all $t_1, t_2 \in r$, if $t_1[X] = t_2[X]$ then $t_1[Y] = t_2[Y]$.*

The satisfaction can be verified using this well-known property:

Property 1. Let r be a relation over $\mathcal{R}$ and $X \to Y$ an FD over R. Then: $r \models X \to Y \Leftrightarrow |\pi_{XY}(r)| = |\pi_X(r)|$

Understanding what tuples prevent a given functional dependency to be satisfied relies on the notion of counterexamples, defined as follows:

Definition 3. *Let r be a relation over R and $X \to Y$ a FD f on R. The set of counterexamples of f over r is denoted by $CE(X \to Y)$ and defined as follows:*

$$CE(X \to Y, r) = \{(t_1, t_2) | t_1, t_2 \in r, \text{ for all } A \in X, t_1[A] = t_2[A] \text{ and there exists } B \in Y, t_1[B] \neq t_2[B]\}$$

The error of the functional dependency in a relation has been addressed in [23], in which three measures are presented, given a functional dependency $X \to Y$ and a relation r. Other measures, based on information theory, are presented in [15], but are out of the scope of this paper.

The first measure, G_1, gives the proportion of counterexamples in the relation:

$$G_1(X \to Y, r) = \frac{|\{(u,v)|u,v \in r, u[X] = v[X], u[Y] \neq v[Y]\}|}{|r|^2}$$

Using Definition 3, this can be rewritten as:

$$G_1(X \to Y, r) = \frac{|CE(X \to Y, r)|}{|r|^2}$$

Following this first measure, it is also possible to determine the proportion of tuples involved in counterexamples. This measure G_2 is given as follows:

$$G_2(X \to Y, r) = \frac{|\{u|u \in r, \exists v \in r : u[X] = v[X], u[Y] \neq v[Y]\}|}{|r|}$$

These two metrics are designed to evaluate the importance of counterexamples in the relation. Similarly, measure G_3 computes the size of the set of tuples in r to obtain a maximal new relation s satisfying $X \to Y$. Contrary to [23] that present this measure as an error, we propose it as follows:

$$G_3(X \to Y, r) = \frac{max(\{|s| | s \subseteq r, s \models X \to Y\})}{|r|}$$

Example 2. Using Table 1, considering the functional dependency $fd = Ticket, Age, Gender \to Survived$, we have:
$CE(fd, Titanic) =$
$\qquad \{(t_1, t_{10}), (t_2, t_5), (t_3, t_8), (t_5, t_6), (t_5, t_9), (t_7, t_8)$
$\qquad (t_{10}, t_1), (t_5, t_2), (t_8, t_3), (t_6, t_5), (t_9, t_5), (t_8, t_7)\}$
As a result:

- $G_1(fd, Titanic) = \frac{12}{100} = 12\%$
- $G_2(fd, Titanic) = \frac{9}{10} = 90\%$
- $G_3(fd, Titanic) = 70\%$

2.2 Supervised Classification in Machine Learning

Traditionally, a supervised classification problem (see [30]) consists in a set of N training examples, of the form
$\{(x_1, y_1), ..., (x_N, y_N)\}$ where x_i is the feature vector of the i-th example and y_i its label. The number of labels (also known as class), k, is limited and usually much smaller than the number of examples ($k = 2$ in binary classification problems). Given the training examples, classification is the task of learning a target function g that maps each example x_i to one of the k classes.

The function g, known as a classifier is an element of some space of possible functions G, usually called the *hypothesis space*. The objective of a learning algorithm is to output the classifier with the lowest possible error rate, which is the portion of misclassified examples according to their ground truth label.

It is sometimes convenient to represent g using a scoring function $f : X \times Y \rightarrow \mathbb{R}$ such that g is defined as returning the y value that gives the highest score:

$$g(x) = \arg\max_y f(x, y)$$

This optimal function can take different forms, depending on the learning algorithm used to define it: polynomial, exponential, sometimes not even expressible using simple formulas (black boxes). This function g is often referred to as the *model* of the classification task.

In the rest of the paper, we will consider a relation r over $\{A_1, \ldots, A_n, C\}$ such that for every tuple $t_i \in r$, $t_i[A_1 \ldots A_n] = x_i$ and $t_i[C] = y_i$.

Evaluating the performances of a classification model is a crucial part in a learning process. It allows to evaluate its quality and how well the model generalizes. It is also useful to compare the performances of different learning algorithms over a given dataset, to choose the most appropriate one given the problem at hand. In this paper, we will focus mainly on *accuracy*, a simple but efficient measure. We refer to [39] for a detailed overview of how to deal with the evaluation of classification models.

Accuracy is a widely used metrics, as it is both informative and easy to compute. Given a classification dataset of N samples, accuracy is the proportion of samples that are correctly classified by the model. This score lies between 0 and 1, and ideally should get as close as possible to 1. Given a model M over a relation r, the accuracy is defined as follows:

$$accuracy(M, r) = \frac{\# \, of \, correct \, predictions}{|r|}$$

3   From Machine Learning to Functional Dependencies

3.1   Existence Versus Determination of a Function

At first sight, supervised classification and functional dependencies do not appear to be two related concepts: they do not apply to the same problems. Both share the well-known concept of *function*, recalled below:

Definition 4. *A function $f : X \rightarrow Y$ is a mapping of each element x of a set X (the domain of the function), to a unique element y of another set Y (the codomain of the function).*

According to the core definition of a classification problem in Sect. 2, a classifier is itself a function: for any input vector, it predicts a unique output value. As a result, classifiers rely on the assumption that there exists a function from the attributes to the class in the dataset.

Functional dependencies also rely heavily on this notion of unique output. Indeed, a relation r satisfies a FD $X \rightarrow Y$ if and only if all tuples that are equal on X are associated with the same unique value on Y. As a result, $r \models X \rightarrow Y$

if and only if there exists a function f from X to Y, on the active domain of r. It should be noted that a functional dependency is a statement of the existence of a function in every possible relation r over R. A classification task can't be defined at the schema level, and requires a dataset to be provided as an input.

If we combine these results, it appears that a classifier determines a function over a relation, whereas a satisfied functional dependency guaranties the existence of a partial function from the active domain of X to the active domain of Y. Therefore, it follows:

Property 2. $r \models A_1, \ldots, A_n \to C \iff$ there exists a function f from $adom(A_1, r) \times \ldots \times adom(A_n, r)$ to $adom(C, r)$

This problem is clearly easier than the associated classification problem: determining the function itself requires more investigation than proving its existence. However, it is interesting to notice that in most classification problems, the existence of the function is assumed but not formally verified. This is surprising, as it could be useful at several steps of the learning process. First, FDs satisfaction in the training set can be used for data cleaning. Indeed, the tuples that are counterexamples of the functional dependency can be used to identify inconsistencies in the dataset, that can have various explanations. Seeing those counterexamples could then assist an analyst during the data cleaning part, to see where those inconsistencies come from: are they normal, or do they correspond to measurement errors that should be corrected? If a few counterexamples can be expected, when their proportion is too high, the classification model might not be trusted. This observation allows the data scientist and the domain expert to stay connected, and to demystify part of the black box aspect of machine learning, by explaining concrete limitations of the model.

To summarize, our first proposition is, given a classification dataset, to verify the satisfaction of the functional dependency *attributes* → *class*. Contrary to many pattern mining problems related to functional dependencies' enumeration, that pose combinatorial complexity, this problem is dramatically simpler, as we only consider one dependency, *attributes* → *class*, with *attributes* $= A_1 \ldots A_n$.

3.2   Upper Bound for Accuracy

In this setting, measure G_3 appears to be of crucial importance for the classification problem, as it represent the proportion of tuples in the dataset, that satisfy the considered functional dependency. In this subset of the original data, there is therefore no counterexample. This means that in the subset s defined for G_3, there exists a function between the left and right hand side of the dependency. Theoretically, it is therefore possible for a classifier to reach a perfect score if it identifies the correct underlying function, independently of its capabilities to generalize from it. On the opposite, the counterexamples to $A_1, \ldots, A_n \to class$ are blocking point for any classification algorithms, as they introduce pairs of tuples for such that the classifier will misclassify at least one of them. As a consequence, we propose the following result:

Proposition 1. *Let* $A_1, \ldots, A_n \to class$ *be a FD over* $\mathcal{R}$, *r a relation on* $\mathcal{R}$, *and* M *a classifier from* $A_1, \ldots, A_n$ *to* C. *Then:*

$$accuracy(M, r) \leq G_3(A_1, \ldots, A_n \to C, r)$$

Proof. Let s be a maximum subset of r such that $s \models A_1, \ldots, A_n \to C$.

For all $(t_i, t_j) \in s$, if $t_i[attributes] = t_j[attributes]$ then $t_i[class] = t_j[class]$.

Let $t_h \in r \setminus s$. Then there exists $t_i \in s$, such that $(t_i, t_j) \in CE(attributes \to class, r)$, otherwise s is not maximal. If only the tuples from $r \setminus s$ are misclassified, and all the tuples from s correctly classified, $accuracy(M, r) = \frac{|s|}{|r|} = G_3(attributes \to class, r)$.

If some tuples are misclassified due to the algorithm itself, this can only lower the accuracy, and thus the result follows.

This upper-bound result is simple but powerful, as it can be applied to any classification dataset, and offer guaranties on the feasibility of classification over it. Moreover, G_3 is closely related to Bayes error [43], allowing to revisit this error through the prism of functional dependencies. The statistical learning theory give theoretical bounds for the capacity of learning of a given type of classifier [44], but these bounds are extremely difficult to compute. Our usage of G3 give an estimation of a high bound which can eventually be attended by a classifier on a given dataset. In addition, we make simpler assumptions by only considering the available data and comparing the given tuples, and do not consider a probability distribution. What we propose is an upper bound, which is only based on the tuples used to evaluate the accuracy, which means that this can be influenced by how the available data is split between training and testing sets for example.

3.3   Validation on Classification Datasets

We propose to compute this upper bound on various classification datasets, to see how state-of-the-art algorithms perform in terms of accuracy, with respect to this upper bound.

G_3 Computation. Contrary to G_1 and G_2 that can be quite easily computed by looking at each pair of tuples, G_3 requires to identify the tuples to be removed from the dataset so that is satisfies the dependency. In addition, the minimum possible number of tuples should be removed. In the general case, this is a NP-complete problem, as it is equivalent to the minimal vertex cover problem for graphs [42].

However, when the data is discrete and when using crisp functional dependencies, the comparison of values is transitive, and it is therefore possible to compute G_3. Following the definition of G_3, in order for s to be maximal, it should keep as many tuples as possible, while removing all the counterexamples of the given functional dependency. As a result, this can be done by grouping all the tuples that share the same left hand side, and then selecting among them the ones that share the same right hand side, and that are the majority. This allows to remove all the counterexamples, while removing the minimum number of counterexamples. The size of s is therefore the sum, for each different left hand side, of the size of the majority right hand side. Therefore, G_3 can be computed with the following proposition:

Proposition 2. *Let r be a relation over $\mathcal{R}$. Then:*

$$G_3(X \to Y, r) = \frac{\sum_{x_i} \max_{y_i} |\pi_{XY}(\sigma_{X=x_i \land Y=y_i}(r))|}{|r|}$$

where $x_i \in \pi_X(r)$ and $y_i \in \pi_Y(\sigma_{X=x_i}(r))$.

Note that $X = x_i$ is a simplification for $A_1 = v_1 \land \ldots \land A_n = v_n$ for $X = \langle A_1..A_n \rangle$ and $x_i = \langle v_1..v_n \rangle$.

To compute this measure, we propose Algorithm 1. It relies on a specific data structure, presented on Fig. 1, with tuples from Table 1 as an example. It is a hash map, with the values over the attributes as key, and another hash map as value. For the second map, the key is the class, and the value the number of times this class appears (for these given attributes). The construction of this map is explained from line 3 to line 14 of Algorithm 1: for each row in the dataset, the corresponding values in the map are filled or created when necessary. Once this data structure is complete, the algorithm looks at each key in the map: it will then retrieve the number of occurrences for the class that has the highest value in the second map. All these maximum values are added to one another, as they correspond to the maximum number of tuples that can be kept, among the ones that share the same attributes value, in order to satisfy the functional dependency. This process is explained though line 15 to 19 in Algorithm 1, with a complexity in $\mathcal{O}(\log |r|)$.

Example 3. Using Fig. 1, measure G_3 can be computed as follows for the Titanic dataset:

$$G_3(Ticket, Age, Gender \to Survived, Titanic) = \frac{2+1+1+3}{10} = \frac{7}{10} = 70\%$$

Experimentations. We decided to perform experimentations, in order to show experimentally the upper bound given by G_3 on the accuracy of classifiers. To do so, we ran experiments on well-known datasets, to compare the state-of-the-art accuracy results for these datasets with their G_3 measure. The datasets and the accuracy measure come from [19], a thorough study on the accuracy of 179 classification algorithms over 121 datasets: the measures we use are therefore the ones given by this study using these algorithms.

The results are presented in Table 2. As expected, for all the datasets, the maximum accuracy measured in [19] is always below our measured G_3 value: the difference between the two values is indicated in the last column of the table, showing some significant differences for some datasets. For some datasets, the G_3 measure is 100%, which is reassuring, as it means that their exists a function between the attributes and the class, and that it does actually make sense to perform classification. It is also interesting that despite the existence

---

Algorithm 1: G_3 computation algorithm

---

1 procedure ComputeG3 (r);
    Input : r the classification dataset,
                $A_1 \ldots A_n \to C$ a functional dependency
    Output: $G_3(A_1 \ldots A_n \to C, r)$
2 map = {}
3 **for** $row \in r$ **do**
4   **if** $row[A_1..A_n] \in map$ **then**
5   **if** $row[class] \in map[row[A_1..A_n]]$ **then**
6 | map[row[$A_1..A_n$]][row[$class$]]+ = 1
7   **else**
8   map[row[$A_1..A_n$]][row[$class$]] = 1
9   **else**
10   map[row[$A_1..A_n$]] = {}
11   map[row[$A_1..A_n$]][$row[class]$] = 1
12 maxsum = 0
13 **foreach** $key \in map$ **do**
14   maxfrequent = max(map[key])
15   maxsum += maxfrequent
16 **return** $\frac{maxsum}{|r|}$

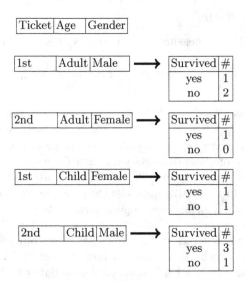

Fig. 1. Data structure for G_3 computation

of a function, the average accuracy is still very low sometimes, such as for the Contract dataset. Finally, the Titanic and the Led display are very interesting datasets, as their G_3 measure is pretty low compared to the other ones. Therefore it is worth questioning the interest of performing classification on these datasets. For the Titanic dataset, the maximum accuracy is strictly equal to G_3, meaning their exists a *perfect* classifier on this dataset, that only failed on tuples from counterexamples.

These results are very interesting, as they show how this paper's result could be used on any given datasets. It indicates both to data scientist whether or not it is worth performing classification, or if there are simply too many counterexamples for the results to be interesting. In addition, depending on the classification's results, it is interesting to see if G_3 is reached or not. Based on these measures, it could also be used to compare various classification methods, in order to see how they influence the accuracy, and if there are methods that are more often that other closer to the upper bound defined by $G3$.

Table 2. Comparison of accuracy and G_3 measure over classification datasets

Dataset	# tuples	# classes	Average accuracy (%)	Max Accuracy	G_3 (%)	$G_3 - max$
Titanic	2201	3	76.6	79.1	79.1	0.0
Breast Cancer	286	9	71.2	76.2	97.8	21.6
Abalone	4177	5	60.1	67,4	100	32.6
Adult	48842	13	81.8	86,2	99.9	13.7
Bank	4521	16	88.4	90,5	100	9.5
Car	1728	6	86	99,2	100	0.8
Contract	1473	9	49.6	57,2	95,5	38.3
Ecoli	336	7	77.6	90,9	100	9.1
Iris	150	4	89.4	99,3	100	0.7
Led-display	1000	7	60.3	74,8	76	1.2
Lenses	24	4	74	95,8	100	4.2
wine-quality-red	1599	11	55.6	69	100	31
yeast	1484	8	52.5	63,7	100	36.3
zoo	101	16	86.5	99.0	100	1.0

4   Generating Difficult Datasets for Classification

In this section, we are interested in generating datasets for classification as hard as possible, using the notion of counterexamples.

4.1　Generation

The idea to generate datasets with a very low G_3 measure, such that any classifier will not be able to perform efficiently on it, as shown in the previous section. Generating such datasets can then be used to test new classifier, or to improve existing one so that they get as close as possible to the theoretical maximum accuracy (i.e. they only misclassify counterexamples).

To generate such datasets, it is necessary to create counterexamples, and to play with their number to increase G_3 error and lower the maximum accuracy. To get very difficult classification datasets, we propose to start with an initial classification relation that does not have any identical tuples, and to duplicate them, by associating each new tuple to a different class at each duplication. This will naturally introduce counterexamples, and their number will increase with the number of duplication.

Table 3. Generation of a difficult dataset

id	A_1	A_2	...	A_{n-1}	A_n	Class	Scaling Factor
1	13	9	...	21	16	1	
2	58	13	...	18	5	2	
⋮	⋮	⋮	⋮	⋮	⋮	⋮	
...	...	...	...	...	...	k	1
...	...	...	...	...	...	1	
⋮	⋮	⋮	⋮	⋮	⋮	⋮	
N	35	9	...	21	11	4	
⋮	⋮	⋮	⋮	⋮	⋮	⋮	⋮
$(j-1) \times N + 1$	13	9	...	21	16	$(t_{((j-1)\times N+1)-N}[Class] + 1)\%k$	
...	...	...	...	...	...	...	
i	$t_{i\%N}[A_1]$	$t_{i\%N}[A_2]$	... $t_{i\%N}[A_{n-1}]$	$t_{i\%N}[A_n]$	$(t_{i-N}[Class] + 1)\%k$	j
...	...	...	...	...	...	...	
$j \times N$	35	9	...	21	11	$(t_{(j\times N)-N}[Class] + 1)\%k$	
⋮	⋮	⋮	⋮	⋮	⋮	⋮	⋮
$(sf-1) \times N + 1$	13	9	...	21	16	$(t_{((sf-1)\times N+1)-N}[Class] + 1)\%k$	
...	...	...	...	...	...	...	sf
$sf \times N$	35	9	...	21	11	$(t_{(sf\times N)-N}[Class] + 1)\%k$	

The generation strategy is illustrated in Table 3. It requires the size N of the initial relation, the number n of attributes of the relation, the number k of classes, and the scaling factor sf (total number of relations after the duplications) used to produce counterexamples. The strategy works as follows: let r be a relation over $R = A_1 \ldots A_n$. Then:

1. Insert N unique tuples t_i for $i \in 1..N$. For each tuple $t_i, i \in 1..N$, add a value for the *class* attribute as follows: $t_i[Class] = i\%k$. This corresponds to the rows 1 to N in Table 3.

2. The duplication process is repeated $sf - 1$ times as follows:
Let j be the current duplication, $2 \leq j \leq sf$. The initial relation is duplicated, generating N new tuples, numbered $t_{(j-1) \times N+1}$ to $t_{j \times N}$. For each duplicated tuple $t_i, (j-1) \times N + 1 \leq i \leq j \times N$, the values do not change over attributes A_1 to A_n, i.e. $t_i[A_1...A_n] = t_{i\%N}[A_1...A_n]$. However, the class value is shifted by one with respect to the previous duplicate, i.e. $t_i[Class] = (t_{i-N}[Class] + 1)\%k$

Algorithm 2: Difficult dataset generation algorithm

---

1 procedure GenerateDifficult (n, N, k, sf);

   Input   : n the number of attributes, N the number of tuples before
                duplication, k the number of classes, and sf the scaling factor

   Output : d a difficult dataset for classification

2 class = 1

3 relation = [N][n+1]

4 **for** $i \in 1..N$ **do**

5   **for** $j \in 1..n$ **do**

6   relation[i][j] = random([0:ln(N)])

7   relation[i][n+1] = class

8   **if** $class == k$ **then**

9   class = 1

10   class += 1

11 **if** $A_1..A_n$ *is not a key ;*   // Check that all rows are unique

12 **then**

13 dataset = relation

14 copy = relation

15 **for** $i \in 2..sf$ **do**

16   copy = Duplicate(copy, k);

17   dataset = $dataset \bigcup$ copy;

18 **return** dataset

19 **Function Duplicate** (r, k)**:**

20   duplicate = []

21   **for** $row \in r$ **do**

22     $new[A_1...A_n] = row[A_1...A_n]$

23     $new[class] = (row[class] + 1)\%k$

24   duplicate += new

25   **return** duplicate

Algorithm 2 give the details of the generation process. Let us mention a few important point not detailed here.

- First, the domain of attributes is to be defined. In Table 3, we use integers for the sake of clarity, but any other type of attribute would work exactly the same. However the data types will have an impact on the classifiers, as for example non-numerical values would require some pre-processing to be used with most classifiers. This also underlines how classification is impacted par features' domains while FDs are not.
- The only limitation on the attribute domain is to have enough values to generate unique rows, at least $\frac{ln(N)}{ln(n)}$ values[1]. Using a really high number of different values will only increase the difficulty for a classifier, as there will be very little redundancy between the values. This is a parameter than can be used to tune the difficulty of the classification dataset. In Algorithm 2 and the experiments, we used $ln(N)$ different values (see line 6 in Algorithm 2).
- In addition, whenever $sf > k$, the dataset contains duplicates that share the same class values, as all values for the class have already been used for duplicates. This introduces redundancy in the data, but does not remove any counterexample. Given the parameters of Algorithm 2, it is possible to compute the exact value of G_3 for the produced dataset:

Proposition 3. *Let r_{hard} be a relation generated using Algorithm 2. Then:*

$$G_3(A_1..A_n \rightarrow Class, r_{hard}) = \frac{1 + \frac{sf - sf\%k}{k}}{sf}$$

Proof. Let $i \in [1..sf]$ denote the i-th duplication of the initial relation. While $i < k$, it only introduces counterexamples. Therefore, for each duplicated tuple, there are i different classes, for each of the N original tuples. As a consequence, if $sf < k$, $G_3 = \frac{N}{N*sf} = \frac{1}{sf}$.

For $i \geq k$, there is redundancy for each duplicate: the duplicated tuples agree with the ones already produced. Therefore, there are as many agreeing tuples as the number of times $i\%k = 1$. The size of the set of agreeing tuples therefore depends of how many times an initial tuple is associated with the same initial class during the sf duplications, which is exactly the quotient of the euclidean division of sf by k, i.e $\frac{N + N * \frac{sf - sf\%k}{k}}{sf*N}$. And the result follows.

4.2   Experimentations

We implemented the generation algorithm, in order to measure the influence of its different parameters. To do so, we generated datasets with different parameters, and used ten different classifiers from the scikit-learn library [32] to estimate their accuracy over the datasets. In order to propose a general comparison over several algorithms, the algorithms are based on the default parameters from the library. All results presented below are averaged over 10 different instances

---

[1] Given $|dom|$ different values, there exists $n^{|dom|}$ different vectors of size n. Therefore it is necessary that $N < n^{|dom|}$ and thus $|dom| > \frac{ln(N)}{ln(n)}$.

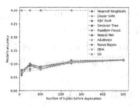 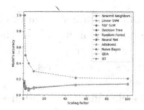 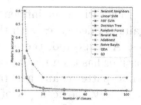

(a) Evolution of classifiers accuracy against the number of tuples the dataset, with respect to G_3 $(k = 5, sf = 10)$

(b) Evolution of classifiers accuracy against the scaling factor of the dataset, with respect to G_3 $(N = 100, k = 5)$

(c) Evolution of classifiers accuracy against the number of classes in the dataset, with respect to G_3 $(N = 100, sf = 10)$

Fig. 2. Classifiers accuracy given the parameters for generating difficult classification datasets, compared to G_3

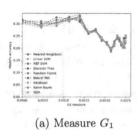 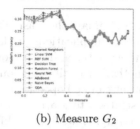 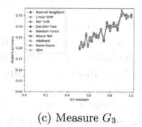

(a) Measure G_1 (b) Measure G_2 (c) Measure G_3

Fig. 3. Evolution of classifiers accuracy given the FD error measure of the dataset

randomly generated using the algorithm. The computing time being below one second, they are not discussed in this paper.

First, the influence of the number of tuples in the original relation (before duplication), was tested. The results are shown on Fig. 2a. It is worth noticing that the accuracy is in any case really low as expected: the maximum accuracy reached is 12%. However, as the initial number of tuples increases, so does the accuracy. Indeed, adding more tuples introduces some redundancy among the values for each attribute, allowing the classifier to find some sort of generalization for some cases. However, the number of counterexamples is way too high to reach good classification measure, and $G3$, which is constant as the number of tuples does not influence it, is also low: it can be seen that the model is far from reaching it.

Then, the influence of the scaling factor sf was tested, and results are presented on Fig. 2b. As it influences $G3$, this measure slowly decreases with the scaling factor, as more and more counterexamples are introduced. For this parameter, the accuracy first drops, before slowly increasing with the scaling ratio. This increase starts as soon as $sf > k$, as explained previously, because there is then some redundancy allowing the classifier to make correct predictions for some tuples.

In addition, the influence of the number of classes is exposed on Fig. 2c. Once again, G_3 decreases with the number of classes, as their are more counterexamples. As expected, the accuracy only drops with the number of classes, as the classifier has then fewer examples for each class, and therefore fewer possibilities to find patterns and generalize.

Finally, the accuracy of the classifiers was evaluated with respect to the error measure of the functional dependency $A_1...A_n \rightarrow class$. The results are shown on Fig. 3. For measures G_1 and G_2 the accuracy drops as the error increases, as the number of counterexamples also increases. On the opposite, when G_3 increases, so does the accuracy, as it means that the set of tuples that would satisfy the functional dependency is getting bigger, allowing the classifier to reach a higher accuracy.

5   Application to Real Life Datasets

Using functional dependency to evaluate the feasibility of classification datasets can be very useful for industrial applications. Indeed, many companies now understand the interest of their data, and are more and more interested in applying machine learning methods to gain value out of their data. Being able to quickly tell the company what can be hoped for as classification results, given their data, is a very useful strategy to start the discussion, and to see what can be done to improve if necessary. However, real-life datasets are known to be often dirty, with null or imprecise values, incoherence and uncertainties. In this setting, we discuss the interest of applying the previous results right before ML techniques in practical scenarios, to let the domain experts in the loop of the construction of their ML model.

5.1   Interest and Limits of G_3 Measure

Measures like G_3 can be seen as an indicator of whether or not the classification should be done, in comparison with the accuracy required by domain experts. Moreover, expressing at a declarative level such a constraint to domain experts offers more guarantee about their understanding of the whole process.

The main problem concerns the inability of crisp functional dependencies to deal with real-life data. Fortunately, many propositions have been made to extend functional dependencies, for example [7,9,12,34]. Indeed, when performing the comparison of tuples on each attribute, the strict equality might not be the best suited for comparing real-life values. When dealing for example with continuous values, it is very less likely for two values to be equal, and therefore all possible functional dependencies are likely to be satisfied in a given dataset. This is especially true for physical measurements, for which the precision of the measure is important to take into account: two values might not be exactly equal, but by considering the interval of measurement uncertainty, actually overlap.

Example 4. On Fig. 5a, the table presents data from a meteorological problem: given the temperature, pressure and humidity of a place, will it be raining the next hour ? All the attributes are measured using instruments that have a measurement uncertainty, well-known from the meteorologists:

- Temperature measurement uncertainty is $\pm 0.5°C$
- Pressure measurement uncertainty is $\pm 1hPa$
- Humidity measurement uncertainty is $\pm 2\%$

Considering this, every possible crisp FD is likely to be satisfied and all of them are thus useless.

We also note that very close values between two tuples but with a different class might confuse the classifier and prevent its generalization. In these situations, feedbacks of domain experts on the dataset is important to understand what it means for two values to be equal or similar on a given attribute.

Main issue: To sum up, we have to take into account some form of similarities between data values, without requiring domain experts to spend times on these time consuming tasks. This will be addressed in Sect. 5.3.

5.2 Interest of Counterexamples

The counterexamples are also very important to understand the score, to see the data that causes conflicts, so that a domain expert can explain their presence, and eventually remove them to improve the classification results. The counterexamples are a powerful notion to avoid the domain expert from being overwhelmed by the data, as she then only have a small but meaningful subset of tuples to study. The counterexamples are therefore a perfect starting point for a discussion between data scientist and domain expert: while the first gain knowledge on data they are not expert on, the others can point out important information more easily. The counterexamples are a way for domain experts to read a concrete information that can have an impact on their day-to-day work.

With respect to counterexamples, not all of them are of equal interest. To help domain experts in exploring them, and especially if there are many of them, it is important to think about how to present them, so that the experts are not overflowed. To do so, several strategies are possible, for example ranking the counterexamples, by computing how much they differ on the class value, which is especially easy for numerical value, by computing the difference between the two values. For other types, a score can be manually defined. In addition, we propose to visualize all of the counterexamples, so that domain experts can see the global picture in one glance. For instance, a graph representation can be built as follows: Let $G = (V, E)$ a graph where V is the set of tuples and $(t_1, t_2) \in E$ if t_1, t_2 are implied in one counterexample. The degree of a node is a first criterion to sort out the tuples to focus on. This modelisation show how the computation of G_3 and the removal of counterexamples can be seen as a graph problem, equivalent to the minimal vertex cover [42].

Example 5. Figure 4 presents such a graph for the Titanic dataset. The degree of t_5 (resp. t_8) is 3 (resp. 2). Clearly t_5 and t_8 cause more counterexamples

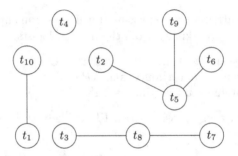

Fig. 4. Counterexamples interaction graph for the Titanic dataset

than the others. By changing the class value for these two tuples, the number of counterexamples drops to 1 (instead of 6).

Such visualizations can be useful for data cleaning, as the most conflictual tuples could then be easily identified and removed, to easily decrease significantly the number of counterexamples. Another solution would be to correct the counterexamples, with a minimal number of correction, by assigning them a class that does not contradict the other tuples. These visualization is also useful to see that finding an optimal solution is not an easy problem. Indeed, the objective is, from the graph, to remove as few vertices as possible, so that there are no more edges. This is known as the minimal vertex problem, which is NP-complete.

Main Issue: To sum up, when it comes to counterexamples enumeration, the main bottleneck lies on the comparison of each pair of tuples, which is quadratic in the number of tuples. This problem appears in different contexts such as deduplication, and several techniques have been proposed to perform such comparison in a reasonable amount of time, such as blocking [4], or parallelization using specific distribution strategies as in [13].

5.3   Similarity-Aware Dataset Reduction for Scaling Counterexamples Enumeration

In order to overcome the problems mentioned in Sects. 5.1 and 5.2, we propose a hybrid approach, that can both scale the counterexamples retrieval, while also allowing to consider similarities between values of a given attribute. Our approach is based on single attribute clustering and dataset reduction. It is a form of discretization, which is a classic approach in machine learning. In this setting, we use it to reduce the size of the dataset on which to evaluate the FD, and to therefore reduce the number of necessary comparisons between pairs of tuples.

The idea is to first group similar values together, so that they are all assigned to a unique same value: this allows to define similarity. Second, as the number of different values is likely to be much smaller, it is possible to "reduce" the dataset by only keeping unique rows. The detailed process is illustrated on Fig. 5, and works as follows:

id	Temp.	Pres.	Hum.	Rain
t_1	27.2	1004.5	98.7	yes
t_2	26.5	1018.4	42.5	no
t_3	15.7	1008.6	78.9	yes
t_4	16.1	1016.9	76.7	no
t_5	25.9	1017.5	43.8	yes
t_6	28.1	1021.7	41.7	no
t_7	4.1	1007.2	74.3	yes
t_8	15.9	1022.3	79.1	no
t_9	27.3	1019.8	39.5	no
t_{10}	3.8	1006.7	71.4	yes

(a) Original data

$\rightarrow$

id	Temp.	Pres.	Hum.	Rain
t_1	1	1	4	yes
t_2	1	2	1	no
t_3	3	1	2	yes
t_4	2	2	2	no
t_5	1	2	1	yes
t_6	1	2	1	no
t_7	3	1	2	yes
t_8	2	2	2	no
t_9	1	2	1	no
t_{10}	3	1	2	yes

(b) Clustered data

$\rightarrow$

id	Temp.	Pres.	Hum.	Rain	#
t'_1	1	1	4	yes	1
t'_2	1	2	1	no	3
t'_3	2	2	2	no	2
t'_4	1	2	1	yes	1
t'_5	3	1	2	yes	3

(c) Reduced data

Fig. 5. Data reduction process

- First, each attribute of the original data is clustered, to group similar values. The clustering algorithm can be adapted to the need, we propose to use k-means [29], using the silhouette coefficient [36] to automatically determine the best value for k. Of course, domain knowledge can also be used if it is available. It should be noted that this can be adapted and fine-tuned to each application, and that specific similarity measures can be defined in this step if necessary. Clustering could also be extended to deal with more than one attribute (not detailed here).
- Once an attribute is clustered, each of its value is replaced by the number of cluster it belongs to. As functional dependencies do not care about the order between values, this does not impact the validity of the dependency.
- Once the data is clustered, as the number of different values for each attribute is equal to the number of clusters, there might be identical rows in the dataset. It is therefore possible to dramatically reduce the size of the original data, by only keeping unique rows, and adding an additional attribute to memorize how many times this row appears in the clustered data.

To perform this process, we propose Algorithm 3: the clustering process is described from line 3 to 9, and the data reduction is performed on line 12.

Example 6. In the reduced dataset given in Fig. 5c, let us consider the counterexample (t'_2, t'_4) of the functional dependency $Temp, Pres, Hum \rightarrow Rain$. Using Fig. 5b, it concerns in fact 4 tuples: t_2, t_6, t_9 and t_5 (cf previous example). It is then possible to go back to the original data in Fig. 5a to see what does that mean on the real values. For example, values $\langle 25.9, 1017.5, 43.8 \rangle$ of t_5 and values $\langle 28.1, 1021.7, 41.7 \rangle$ of t_6 are considered similar and then, both tuples form a counterexample.

5.4 Experimentations

We evaluate both the data reduction technique and the scalability of counterexamples enumeration. We first looked at how the data is reduced. We took the 4

Algorithm 3: Scaling algorithm

---

1 procedure Reduce (r) over attributes $A_1..A_n$;
   Input : r the classification dataset
   Output: A clustered and reduced dataset of integers
2 d = []
3 **for** $A \in \{A_1..A_n\}$ **do**
4   **if** A *is continuous* **then**
5 $k = max_{silhouette}(r[A])$
6   clusters $= cluster(r[A], k)$
7   d[A] = clusters
8   **else**
9   d[A] = $r[A]$
10 d[class] = r[class]
11 $r_{reduced}$ =Select $A_1 \ldots A_n, C, count(*)$ as $'\#'$ From d Group By $A_1 \ldots A_n, C$
12 **return** $r_{reduced}$

---

biggest datasets from Table 2, and computed their reduction ratio, when applying our algorithm. In this situation, we used the silhouette coefficient [36] to determine the most appropriate number of clusters for each attribute. The results are presented in Table 4. It shows that the ratio differs from one dataset to another, with some very significant drops for some datasets such as Titanic, indicating their must be many redundant values. We then evaluated how well the data reduction technique improves the counterexamples retrieval time, to see how the approach would scale on large datasets. We evaluated it on astrophysical data from the Large Synoptic Survey Telescope[2] containing 500 000 tuples over 25 attributes. For different sizes of datasets, we compute:

- The reducing ratio, i.e how much the initial dataset is reduced:

$$ratio = \frac{|r| - |r_{reduced}|}{|r|}$$

Where $r_{reduced}$ is the reduced dataset.
- The computation time for counterexamples retrieval on the original data.
- The computation time for counterexamples retrieval on the reduced data.

The results of these experimentations are presented on Fig. 6. The first observation is that on the original data, the computing time is quickly too long even on relatively small instances. On the opposite, on the reduced data, it increases very slowly with the number of tuples, allowing for a reasonable time for retrieving the counterexamples. This is tightly linked with the reducing ratio, that increases significantly with the number of tuples: the more tuples there are, the more the original data is reduced with respect to its original size.

---

[2] https://www.lsst.org/.

On datasets on which our approach would not be sufficient to scale, it is always possible to apply blocking [4] or parallelization [13], but this is out of the scope of this paper.

Table 4. Reduction ratio for some datasets from Table 2

Dataset	#tuples before	#tuples after	Reduction ratio
Titanic	2201	24	98.9%
Abalone	4177	242	94.2%
Adult	48842	10176	79.2%
Bank	4521	4031	10.8%

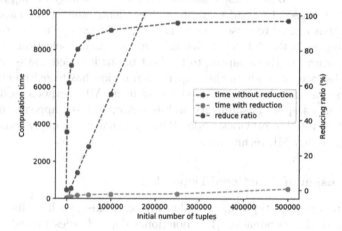

Fig. 6. Validation of G_3 computing time, on both original and reduced data, in parallel with the reducing ratio

6 Related Work

This related work section has been organized according to three axes: data dependencies for machine learning, extension of functional dependencies and data dependencies for data cleaning.

6.1 Data Dependencies for Machine Learning

Many research papers make use of principles from the database community to tackle machine learning problems, and vice versa (see for example [1,3,6]).

Recently, relational learning has been proposed [20,25], an alternative machine learning approach based on declarative relational representations paired with probabilistic models.

Functional dependencies are used in [27] to build decision trees, leading to more accurate classifiers with a more compact structure. In [1], the authors propose to perform in-database learning, and use functional dependencies to tackle optimization problems. More generally, there is a raising interest for integrated key database theory concepts into machine learning, such as in [41] that builds least squares regression models over training datasets defined by arbitrary join queries on database table. It is also worth mentioning [50] where an entire machine learning library has been adapted so that it is compatible with a storage of data in a DBMS. There is also [45] which is a SQL extension for data mining. Similar approach was used in [31] with an implementation of the K-means algorithm using SQL queries.

In [26], the authors show that if there is a functional dependency between features, it is likely to affect the classifier negatively. Similarly in [40], functional dependency are used to build a graph of dependency among the classification attributes, that is used to cluster the attributes, and therefore reduce total number of attributes in the dataset, which is a form of feature selection.

In comparison to these papers, to the best of our knowledge, we notice that the main observation made in this paper – a function has to exist between the features and the class to be predicted before using ML methods to determine that function – despite its simplicity and its common sense, appears to be new, not explicitly stated in previous works. We argue that it has many consequences for trusting trendy ML techniques.

6.2   Extension of Functional Dependencies

Although many other types of data dependencies exist, such as inclusion [10] and multivalued dependencies [17], functional dependencies proved to be the most appropriate for the given problem, as they capture the notion of function between two sets of attributes.

Many extensions of functional dependencies exist, among which we quote [7,11,12,22,34]. Approximate functional dependencies [22] allow to define dependencies that almost hold in a relation, so that not all tuples have to be looked at, as long as enough support the dependency. Relaxed functional dependencies [9] and RQL [12] are general frameworks to extend functional dependencies. Fuzzy functional dependencies [7,34] introduce a *fuzzy* resemblance measure to compare two values on the same domain. Similarly, [11] defines similarity over complex attributes over a multimedia database.

In comparison, our clustering technique on every attribute appears as a trick allowing to both 1/ take into account complex similarities, that can be fully automated if the domain expert does not exactly know how to define the similarity and 2/ reduce the size to the database to enumerate efficiently counterexamples.

6.3   Data Dependencies for Data Cleaning

Data cleaning is a crucial part in most of data science application, as data scientist actually spend around 80% of their time on cleaning the data [49]. As a consequence, many research has be done on addressing this problem [33]. For instance, [47] proposes a semantic data profiler that can compute samples that satisfy the same constraints than a given dataset. As the limited expressiveness of functional dependencies did not always adapt well to the need of data cleaning on real datasets, specific dependencies have been proposed to identify inconsistencies in a dataset, and eventually repair it. Conditional dependencies [5] are functional dependencies that hold only on a subset of the dataset. Matching dependencies [18] for data repairing uses matching rules to relax the equality on functional dependencies and assign values for data repairing. In Holoclean [35], dependencies are used to clean automatically a dataset. In [37], a formal framework is proposed to bridge the gap between database theory and learnability theory, and is applied to three applications: data cleaning, probabilistic query answering, and learning. It can even be used to clean dataset in order to provide *fairness* [38]. [14] introduces denial constraints, allowing to declaratively specify logical formulae to exclude counterexamples. This work acknowledges the importance of counterexamples for data cleaning, in collaboration with domain experts.

There is a tight relationship between denial constraints and our counterexamples. Indeed, counterexamples of functional dependencies are no more than a special case of denial constraints, i.e. $\not\exists t_1, t_2$ such that $t_1[X] = t_2[X]$ and $t_1[Y] \neq t_2[Y]$. Due to our data reduction techniques, our counterexamples are clearly much more general and complex than those of crisp FDs. Interestingly, we do not rely on expert users to specify logical statements for defining denial constraints, and thus counterexamples. Our proposition is fully automatic, and the counterexamples we provide at the end are complex and do not require any user input. The price to be paid is that we cannot express the induced denial constraints.

7   Conclusion

In this paper, we have proposed to estimate the feasibility of a classification over a given dataset. To do so, we have used functional dependencies, a well-known concept in the database community, and checked whether the dataset satisfies a dependency between the features and the class to predict. When it does not, which is not unusual for real life datasets, measures exist to estimate the proportion of counterexamples to the dependency, and therefore estimate whether or not it is reasonable to perform classification on the dataset. We argue that this is a way to bring more interpretability to classification, by explaining to domain experts the limitations of the model, that come from the dataset itself. This could help them to better accept the produced model, by demystifying their performances.

In addition, we have provided a tight upper-bound for the accuracy any classifier could reach on the dataset. We have proposed an algorithm and showed consistent results on well-known classification datasets. In addition, we have devised an algorithm to generate difficult datasets for classification. Finally, we have designed a hybrid approach based on single attribute clustering and on a data reduction technique, allowing to both deal with dirty data and scale the enumeration of counterexamples. Experimental results have been conducted with very good compression ratio and scalability.

The results obtained in this paper provide guarantees on the classification dataset. They can be used to decide whether or not it is worth trying to fit a model, or if more time should be spent on the dataset itself. This is very useful for companies starting with new classification problems on data that might not be yet ready for classification. In addition, the counterexamples of functional dependencies are very useful to engage the discussion with domain experts, to understand the dataset into details, and therefore give them a better understanding of what can be done classification-wise.

Acknowledgment. The authors would like to thank the anonymous reviewers for their valuable remarks that helped improve and clarify this manuscript.

References

1. Abo Khamis, M., Ngo, H.Q., Nguyen, X., Olteanu, D., Schleich, M.: In-database learning with sparse tensors. In: Proceedings of the 35th ACM SIGMOD-SIGACT-SIGAI Symposium on Principles of Database Systems, pp. 325–340. ACM (2018)
2. Armstrong, W.W.: Dependency structures of database relationship. Inf. Process. **74**, 580–583 (1974)
3. Berlin, J., Motro, A.: Database schema matching using machine learning with feature selection. In: Pidduck, A.B., Ozsu, M.T., Mylopoulos, J., Woo, C.C. (eds.) CAiSE 2002. LNCS, vol. 2348, pp. 452–466. Springer, Heidelberg (2002). https://doi.org/10.1007/3-540-47961-9_32
4. Bilenko, M., Kamath, B., Mooney, R.J.: Adaptive blocking: learning to scale up record linkage. In: Sixth International Conference on Data Mining (ICDM 2006), pp. 87–96. IEEE (2006)
5. Bohannon, P., Fan, W., Geerts, F., Jia, X., Kementsietsidis, A.: Conditional functional dependencies for data cleaning. In: 2007 IEEE 23rd International Conference on Data Engineering, pp. 746–755. IEEE (2007)
6. Bonifati, A., Ciucanu, R., Staworko, S.: Interactive inference of join queries (2014)
7. Bosc, P., Dubois, D., Prade, H.: Fuzzy functional dependencies and redundancy elimination. J. Am. Soc. Inf. Sci. **49**(3), 217–235 (1998)
8. Bratko, I.: Machine learning: between accuracy and interpretability. In: Della Riccia, G., Lenz, H.-J., Kruse, R. (eds.) Learning, Networks and Statistics. ICMS, vol. 382, pp. 163–177. Springer, Vienna (1997). https://doi.org/10.1007/978-3-7091-2668-4_10

9. Caruccio, L., Deufemia, V., Polese, G.: Relaxed functional dependencies–a survey of approaches. IEEE Trans. Knowl. Data Eng. **28**(1), 147–165 (2015)
10. Casanova, M.A., Fagin, R., Papadimitriou, C.H.: Inclusion dependencies and their interaction with functional dependencies. J. Comput. Syst. Sci. **28**(1), 29–59 (1984)
11. Chang, S.K., Deufemia, V., Polese, G., Vacca, M.: A normalization framework for multimedia databases. IEEE Trans. Knowl. Data Eng. **19**(12), 1666–1679 (2007)
12. Chardin, B., Coquery, E., Pailloux, M., Petit, J.: RQL: a query language for rule discovery in databases. Theoret. Comput. Sci. **658**, 357–374 (2017). https://doi.org/10.1016/j.tcs.2016.11.004
13. Chu, X., Ilyas, I.F., Koutris, P.: Distributed data deduplication. Proc. VLDB Endow. **9**(11), 864–875 (2016)
14. Chu, X., Ilyas, I.F., Papotti, P.: Discovering denial constraints. Proc. VLDB Endow. **6**(13), 1498–1509 (2013)
15. Dalkilic, M.M., Roberston, E.L.: Information dependencies. In: Proceedings of the Nineteenth ACM SIGMOD-SIGACT-SIGART Symposium on Principles of Database Systems, pp. 245–253. ACM (2000)
16. Doshi-Velez, F., Kim, B.: Towards a rigorous science of interpretable machine learning. arXiv preprint arXiv:1702.08608 (2017)
17. Fagin, R.: Multivalued dependencies and a new normal form for relational databases. ACM Trans. Database Syst. (TODS) **2**(3), 262–278 (1977)
18. Fan, W.: Dependencies revisited for improving data quality. In: Proceedings of the Twenty-Seventh ACM SIGMOD-SIGACT-SIGART Symposium on Principles of Database Systems, pp. 159–170. ACM (2008)
19. Fernández-Delgado, M., Cernadas, E., Barro, S., Amorim, D.: Do we need hundreds of classifiers to solve real world classification problems? J. Mach. Learn. Res. **15**(1), 3133–3181 (2014)
20. Getoor, L.: The power of relational learning (invited talk). In: 22nd International Conference on Database Theory, ICDT 2019, Lisbon, Portugal, 26–28 March 2019, pp. 2:1–2:1 (2019). https://doi.org/10.4230/LIPIcs.ICDT.2019.2
21. Han, J.: Data Mining: Concepts and Techniques. Morgan Kaufmann Publishers Inc., San Francisco (2005)
22. Huhtala, Y., Kärkkäinen, J., Porkka, P., Toivonen, H.: TANE: an efficient algorithm for discovering functional and approximate dependencies. Comput. J. **42**(2), 100–111 (1999)
23. Kivinen, J., Mannila, H.: Approximate inference of functional dependencies from relations. Theoret. Comput. Sci. **149**(1), 129–149 (1995)
24. Kivinen, J., Mannila, H.: Approximate inference of functional dependencies from relations. Theoret. Comput. Sci. **149**(1), 129–149 (1995). https://doi.org/10.1016/0304-3975(95)00028-U
25. Koller, D., et al.: Introduction to Statistical Relational Learning. MIT Press, Cambridge (2007)
26. Kwon, O., Sim, J.M.: Effects of data set features on the performances of classification algorithms. Expert Syst. Appl. **40**(5), 1847–1857 (2013). https://doi.org/10.1016/j.eswa.2012.09.017
27. Lam, K.W., Lee, V.C.: Building decision trees using functional dependencies. In: 2004 Proceedings of the International Conference on Information Technology: Coding and Computing. ITCC 2004. vol. 2, pp. 470–473. IEEE (2004)

28. Levene, M., Loizou, G.: A Guided Tour of Relational Databases and Beyond. Springer, Heidelberg (2012). https://doi.org/10.1007/978-0-85729-349-7
29. Lloyd, S.: Least squares quantization in PCM. IEEE Trans. Inf. Theory **28**(2), 129–137 (1982)
30. Mohri, M., Rostamizadeh, A., Talwalkar, A.: Foundations of Machine Learning. MIT Press, Cambridge (2018)
31. Ordonez, C.: Integrating k-means clustering with a relational DBMS using SQL. IEEE Trans. Knowl. Data Eng. **18**(2), 188–201 (2006). https://doi.org/10.1109/TKDE.2006.31
32. Pedregosa, F., et al.: Scikit-learn: machine learning in Python. J. Mach. Learn. Res. **12**, 2825–2830 (2011)
33. Rahm, E., Do, H.H.: Data cleaning: problems and current approaches. IEEE Data Eng. Bull. **23**(4), 3–13 (2000)
34. Raju, K., Majumdar, A.K.: Fuzzy functional dependencies and lossless join decomposition of fuzzy relational database systems. ACM Trans. Database Syst. (TODS) **13**(2), 129–166 (1988)
35. Rekatsinas, T., Chu, X., Ilyas, I.F., Ré, C.: Holoclean: holistic data repairs with probabilistic inference. Proc. VLDB Endow. **10**(11), 1190–1201 (2017)
36. Rousseeuw, P.J.: Silhouettes: a graphical aid to the interpretation and validation of cluster analysis. J. Comput. Appl. Math. **20**, 53–65 (1987)
37. Sa, C.D., Ilyas, I.F., Kimelfeld, B., Ré, C., Rekatsinas, T.: A formal framework for probabilistic unclean databases. In: 22nd International Conference on Database Theory, ICDT 2019, Lisbon, Portugal, 26–28 March 2019, pp. 6:1–6:18 (2019). https://doi.org/10.4230/LIPIcs.ICDT.2019.6
38. Salimi, B., Rodriguez, L., Howe, B., Suciu, D.: Interventional fairness: causal database repair for algorithmic fairness. In: Proceedings of the 2019 International Conference on Management of Data, pp. 793–810. ACM (2019)
39. Santafe, G., Inza, I., Lozano, J.A.: Dealing with the evaluation of supervised classification algorithms. Artif. Intell. Rev. **44**(4), 467–508 (2015). https://doi.org/10.1007/s10462-015-9433-y
40. Santanu, P., Jaya, S., Das, A.K., et al.: Feature selection by attribute clustering of infected rice plant images. Int. J. Mach. Intell. **3**(2), 74–88 (2011)
41. Schleich, M., Olteanu, D., Ciucanu, R.: Learning linear regression models over factorized joins. In: Proceedings of the 2016 International Conference on Management of Data, pp. 3–18. ACM (2016)
42. Song, S., Chen, L.: Differential dependencies: reasoning and discovery. ACM Trans. Database Syst. (TODS) **36**(3), 1–41 (2011)
43. Tumer, K., Ghosh, J.: Estimating the Bayes error rate through classifier combining. In: Proceedings of 13th International Conference on Pattern Recognition, vol. 2, pp. 695–699. IEEE (1996)
44. Vapnik, V., Levin, E., Cun, Y.L.: Measuring the VC-dimension of a learning machine. Neural Comput. **6**(5), 851–876 (1994)
45. Wang, H., Zaniolo, C., Luo, C.R.: Atlas: a small but complete SQL extension for data mining and data streams. In: Proceedings of the 29th International Conference on Very Large Data Bases, vol. 29, pp. 1113–1116. VLDB Endowment (2003)
46. Wang, T., Rudin, C., Velez-Doshi, F., Liu, Y., Klampfl, E., MacNeille, P.: Bayesian rule sets for interpretable classification. In: 2016 IEEE 16th International Conference on Data Mining (ICDM), pp. 1269–1274. IEEE (2016)
47. Wei, Z., Link, S.: DataProf: semantic profiling for iterative data cleansing and business rule acquisition. In: Proceedings of the 2018 International Conference on Management of Data, pp. 1793–1796. ACM (2018)

48. Zeng, J., Ustun, B., Rudin, C.: Interpretable classification models for recidivism prediction. J. Roy. Stat. Soc.: Ser. A (Stat. Soc.) **180**(3), 689–722 (2017)
49. Zhang, S., Zhang, C., Yang, Q.: Data preparation for data mining. Appl. Artif. Intell. **17**(5–6), 375–381 (2003)
50. Zou, B., Ma, X., Kemme, B., Newton, G., Precup, D.: Data mining using relational database management systems. In: Ng, W.-K., Kitsuregawa, M., Li, J., Chang, K. (eds.) PAKDD 2006. LNCS (LNAI), vol. 3918, pp. 657–667. Springer, Heidelberg (2006). https://doi.org/10.1007/11731139_75

Enabling Decision Support Through Ranking and Summarization of Association Rules for TOTAL Customers

Idir Benouaret[1]([✉]), Sihem Amer-Yahia[1], Senjuti Basu Roy[2],
Christiane Kamdem-Kengne[3], and Jalil Chagraoui[3]

[1] CNRS, Univ. Grenoble Alpes, Grenoble, France
`{idir.benouaret,sihem.amer-yahia}@univ-grenoble-alpes.fr`
[2] New Jersey Institute of Technology, Neward, NJ, USA
`senjutib@njit.edu`
[3] TOTAL, Paris, France
`{christiane.kamdem-kengne,jalil.chagraoui}@total.com`

Abstract. Our focus in this experimental analysis paper is to investigate existing measures that are available to rank association rules and understand how they can be augmented further to enable real-world decision support as well as providing customers with personalized recommendations. For example, by analyzing receipts of TOTAL customers, one can find that, customers who buy windshield wash, also buy engine oil and energy drinks or middle-aged customers from the South of France subscribe to a car wash program. Such actionable insights can immediately guide business decision making, e.g., for product promotion, product recommendation or targeted advertising. We present an analysis of 30 million unique sales receipts, spanning 35 million records, by almost 1 million customers, generated at 3,463 gas stations, over three years. Our finding is that the 35 commonly used measures to rank association rules, such as Confidence and Piatetsky-Shapiro, can be summarized into 5 synthesized clusters based on similarity in their rankings. We then use one representative measure in each cluster to run a user study with a data scientist and a product manager at TOTAL. Our analysis draws actionable insights to enable decision support for TOTAL decision makers: rules that favor Confidence are best to determine which products to recommend and rules that favor Recall are well-suited to find customer segments to target. Finally, we present how association rules using the representative measures can be used to provide customers with personalized product recommendations.

Keywords: Data mining · Association rules · Recommendation

I. Benouaret and S. Amer-Yahia—Our work is funuded by a grant from TOTAL.

A. Hameurlain et al. (Eds.) TLDKS XLIV, LNCS 12380, pp. 160–193, 2020.
https://doi.org/10.1007/978-3-662-62271-1_6

1   Introduction

Association rule mining [1] is one of the most frequently used techniques to analyze customers' shopping behavior and derive actionable insights to enable decision support. Like many others in the retail industry, marketers and product managers at TOTAL conduct regular studies of customer preferences and purchasing habits. The goal of those studies is to determine two main decisions: *which products to bundle together in a promotional offer and which customers to target.* Those studies usually focus on unveiling the interest of customers for *specific products or categories* (e.g., *tire service, gas, food*) or the behavior of *pre-defined customer segments.* However, when the underlying dataset is extremely large, such as the one we use for our analysis from TOTAL (30 million receipts spanning 35 million records), it can create an explosion of association rules; therefore one has to make use of existing ranking measures of association rules, such as, *Support, Confidence, Piatetsky-Shapiro, Lift,* etc to rank the rules. Even after that, as there exists many ranking measures (as many as 35) [4,12], there may not be enough guideline to understand which ranking measure is to be leveraged for what types of decision making task, unless these ranking measures are further summarized.

To address that, we leverage the power of association rule mining and ranking measures for marketers to extract actionable insights from large volumes of consumer data. To make the outcome tightly aligned with the practitioners need, our workflow consists of the following 4 steps: **Step 1:** We empower non-scientist domain experts with the ability to express and analyze association rules of interest. **Step 2:** we summarize the ranking measures into a set of synthesized clusters or groups. The outcome of this process is a 5 synthesized clusters (or groups) that summarize the ranking measures effectively. **Step 3:** We allow the domain expert non-scientists to provide feedback on the synthesized clusters. **Step 4:** We show how this process can *provide actionable insights and enable decision support for virtually any customer segment* and *any product.* Our analysis shows: rules that favor Confidence are best to determine which products to promote and rules that favor Recall are well-suited to find customer segments to target.

To the best of our knowledge, this work is the first to run a large-scale empirical evaluation of insights on customer purchasing habits in the *oil* and *gas* retail domain. We summarize our contributions as follows: (i) a reproducible methodology for experimenting with different association rule ranking methods; (ii) several insights on real large-scale datasets; (iii) how to use association rules and interestingness measures in computing recommendations.

1.1   Empowering Domain Experts

When analysts seek to determine which products to run a promotion for or which customers to target, they conduct small to medium-scale market analysis studies. Such studies are expensive, time-consuming and hardly reproducible. We use association rule mining to unveil valuable information about any customer segment and any product. Our collaboration with analysts at TOTAL resulted in the formalization of two kinds of purchasing patterns: those representing associations between a set of products and a single product (*customers who wash their cars and purchase wipes also purchase a windshield washer*), and those associating customer segments to a product category (*young customers in the south of France who frequently wash their cars*).

Our dataset contains 30 million unique receipts, spanning 35 million records, generated at by 1 million customers at 3,463 gas stations , over three years (from January 2017 to December 2019). The ratio 30/35 is due to the fact that, unlike in regular retail such as shopping grocery stores [12], most customers at gas stations purchase *gas* only, and a few purchase additional products such as *car wash*, *drinks* and *food* items.

Based on our initial discussion with TOTAL analysts, we propose two mining scenarios to capture desired purchasing patterns. The goal is to help analysts who are not necessarily tech-savvy, express their needs. In the first scenario, prod_assoc, the analyst specifies a target product and expects rules of the form *set of products* ↪ *target product*. In the second scenario, demo_assoc, the analyst specifies a target product category and expects rules of the form *customer segment* ↪ *category*, i.e. customers who purchase products in that category. Each scenario requires to ingest and prepare data as a set of transactions. The transactions are fed to jLCM [16], our open-source parallel and distributed pattern mining algorithm that runs on MapReduce [13], to compute association rules. To cope with the skewed distribution of our transactions, jLCM is parameterizable and is used to mine per-item top-k itemsets.

1.2   Ranking and Summarization of Association Rules

Regardless of the mining scenario, the number of resulting rules can quickly become overwhelming. As an example, for a single target product: *TOTAL wash* and with a 1,000 minimum support, jLCM mines 4,243 frequent rules of the form *set of products* ↪ *TOTAL wash*. Out of these, 805 have a *Confidence* of 50% or higher. Table 1 shows a ranking of the top-5 rules for the product category *Lubricants* and the top-5 rules for the product *Coca Cola*, sorted using 2 different interestingness measures proposed in the literature [4]. Given the rule $\mathcal{A} \rightarrow \mathcal{B}$, *Confidence* is akin to precision and is defined as the probability to observe $\mathcal{B}$ given that we observed $\mathcal{A}$, i.e., $P(\mathcal{B}|\mathcal{A})$. *Piatetsky-Shapiro* [22] combines how $\mathcal{A}$ and $\mathcal{B}$ occur together with how they would if they were independent, i.e., $P(\mathcal{AB}) - P(\mathcal{A})P(\mathcal{B})$. *Recall* is defined as the probability to observe $\mathcal{A}$ given that we observed $\mathcal{B}$. Clearly, different measures yield different rule rankings for both prod_assoc and demo_assoc.

To ease the burden on analysts, we propose to examine the rankings induced by existing measures (exactly 35 measures [4]) and attempt to reduce them based on similarities in rankings. We run our measures to rank association rules for 228 representative products in prod_assoc and for 16 representative product categories in demo_assoc. In each case, we use hierarchical clustering to summarize or group the rule rankings based on their similarities (we use multiple list

Table 1. Top-5 demographics association rules, Top-5 products association rules, according to different interestingness measures. For `demo_assoc`, rules are denoted {age, gender, region} → *target category*. Product category was translated to English, French regions were left unchanged. For `prod_assoc`, rules are denoted {set of products} → *target product*. Products were translated to English.

By confidence		By Piatetsky-Shapiro [22]	
{50–65, M,Ile-de-France}	→ *Lubricants*	*{50-65, M, ∗}*	→ *Lubricants*
{50–65, ∗, Ile-de-France}	→ *Lubricants*	*{∗, M,Ile-de-France}*	→ *Lubricants*
{>65, M,Ile-de-France }	→ *Lubricants*	*{∗, ∗,Ile-de-France }*	→ *Lubricants*
{>65, M, ∗}	→ *Lubricants*	*{∗, F, ∗}*	→ *Lubricants*
{50–65 , M,Hauts-de-France }	→ *Lubricants*	*{∗, M, ∗}*	→ *Lubricants*
{ Bbq chips, Ham sandwish }	→ *Coca Cola*	*{Coffee }*	→ *Coca Cola*
{Cheese sandwish, Bbq chips }	→ *Coca Cola*	*{Fuze Peche }*	→ *Coca Cola*
{Bbq chips, Salted chips }	→ *Coca Cola*	*{Insulated bottle}*	→ *Coca Cola*
{Chicken sandwish, Salted chips }	→ *Coca Cola*	*{Mars legend }*	→ *Coca Cola*
{Chicken sandwish, Bbq chips }	→ *Coca Cola*	*{ Snickers }*	→ *Coca Cola*

similarities to compare rankings). Our finding is that existing measures can be clustered into 5 similar synthesized groups regardless of the mining scenario. The clusters we obtained are summarized in Table 3. They differ in their emphasis on *Confidence* and *Recall*. In the case of `prod_assoc`, we observe high *Confidence* and low *Recall* for G_1 which contains 18 measures among which *Lift*, and for G_2 which contains 3 measures among which *Accuracy*. G_3 which contains 7 measures among which *J-measure*, achieves a good tradeoff between *Confidence* and *Recall*. G_4 contains 5 measures among which *Piatetsky-Shapiro* and achieves average *Confidence* and high *Recall*. G_5 contains 2 measures among which *Recall* and is characterized by the lowest *Confidence* and highest *Recall* among all groups. In the case of `demo_assoc`, we observe the same groups G_1 and G_2 with also a high *Confidence* and low *Recall*. G_3' which contains 7 measures among which *Klosgen*, achieves a good tradeoff between *Confidence* and *Recall*. G_4' contains 3 measures among which *Two-way support variation* and achieves low *Confidence* and high recall. Finally, G_5' contains 4 measures among which *Recall* and is characterized by the lowest *Confidence* and the highest *Recall* overall.

1.3 Gathering Feedback

The reduction of the number of interestingness measures to rank rules enabled us to conduct a user study with 2 analysts, one data scientist and one product manager (co-authors of this paper), at TOTAL to address the following question: **out of the 5 groups of similar interestingness measures, which ones return actionable rules?** Actionable rules are ones that can be used by analysts either to promote products or to find customer segments to target. Our study lets analysts compare 2 (hidden) ranking measures at a time for a given scenario and a given target product or category. Our first deployment was deemed "reassuring" and "unsurprising". A joint examination of the results identified two issues: (1) rules contained many "expected associations", i.e., those resulting from promotional offers that already occurred; (2) many rules were featuring "familiar" items, i.e., frequently purchased ones. After filtering unwanted items such as *gas, plastic bags, etc* and offers, we ran a second deployment with our analysts. Their interactions with returned association rules (of the form $\mathcal{A} \rightarrow \mathcal{B}$, where $\mathcal{B}$ is a product or a category) were observed and their feedback recorded. This deployment yielded two insights: rankings that favor *Confidence*, i.e., $P(\mathcal{B}|\mathcal{A})$, are best to determine which products to promote while rankings that favor *Recall*, i.e., $P(\mathcal{A}|\mathcal{B})$, are well-suited to find which customer segments to target. Confidence represents how often the consequent is present when the antecedent is, that is, $P(\mathcal{B}|\mathcal{A})$, and confidence-based ranking can be used to determine which A products to bundle with a target product $\mathcal{B}$ to promote $\mathcal{B}$. Recall represents the proportion of target items that can be retrieved by a rule, that is, $P(\mathcal{A}|\mathcal{B})$, and recall-based ranking can be used to determine which customer segments $\mathcal{A}$ to target with $\mathcal{B}$.

1.4 Product Recommendation

Finally, we show how association rules can effectively be used to perform product recommendation using different interestingness measures. Clustering the overwhelming number of interestingness measures into 5 synthesized clusters enabled us to conduct an offline experiment to test the effectiveness of each cluster of measures to generate accurate product recommendations. We split our data using the available timestamps into a training set (transactions from January 2017 to December 2018) and a test set (transactions from January 2019 to December 2019), i.e., we extract association rules based on past purchases to predict future purchases. The obtained accuracy results are consistent with our clustering as well as the preference of our analysts for measures that favor *Confidence* for product recommendation.

In summary, this paper presents a joint effort between researchers in academia and analysts at TOTAL. We leverage the power of association rule mining and augment them with the power of rule ranking and summarization to guide decision support as well as the ability of performing product recommendation. The rest of the paper could be summarized as follows: The background and the goal of the work are provided in Sect. 2. Our underlying process using TOTAL datasets is described in Sect. 3. In Sect. 4, we describe how we summarize (cluster) interestingness measures based on similarities in rule rankings. These clusters are then evaluated by analysts in Sect. 5 leading to insightful findings. We discuss how to turn use our findings into product recommendation through association rule ranking in Sect. 6. The related work is summarized in Sect. 7. We conclude in Sect. 8.

2   Background and Overall Goal

We describe the TOTAL dataset, the mining scenarios, and interestingness measures used to rank association rules, and finally we state our goal.

2.1   Dataset

Our dataset represents customers purchasing products at different gas stations that are geographically distributed in France, for a period of two years (from January 2017 to December 2018). The dataset $\mathcal{D}$ is a set of records of the form $\langle t, c, p \rangle$, where t is a unique receipt identifier, c is a customer, and p is a product purchased by c. The set of all receipt identifiers is denoted T. Each receipt identifier is associated with a unique customer, and multiple receipt identifiers can be associated with the same customer according to his/her visits to different gas stations. When a customer purchases multiple products in the same visit to a gas station, several records with the same receipt identifier t are generated.

The complete dataset contains over 30 million unique receipts, spanning 35 million records, generated at 3, 463 gas stations, over three years. The ratio 30/35 in our dataset is due to the fact that, unlike regular retail such as shopping grocery stores [12], most customers at gas stations purchase *gas* only, and a few of them purchase additional products such as car services (*oil change, car wash*), *drinks* and *food* items.

The set of customers, $\mathcal{C}$, contains over 1 million unique records. Each customer has demographic attributes. In this study, we focus on 3 attributes: *age, gender* and *location*. The attribute *age* takes values in $\{<35, 35 - 49, 50 - 65, >65\}$ and the attribute *location* admits French regions as values. We use *demographics*(c) to refer to the set of attribute values a customer c belongs to. For example, $\{<35, F, Ile-de-France\}$ represents a 28 years old *female* from the *Ile-de-France* region, whom we will refer to as *Mary*. The attributes are used to form customer segments. Each segment is described by a set of user attribute values that are interpreted in the usual conjunctive manner. For example, the segment $\{<35, *, Ile-de-France\}$ refers to young customers from the *Ile-de-France* region and the segment $\{>65, M, Normandie\}$ refers to Senior Male customers from the *Normandie* region.

The set of products $\mathcal{P}$ contains over 37, 556 entries, out of which 976 have been sold more than a thousand times. Each product p is associated with a product category. Our dataset contains 54 different categories including *gas, lubricants, car wash, hot drinks,* and *sweets.* We use *cat*(p) to denote the category of a product p.

2.2   Mining Customer Receipts

We describe our data preparation process - that is how to translate the sale receipts to a transactional dataset that could be further injected to the mining process. We then describe the mining scenarios and present interestingness measures to rank association rules.

Table 2. Our mining scenarios and example association rules.

Target Associations	Associations and $\mathcal{T}$
demo_assoc:	$\{demo(c) \cup cat(p)|\langle t, c, p \rangle \in \mathcal{D}\}$
$segment \rightarrow category$	min support is 1,000
prod_assoc:	$\{\cup_{\langle t_j, c, p_i \rangle \in \mathcal{D}} p_i | c \in \mathcal{C}\}$
$product(s) \rightarrow product$	min support is 1,000

Target Associations	Desired Association Rules
demo_assoc:	A segment of customers who are
	likely to purchase products in a given category
$segment \rightarrow category$	$\{< 35, F, *\} \rightarrow car\ wash$
prod_assoc:	Customers who purchase a set of
	products and are likely to purchase the target product
$product(s) \rightarrow product$	$\{Bbq\ Chips, Snickers\ Bar\} \rightarrow Coca\ Cola$

Dataset Preparation. Figures 1, 2 and 3 report statistics on one month in the dataset which contains $407,212$ sales records generated by $257,102$ customers for $5,479$ products at $3,079$ gas stations. For confidentiality reasons, we do not report the statistics of the full dataset. We can however state that other periods in the dataset exhibit similar distributions. The statistics clearly show that the most purchased items are *gas* and that most transactions are short.

To gain an understanding of customers' buying habits and provide them with relevant offers, analysts from TOTAL are interested in studying two kinds of purchasing patterns: those associating a set of products to a single product (*customers who wash their cars and purchase wipes also purchase a windshield washer*) and those representing associations between customer segments and a product category (*young customers in the south of France who frequently wash their cars*). In all cases the analyst specifies a rule target $\mathcal{B}$ which corresponds to a product or a product category, and expects rules of the form $\mathcal{A} \rightarrow \mathcal{B}$.

In the first scenario, that we denote prod_assoc, the analyst specifies a target product and is shown rules of the form *set of products $\rightarrow$ target product*, i.e. customers who purchase the set of products are likely to purchase the target product. In the second scenario, that we denote demo_assoc, the analyst specifies a target category, and is shown rules of the form *customer segment $\rightarrow$ target category*, i.e. customers who belong to some segment are likely to purchase products in the target category.

In both scenarios, the original dataset $\mathcal{D}$ is mapped into a collection of transactions $\mathcal{T}$ that is given as input to the mining process, as summarized in Table 2. The set $\mathcal{T}$ is built differently according to each scenario.

In the first scenario prod_assoc, we generate the set of transactions $\mathcal{T}$ by grouping records in $\mathcal{D}$ by customer identifiers. For each customer c, we generate a single transaction containing the set of all products ever purchased by c $\{p|\langle t, c, p \rangle \in \mathcal{D}\}$. We obtain $|\mathcal{C}|$ transactions, each of which is a subset of $\mathcal{P}$.

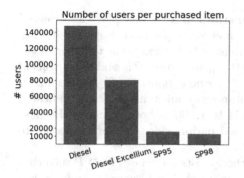

Fig. 1. Most purchased items

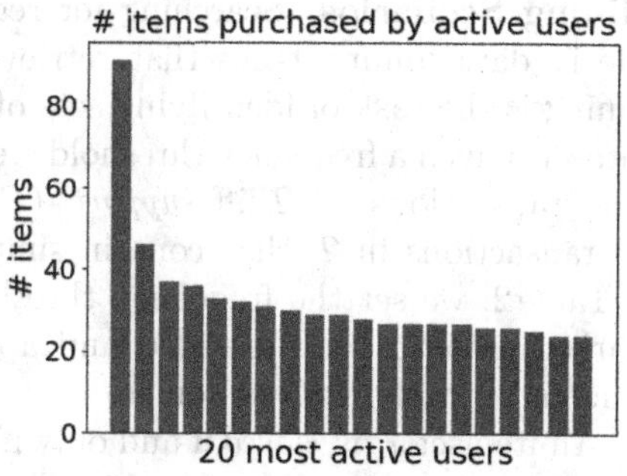

Fig. 2. Most active users

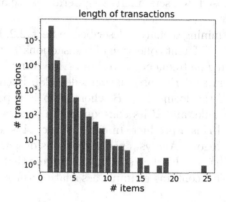

Fig. 3. Length of transactions

This enables the discovery of customer patterns occurring over several visits to a station. The number of transactions in `prod_assoc` is 1,083,901, where each transaction contains 7 products on average.

In the second scenario `demo_assoc`, a transaction is a tuple built for each record $\langle t, c, p \rangle$ by associating the customer segment $demographics(c)$ with the corresponding category of the product $cat(p)$. For example, an entry in the raw data consisting of the record $\langle 4523768, Mary, tea \rangle$ is mapped to the transaction $\langle\ {<}35, F, \mathit{Ile\text{-}de\text{-}France}, hot\ drinks\ \rangle$. We obtain $|\mathcal{D}|$ transactions, and each transaction contains the segment a customer belongs to, and the category of the purchased product.

Mining Scenarios. Searching for regularities in a dataset plays an essential role in data mining tasks that retrieve interesting patterns. Frequent itemset mining is the task of identifying sets of items which often occur together in the dataset. Given a frequency threshold $\varepsilon \in [1, n]$, an itemset P is said to be *frequent* in a transactions set $\mathcal{T}$ iff $support_{\mathcal{T}}(P) \geq \varepsilon$ where $support_{\mathcal{T}}(P)$ is the number of transactions in $\mathcal{T}$ that contain simultaneously all items in P. As indicated in Table 2, we set the frequency threshold to 1,000 in both scenarios. Because marketing actions are decided and applied nation-wide, they are expected to concern at least 1,000 customers.

An itemset P is *closed* if and only if there exists no itemset $P' \supset P$ such that $support_{\mathcal{T}}(P) = support_{\mathcal{T}}(P')$ [20]. The number of closed itemsets can be orders of magnitude less important than the number of itemsets, while providing the same amount of information on $\mathcal{T}$. Several algorithms, including ours, focus on extracting frequent closed itemsets, increasing performance and avoiding redundancy in results [21,30].

We consider our 2 mining scenarios described in Sect. 2.2. Each scenario leads to the construction of a different collection of transactions $\mathcal{T}$, where a transaction is a set of items. Given $\mathcal{T}$, a frequency threshold ε, we retrieve all closed frequent itemsets, and use them to derive association rules [28]. Each itemset P implies an association rule of the form $\mathcal{A} \rightarrow \mathcal{B}$ where $\mathcal{A}, \mathcal{B}$ is a partition of P. $\mathcal{A}$ is the antecedent of the rule, and $\mathcal{B}$ its consequent. In `prod_assoc`, $\mathcal{A}$ is a set of products ($\mathcal{A} \subseteq \mathcal{P}$) and $\mathcal{B}$ is a product. In `demo_assoc`, $\mathcal{A}$ is a customer segment and $\mathcal{B}$ is a product category. Analysts generally focus on particular products or product categories. That is why they specify the targets that they are interested in each scenario. Table 2 contains example association rules extracted from our dataset.

Interestingness Measures. The ability to identify valuable rules is of utmost importance to avoid drowning analysts in useless information. Association rules $\mathcal{A} \rightarrow \mathcal{B}$ were originally selected using thresholds for *Support* ($support_{\mathcal{T}}(\mathcal{A} \cup \mathcal{B})$) and *Confidence* ($\frac{support_{\mathcal{T}}(\mathcal{A} \cup \mathcal{B})}{support_{\mathcal{T}}(\mathcal{A})}$) [1]. However, using two separate values, and guessing the right threshold is not natural. Furthermore, support and confidence do not always coincide with the interest of analysts. Hence, a number of interestingness measures that serve different analyses were proposed in the literature [4,19]. Table 3 summarizes the measures we use in this work. The first column contains the name of the measure, the second its expression. Table 4 describes the group and description of each measure and will refer to it later in the paper.

Table 3. Interestingness measures of a rule $A \to B$. $\Diamond$, $\dagger$, $\ominus$, $\otimes$ indicate measures that always produce the same rule ranking. $|\mathcal{T}|$ is the number of transactions. $P(A) = support(A)/|\mathcal{T}|$.

Measure	Formula
One-way support	$P(B\|A) \times log_2 \frac{P(AB)}{P(A)P(B)}$
Relative risk	$P(B\|A)/P(B\|\neg A)$
Odd multiplier $\triangleright$	$(P(AB)P(\neg B))/(P(B)P(A\neg B))$
Zhang $\triangleright$	$\frac{P(AB)-P(A)P(B)}{max(P(AB)P(\neg B),P(B)P(A\neg B))}$
Yule's Q $\Diamond$	$\frac{P(AB)P(\neg A\neg B)-P(A\neg B)P(B\neg A)}{P(AB)P(\neg A\neg B)+P(A\neg B)P(B\neg A)}$
Yule's Y $\Diamond$	$\frac{\sqrt{P(AB)P(\neg A\neg B)}-\sqrt{P(A\neg B)P(B\neg A)}}{\sqrt{P(AB)P(\neg A\neg B)}+\sqrt{P(A\neg B)P(B\neg A)}}$
Odds ratio $\Diamond$	$(P(AB)P(\neg A\neg B))/(P(A\neg B)P(B\neg A))$
Information gain $\ominus$	$log(P(AB)/(P(A)P(B)))$
Lift $\ominus$	$P(AB)/(P(A)P(B))$
Added value $*$	$P(B\|A) - P(B)$
Certainty factor $*$	$(P(B\|A) - P(B))/(1 - P(B))$
Confidence $*$	$P(B\|A)$
Laplace correction$*$	$(support(AB) + 1)/(support(A) + 2)$
Loevinger $\dagger$	$1 - P(A\neg B)/P(A)P(\neg B)$
Conviction $\dagger$	$P(A)P(\neg B)/P(A\neg B)$
Example and counter-example rate$\otimes$	$1 - P(A\neg B)/P(AB)$
Sebag-Schoenauer $\otimes$	$P(AB)/P(A\neg B)$
Leverage	$P(B\|A) - P(A)P(B)$
Least contradiction	$(P(AB) - P(A\neg B))/P(B)$
Accuracy	$P(AB) + P(\neg A\neg B)$
Gini index	$P(A) \times (P(B\|A)^2 + P(\neg B\|A)^2) + P(\neg A) \times (P(B\|\neg A)^2 + P(\neg B\|\neg A)^2) - P(B)^2 - P(\neg B)^2$

(*continued*)

Table 3. (*continued*)

Measure	Formula
Pearson's χ^2	$\|\mathcal{T}\| \times \left(\frac{(P(AB)-P(A)P(B))^2}{P(A)P(B)} + \frac{(P(\neg AB)-P(\neg A)P(B))^2}{P(\neg A)P(B)} \right)$
	$+\|\mathcal{T}\| \times \left(\frac{(P(A\neg B)-P(A)P(\neg B))^2}{P(A)P(B)} + \frac{(P(\neg A\neg B)-P(\neg A)P(\neg B))^2}{P(\neg A)P(\neg B)} \right)$
J-measure	$P(AB)log(\frac{P(B\|A)}{P(B)}) + P(A\neg B)log(\frac{P(\neg B\|A)}{P(\neg B)})$
Φ Linear correlation coefficient	$(P(AB) - P(A)P(B))/\sqrt{P(A)P(B)P(\neg A)P(\neg B)}$
Two-way support variation	$P(AB) \times log_2\frac{P(AB)}{P(A)P(B)} + P(A\neg B) \times log_2\frac{P(A\neg B)}{P(A)P(\neg B)}+$
	$P(\neg AB) \times log_2\frac{P(\neg AB)}{P(\neg A)P(B)} + P(\neg A\neg B) \times log_2\frac{P(\neg A\neg B)}{P(\neg A)P(\neg B)}$
Implication index	$\sqrt{\mathcal{T}} \times \frac{P(A\neg B)-P(A)P(\neg B)}{\sqrt{P(A)P(\neg B)}}$
Klosgen	$\sqrt{P(AB)}max(P(B\|A) - P(B), P(A\|B) - P(A))$
Cosine	$P(AB)/\sqrt{P(A)P(B)}$
Jaccard	$P(AB)/(P(A) + P(B) - P(AB))$
Kappa	$\frac{P(B\|A)P(A)+P(\neg B\|\neg A)-P(A)P(B)-P(\neg A)P(\neg B)}{1-P(A)P(B)-P(\neg A)P(\neg B)}$
Piatetsky-Shapiro	$P(AB) - P(A)P(B)$
Two-Way Support	$P(AB) \times log_2\frac{P(AB)}{P(A)P(B)}$
Specificity	$P(\neg B\|\neg A)$
Recall	$P(A\|B)$
Collective Strength	$\frac{P(AB)+P(\neg B\|\neg A)}{P(A)P(B)+P(\neg A)P(\neg B)} \times \frac{1-P(A)P(B)-P(\neg A)P(\neg B)}{1-P(AB)-P(\neg B\|\neg A)}$

2.3 Goal

Our goal is to help analysts test and compare the rankings produced by different interestingness measures on rules extracted from $\mathcal{D}$. An analyst can specify one of 2 mining scenarios, prod_assoc and demo_assoc, and one or several targets (products in the case of prod_assoc, categories in the case of demo_assoc), and the system generates as many rule rankings as the number of interestingness measures.

Table 4. Group and description of interestingness measures.

Measure	Group and description	
One-Way Support		
Relative Risk		
Odd Multiplier ▷		
Zhang ▷		
Yule's Q ◊		
Yule's Y ◊		
Odds Ratio ◊		
Information Gain ⊖		Highest confidence
Lift ⊖	G_1	Very low recall
Added Value ∗		
Certainty Factor ∗		
Confidence ∗		
Laplace Correction∗		
Loevinger †		
Conviction †		
Example and counter-example rate⊗		
Sebag-Schoenauer ⊗		
Leverage		
Least Contradiction	G_2	Very high confidence
Accuracy		Very low recall
Gini Index		
Pearson's χ^2		
J-measure		Average confidence
Φ Linear Correlation Coefficient		Average recall
Two-Way Support Variation	G_3	
Implication Index		
Klosgen		
Cosine		
Jaccard		
Kappa		Average confidence
Piatetsky-Shapiro		High recall
Two-Way Support	G_4	
Specificity		
Recall	G_5	Lowest confidence
Collective Strength		Highest recall

3 Data Acquisition, Curation and Mining

3.1 Acquisition and Storage

Each of the 3, 463 gas stations maintains a log of all customer transactions completed during one day. Whenever a customer authenticates her purchases using her loyalty card, a receipt containing the list of purchased products, their price, their category, as well as potential promotional offers, is generated. For each purchased product a record containing the receipt id, product id and customer id, is generated. These receipts are logged as $\langle r, c, p \rangle$ triples and stored in write-ahead log. Once a day, at closing time of each gas station, this log is transferred to the main data store. We have access to an SQL database containing the *sales* table where sales records are stored. Each customer is an entry in the *customers* table, which records the information she provided in her loyalty card (age, gender, region). Note that we do not have access to confidential information such name and phone number.

3.2 Data Curation and Preparation

We first query the *sales* table to retrieve the full raw sales records. We also query the *customers* table to retrieve for each customer the corresponding segment attributes. At the end of this step, we generate two text files. Each line in the *sales* file is a triple $\langle r, c, p \rangle$, and each line in the *customers* file is a quadruple $\langle c, age, gender, region \rangle$.

As described in Sect. 2.2, mining customer receipts starts with the construction of a transactions dataset $\mathcal{T}$ according to the mining scenario specified by the analyst. We rely on Apache Spark and MapReduce operations to build the dataset $\mathcal{T}$ for each mining scenario. The *sales* file is loaded as a resilient distributed dataset. We maintain a HashMap that associates to each customer her segment, and another HashMap that associates to each product its corresponding category. In the case of `prod_assoc`, the products bought by a given customer are grouped by customer identifier using a groupByKey operation. In the case of `demo_assoc`, a single *map* operation is sufficient. For each row $\langle r, c, p \rangle$ in the dataset, the map operation constructs a transaction $\langle age, gender, region, cat(p) \rangle$.

In both cases, a dataset $\mathcal{T}$ is created as a text file, with one line per transaction. In `prod_assoc`, an example of a line is *gas, car wash, cafe, sandwich* that represents all products ever purchased by a single customer. In `demo_assoc`, an example of a line is $\langle >65, M, \text{Ile-de-France}, \text{Soft drinks} \rangle$. Given a dataset $\mathcal{T}$, we can now perform the mining process.

3.3 Mining

Extracting Itemsets Using jLCM. Generating association rules, presented in Sect. 2.2, requires to first extract frequent itemsets from $\mathcal{T}$. We use jLCM [16], our open-source parallel and distributed pattern mining algorithm that runs on MapReduce [13]. Mining frequent itemsets is done in two steps. We scan the input dataset $\mathcal{T}$ once and build a filtered dataset limited to transactions containing the target $\mathcal{B}$ specified by the analyst: $\mathcal{T}_\mathcal{B} = \{\mathcal{E} \in \mathcal{T}, \mathcal{B} \in \mathcal{E}\}$. Then, we execute jLCM on the filtered dataset. jLCM is a recursive algorithm that retrieves frequent itemsets and computes their frequency. Closed itemsets are returned along with their corresponding support, except for singletons that cannot be used to produce association rules. This extraction allows us to quickly obtain itemsets that satisfy our constraint., i.e, all extracted itemsets contain the specified target $\mathcal{B}$.

Mining Rules. Our analysts aim at uncovering interesting association rules expressed as $\mathcal{A} \rightarrow \mathcal{B}$ where $\mathcal{B}$ is the specified target. Evaluating the interestingness of an association rule requires computing the support of itemsets $\mathcal{A}$, $\mathcal{B}$ and $\mathcal{A} \cup \mathcal{B}$ in $\mathcal{T}$. The standard method for mining association rules consists in finding all frequent itemsets in the dataset, and then generating the rules. Given that our analyst specifies a single target $\mathcal{B}$ at a time, this approach would be wasteful. This motivates using jLCM on the filtered dataset limited to transactions containing the target $\mathcal{B}$. The result of the itemsets extraction using jLCM contains the support of $\mathcal{B}$ and $\mathcal{A} \cup \mathcal{B}$ for all association rules we are interested in. At this point, we need to calculate the support of each antecedent itemset $\mathcal{A}$. Thus, in a post-processing step, we scan the dataset $\mathcal{T}$ once and compute the support of all antecedents $\mathcal{A}$. This two-step approach avoids the computation of many itemsets that will never appear as a rule antecedent.

Evaluating Relevant Rules. To evaluate the interestingness of an association rule $\mathcal{A} \rightarrow \mathcal{B}$, we only need to compute $P(\mathcal{A})$, $P(\mathcal{B})$ and $P(\mathcal{A} \cup \mathcal{B})$ because given the number of all transactions $|\mathcal{T}|$, other probabilities such as $P(\mathcal{B}|\mathcal{A})$ and $P(\mathcal{A}\neg\mathcal{B})$ can be derived. Therefore, we denormalize the results of the mining phase to store those three probabilities with each $\mathcal{A}$ and $\mathcal{B}$. The support of all rules' antecedents (used to compute $P(\mathcal{A})$) are added to the results of the mining phase (used to compute $P(\mathcal{B})$ and $P(\mathcal{A} \cup \mathcal{B})$). We create a dataframe where each row represents an association rule and has enough information to compute its interestingness. For instance, in the case of `prod_assoc`, the system computes three values for each rule. As an example, for a rule like *Coffee* $\rightarrow$ *Water*, it computes 3 values: *Support* (number of customers who purchased both *Coffee* and *Water*), *Confidence* (fraction of *Coffee* buyers who also bought *Water*) and *Recall* (fraction of *Water* buyers who also bought *Coffee*). This dataframe is augmented with 35 columns, one for each implemented measure listed in Table 3.

4   Ranking and Summarization

Our goal, stated in Sect. 2.3, is to assist analysts in selecting the most actionable rules, those that can be used to promote products or target specific customers. In this section, we present an empirical evaluation of the 35 measures for association rules introduced in Sect. 2.2. The main goal of our evaluation is to compare the rankings of association rules produced by those measures on our dataset, and study their similarities. This lets us summarize ranking measures into similar clusters. We explain obtained clusters in Sect. 4.2 and 4.3 and discuss their differences. This empirical evaluation automatically reduces the number of candidate measures to present to analysts in the user study.

4.1   Ranking Similarity Measures

We rely on the methods used in [12] to compare ranked lists of rules produced by different interestingness measures. The first three methods are taken from the literature. The last one *NDCC* is a parameter-free measure defined in [12] to emphasize differences at the top of the rankings.

We are given a set of association rules $\mathcal{R}$ to rank. Each measure, m, is seen as a function that receives a rule and generates a score, $m : \mathcal{R} \to \mathbb{R}$. We use $L_{\mathcal{R}}^m$ to denote an ordered list composed of rules in $\mathcal{R}$, sorted by decreasing score. Thus, $L_{\mathcal{R}}^m =< r_1, r_2, \dots >$ s.t. $\forall i > i'\ m(r_i) < m(r_{i'})$. We generate multiple lists, one for each measure m, from the same set $\mathcal{R}$. $L_{\mathcal{R}}^m$ denotes a ranked list of association rules according to measure m where the rank of rule r is given as $rank(r, L_{\mathcal{R}}^m) = |\{r'|r' \in \mathcal{R},\ m(r') \geq m(r)\}|$. To assess dissimilarity between two measures, m and m', we compute dissimilarity between their ranked lists, $L_{\mathcal{R}}^m$ and $L_{\mathcal{R}}^{m'}$. We use r^m as a shorthand notation for $rank(r, L_{\mathcal{R}}^m)$.

Spearman's Rank Correlation Coefficient. Given two ranked lists $L_{\mathcal{R}}^m$ and $L_{\mathcal{R}}^{m'}$, *Spearman's rank correlation* [3] computes a linear correlation coefficient that varies between 1 (identical lists) and −1 (opposite rankings) as shown below.

$$Spearman(L_{\mathcal{R}}^m, L_{\mathcal{R}}^{m'}) = 1 - \frac{6 \sum_{r \in \mathcal{R}} (r^m - r^{m'})^2}{|\mathcal{R}|(|\mathcal{R}|^2 - 1)}$$

This coefficient depends only on the difference in ranks of the element (rule) in the two lists, and not on the ranks themselves. Hence, the penalization is the same for differences occurring at the beginning or at the end of the lists.

Kendall'sτ Rank Correlation Coefficient. *Kendall's τ rank correlation coefficient* [10] is based on the idea of agreement among element (rule) pairs. A rule pair is said to be *concordant* if their order is the same in $L_{\mathcal{R}}^m$ and $L_{\mathcal{R}}^{m'}$, and *discordant* otherwise. τ computes the difference between the number of concordant and discordant pairs and divides by the total number of pairs as shown below.

$$\tau(L_{\mathcal{R}}^m, L_{\mathcal{R}}^{m'}) = \frac{|C| - |D|}{\frac{1}{2}|\mathcal{R}|(|\mathcal{R}| - 1)}$$

$$C = \{(r_i, r_j)|r_i, r_j \in \mathcal{R} \wedge i < j \wedge$$
$$sgn(r_i^m - r_j^m) = sgn(r_i^{m'} - r_j^{m'})\}$$
$$D = \{(r_i, r_j)|r_i, r_j \in \mathcal{R} \wedge i < j \wedge$$
$$sgn(r_i^m - r_j^m) \neq sgn(r_i^{m'} - r_j^{m'})\}$$

Similar to *Spearman's*, τ varies between 1 and −1, and penalizes uniformly across all positions.

Overlap@k. Overlap@k is another method for ranked lists comparison widely used in Information Retrieval. It is based on the premise that in long ranked lists, the analyst is only expected to look at the top few results that are highly ranked. While *Spearman* and τ account for all elements uniformly, Overlap@k compares two rankings by computing the overlap between their top-k elements only.

$$Overlap@k(L_{\mathcal{R}}^m, L_{\mathcal{R}}^{m'}) = \frac{|\{r \in \mathcal{R} \mid r^m \leq k \wedge r^{m'} \leq k\}|}{k}$$

Normalized Discounted Correlation Coefficient. Overlap@k, *Spearman's* and τ sit at two different extremes. The former is conservative in that it takes into consideration only the top k elements of the list and the latter two take too liberal an approach by penalizing all parts of the lists uniformly. In practice, we aim for a good tradeoff between these extremes.

To bridge this gap, we use *NDCC* (*Normalized Discounted Correlation Coefficient*), a ranking correlation measure proposed in [12]. *NDCC* draws inspiration from *NDCG*, *Normalized Discounted Cumulative Gain* [9], a ranking measure commonly used in Information Retrieval. The core idea in *NDCG* is to reward a ranked list $L_{\mathcal{R}}^m$ for placing an element r of relevance rel_r by $\frac{rel_r}{\log r^m}$.

The logarithmic part acts as a smoothing discount rate representing the fact that as the rank increases, the analyst is less likely to observe r. In our setting, there is no ground truth to properly assess rel_r. Instead, we use the ranking assigned by m' as a relevance measure for r, with an identical logarithmic discount. When summing over all of $\mathcal{R}$, we obtain DCC, which presents the advantage of being a symmetric correlation measure between two rankings $L_{\mathcal{R}}^m$ and $L_{\mathcal{R}}^{m'}$.

$$DCC(L_{\mathcal{R}}^m, L_{\mathcal{R}}^{m'}) = \sum_{r \in \mathcal{R}} \frac{1}{\log(1 + r^{m'})\log(1 + r^m)}$$

We compute *NDCC* by normalizing *DCC* between 1 (identical rankings) and -1 (reversed rankings).

$$NDCC(L_{\mathcal{R}}^m, L_{\mathcal{R}}^{m'}) = \frac{dcc - avg}{max - avg}$$

$$\text{where } dcc = DCC(L_{\mathcal{R}}^m, L_{\mathcal{R}}^{m'}), \ max = DCC(L_{\mathcal{R}}^{m'}, L_{\mathcal{R}}^{m'})$$
$$min = DCC(L_*, L_{\mathcal{R}}^{m'}), \ L_* = rev(L_{\mathcal{R}}^{m'})$$
$$avg = (max + min)/2$$

Rankings Comparison by Example. We illustrate similarities between all ranking correlation measures with an example in Table 5. This shows correlation of a ranking L^1 with 3 others, according to each measure. *NDCC* does indeed penalize differences at higher ranks, and is more tolerant at lower ranks.

We perform a comparative analysis of the 35 interestingness measures applied to our two mining scenarios summarized in Table 2. We report the results of this comparison for prod_assoc in Sect. 4.2 and for demo_assoc in Sect. 4.3. Overall

Table 5. Example rankings and correlations

Ranking	Content
L^1	r_1, r_2, r_3, r_4
L^2	r_2, r_1, r_3, r_4
L^3	r_1, r_2, r_4, r_3
L^4	r_2, r_3, r_1, r_4

	Spearman	τ	Overlap@2	NDCC
L^2	0.80	0.67	1	0.20
L^3	0.80	0.67	1	0.97
L^4	0.40	0.33	0.5	−0.18

we identify 5 clusters of similar interestingness measures with some differences between the two scenarios. This confirms the need for a data-driven clustering of interestingness measures in each scenario.

4.2 Rankings Comparison for Prod_assoc

For prod_assoc, we generate a set of association rules $\mathcal{A} \rightarrow \mathcal{B}$, where $\mathcal{B}$ is a single product among a set of 228 representative products that were selected by our analysts. For each product $\mathcal{B}$, analysts seek to make one of two decisions: *which products $\mathcal{A}$ to bundle $\mathcal{B}$ with in an offer, and who to target for product $\mathcal{B}$ (customers who purchase products in $\mathcal{A}$).* Overall we obtain $253, 334$ association rules. We compute one rule ranking per target product and per interestingness measure.

While all measures are computed differently, we notice that some of them always produce the same ranking of association rules. We identify them in Table 3 using special symbols. For example, it is easy to see that *Information gain = $log_2(Lift)$*. *Information gain* is a monotonically increasing transformation of *Lift*, so they are returning exactly the same rankings. It is also easy to see that *Loevinger* $= 1 - \frac{1}{Conviction}$. Thus the higher the rank of any association rule r according to *Conviction*, the higher its rank according to *Loevinger*, which leads to the exactly same rule rankings for these two measures. In addition, some of the measures that always return the same rule rankings can be easily explained analytically. Since our analyst specifies a single target product at a time, for a given ranking $P(\mathcal{B})$ is constant, which eliminates some of the differences between the considered interestingness measures. We provide on Sect. 4.5 a discussion about the existing relationships between all the studied measures.

Comparative Analysis. We now evaluate the correlation between interestingness measures that do not return the same rankings. We compute a correlation matrix of all rankings according to each correlation measure described in Sect. 4.1, and average them over the 228 target products that were chosen by analysts. This gives us a ranking correlation between all pairs of measures.

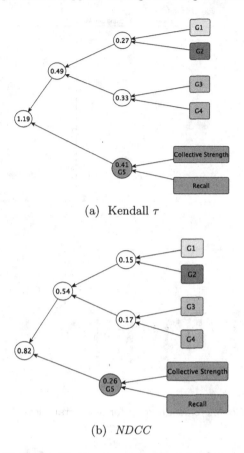

(a) Kendall τ

(b) $NDCC$

Fig. 4. Summarization of interestingness measures through hierarchical clustering for prod_assoc (clusters are described in Table 3)

The correlation matrix is then transformed to a distance matrix $\mathcal{M}$, i.e., the higher the correlation, the smaller the distance. Given the distance matrix $\mathcal{M}$, we can proceed to cluster interestingness measures. We choose to use hierarchical agglomerative clustering with average linkage [27]. Indeed, one of the advantages of hierarchical clustering is that it produces a complete sequence of nested clusterings, by starting with each measure in its own cluster and successively merging the two closest clusters into a new cluster until a single cluster containing all of the measures is obtained. For our hierarchical clustering implementation, we rely on the *cluster.hierarchy* function available from the *scipy* statistics package of Python. We obtain a dendrogram of interestingness measures and analyze their similarities. The dendrograms for $NDCC$ and τ are presented in Fig. 4.

Figure 5 shows the complete dendrogram for all interestingness measures using hierarchical clustering. To describe the results more easily, we partition the interestingness measures into 5 clusters, as indicated in the third column in

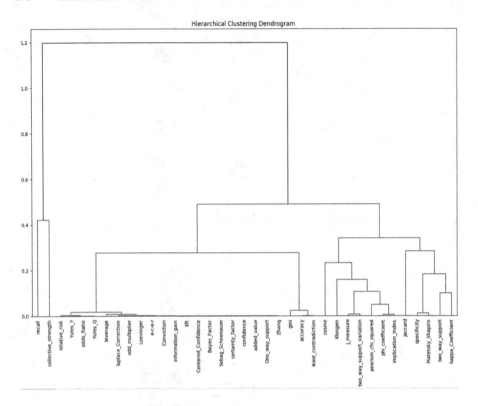

Fig. 5. Complete dendrogram for our hierarchical clustering

Table 3. G_1 is by far the largest cluster and contains 18 measures (among which *Lift, Confidence, Added value*) that produce very similar rankings, among them 6 clusters of measures always generate the same rankings. A second cluster G_2 comprising 3 measures (*Accuracy, Gini index, Least contradiction*) is similar to G_1 according to τ. But this similarity between G_1 and G_2 is higher according to $NDCC$, which shows that it is mostly caused by high ranks. A third cluster G_3 containing 7 measures (among which *J-measure*) emerges, as well as a fourth cluster G_4 containing 5 measures (among which *Piatetsky-Shapiro*), which is very similar to G_3 according to $NDCC$ as their average distance is 0.17. Finally, we have a fifth cluster G_5 containing only two measures: *Recall* and *Collective strength*.

Interestingly, we observe from the dendrograms in Fig. 4 that according to $NDCC$, G_1 and G_2 are very similar. The same is true for G_3 and G_4. This difference between ranking measures illustrates the importance of accounting for rank positions. When the top of the ranked association rules is considered more important, some similarities between clusters emerge. We illustrate this behavior in Fig. 6 by displaying the average rank difference between *Confidence*(G_1) and both *Accuracy*(G_2) and *Gini*(G_2). This experiment clearly shows that when

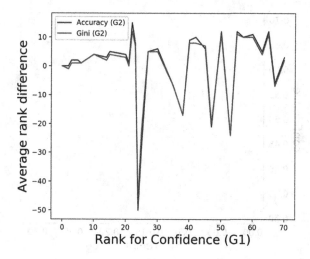

Fig. 6. Rank correlations

focusing on the top-20 (*Overlap@20*) rules the average rank difference between *Confidence* and both *Accuracy*(G_2) and *Gini*(G_2) is small. The same situation occurs between rankings obtained by $G3$ and $G4$. This explains the differences that emerge in clustering interestingness measures when using $NDCC/Overlap$ and $\tau/Spearman$.

Explaining Clusters. While using hierarchical clustering on interestingness measures allows the discovery of clusters of similar measures, it does not fully explain which types of results are favored by each of them. We propose to compare the output clusters according to the two most basic and intuitive interestingness measures used in data mining: *Confidence* and *Recall*. *Confidence* represents how often the consequent is present when the antecedent is, that is, $P(\mathcal{B}|\mathcal{A})$. Its counterpart, *Recall* represents the proportion of target items that can be retrieved by a rule, that is, $P(\mathcal{A}|\mathcal{B})$.

We present in Fig. 7, the average *Confidence* and *Recall* values obtained on the top-20 rules ranked according to each interestingness measure. The cluster G_1 containing *Confidence* scores the highest on this dimension, but achieves a really low *Recall*. G_2 is extremely close to G_1, but achieves a slightly lower *Confidence* and *Recall*. After that, we have in order of increasing *Recall* and decreasing *Confidence* G_3 and G_4. Finally, G_5 which contains *Recall* achieves the highest value on this dimension while having the smallest *Confidence*. Figure 7 also shows that executing a Euclidean distance-based clustering, such as $k - means$, with the $Recall/Confidence$ coordinates leads to similar results as with hierarchical clustering. These results are summarized in Table 4.

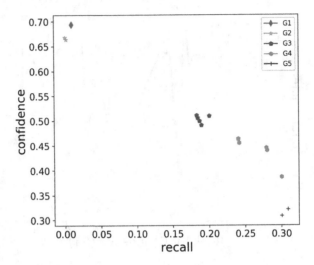

Fig. 7. Average recall/confidence of the top-20 results of interestingness measures

4.3 Rankings Comparison for Demo_assoc

For demo_assoc, we adopt exactly the same protocol as for prod_assoc. We generate a set of association rules $\mathcal{A} \rightarrow \mathcal{B}$, where $\mathcal{B}$ is a product category among a set of 16 representative categories that were selected by our analysts. For each product category $\mathcal{B}$, analysts seek to answer the following question: *which customer segments $\mathcal{A}$ to target with products in category $\mathcal{B}$*. Overall we obtain 7,616 association rules. We compute one rule ranking per combination of target category and interestingness measure.

Similarly to prod_assoc, our summarization results in 5 clusters (we omit the figure due to space limitations). The first two clusters G_1 and G_2 remain unchanged. A third cluster G'_3 contains 7 measures (including *Klosgen* and *Implication index*) is very similar to G_1 according to $NDCC$ (due to accounting for high ranks). We obtain a fourth cluster G'_4 containing 3 measures (*Pearson's χ^2, J-measure* and *Two-way support variation*) and a fifth cluster G'_5 containing 4 measures (*Recall, Collective strength, Cosine, Jaccard*). Our hypothesis is that the observed difference between clusterings obtained for demo_assoc and prod_assoc is mainly due to high values of $P(\mathcal{A})$ in demo_assoc unlike the prod_assoc scenario.

4.4 Running Time and Memory Consumption

Our development environment is comprised of Python 3.7.0 that invokes *j*LCM (implemented in JDK 7), for each target product or category on a 2.7 GHz Intel Core i7 machine with a 16 GB main memory, running OS $\times$ 10.13.6. Table 6) presents the average running time as well as the memory consumption of prod_assoc over 228 target products and that of demo_assoc over 16 categories.

We note that demo_assoc runs slower than prod_assoc. This is mainly due to the difference in cardinalities of the constructed transactional datasets: 35,377,345 transactions in demo_assoc and 1,083,901 transactions in prod_assoc. We notice a similar trend regarding memory consumption.

Table 6. Average run time and memory consumption for mining association rules for a target product/category

Mining scenario	Average run time	Average memory usage
prod_assoc	12,72 s	111,17 Mo
demo_assoc	40,94 s	306.83 Mo

4.5 Rules that Produce the Same Rankings

We report in this section measures that produce exactly the same rankings. Recall that we are given a set of association rules $\mathcal{R}= \{r_1, r_2, ..., r_n\}$ to rank. Given two measures m_1 and m_2 and their corresponding ranked lists of association rules $L_{\mathcal{R}}^{m_1}$ and $L_{\mathcal{R}}^{m_2}$, m_1 and m_2 produce exactly the same ranking iff $L_{\mathcal{R}}^{m_1} = L_{\mathcal{R}}^{m_2}$. More formally, for any two rules r_i and $r_j \in \mathcal{R}$, if m_1 ranks r_i before r_j then m_2 also ranks r_i before r_j, i.e., in order to prove that two measures m_1 and m_2 always produce the exact same ranking, one have to prove that:

$$\forall r_i, r_j \in \mathcal{R} : r_i^{m_1} \leq r_j^{m_1} \iff r_i^{m_2} \leq r_j^{m_2}$$

where r^m is the rank of the rule r according to measure m. These theoretical dependencies between interestingness measures are studied in both *C. Tew et al.* [29] and *Dhouha* [5]. Here, we summarize the group of measures that theoretically produce indistinguishable rankings and give the existing relationship between measures. We do not provide the details of the proofs and kindly refer the reader to *C. Tew et al.* [29] and *Dhouha* [5] for the detailed proofs.

– **{Yule's Q , Yule's Y and Odds Ratio}:**

$$Yule's\,Q = \frac{Odds\,Ratio - 1}{odds\,Ratio + 1}$$

and

$$Yule's\,Q = \frac{\sqrt{Odds\,Ratio} - 1}{\sqrt{odds\,Ratio} + 1}$$

– **{ Lift, Information gain }:**
   It is easy to see that:

$$Information\,gain = log_2(lift)$$

Information Gain is a monotonically increasing transformation of Lift, so they are returning exactly the same rankings.

- **{ Conviction, Loevinger }:**

$$Loevinger = 1 - \frac{1}{Conviction}$$

- **{ Example and Counter-example Rate, Sebag-Schoenauer }:**

$$ECR = 1 - \frac{1}{Sebag\ Schoenauer}$$

- **{Odd Multiplier, Zhang }:**

$$Zhang = \frac{Odd\ Multiplier - 1}{max(1, Odd\ Multiplier)}$$

In addition to these relationships, some others can be found in the special case when the target B is fixed. Since our analyst specifies a single target product at a time, for all ranking measures we have $P(\mathcal{B})$ constant. This eliminates some of the differences between the considered interestingness measures. Here, we highlight the measures that give exact rankings when the target is specified.

- **{Information gain, Lift, Added Value, Certainty factor, Confidence, Laplace correction }**

When, the target B is fix some dependencies can easily be proven analytically. For example, we can easily notice that:

$$Lift(A \rightarrow B) = Confidence(A \rightarrow B)/P(B)$$

Given that $P(B)$ is constant, we have the result that Lift and Confidence give exact association rule ranking. Similar observations appear between other measures. For instance,:

$$Added\ value(A \rightarrow B) = Confidence(A \rightarrow B) - P(B)$$

$$Certainty\ factor(A \rightarrow B) = \frac{Added\ value(A \rightarrow B)}{1 - P(B)}$$

5   User Study

We now report the results of a user study with domain experts at TOTAL. The goal of this study is to assess the ability of interestingness measures to rank association rules according to the needs of an analyst. More specifically, we would like to identify which of the interestingness measures are most preferred by our analysts.

As explained in Sect. 4, we identified 5 clusters of similar measures, and selected a representative measure in each cluster for the user study (their names are in bold in Table 3). Representative measures are selected as the ones that most represents each clusters of measures (i.e., with the highest average similarity).

We rely on the expertise of our industrial partner to determine, for each analysis scenario, which family produces the most actionable results. Actionable is interpreted as the most likely to lead to relevant recommendations. This experiment involved 2 experienced analysts: one data scientist and one product manager (co-authors of this paper).

For each mining scenario, prod_assoc and demo_assoc, we sampled target products and target categories respectively. Each analyst picks a mining scenario among prod_assoc and demo_assoc for which a target product or a target category must be chosen, respectively. The analyst receives a ranked list of rules. Neither the name of the measure nor its computed values for association rules are revealed because we wanted analysts to evaluate rankings without knowing how they were produced.

For a given scenario and a target product or category, our analysts completed 20 comparative evaluations showing two rankings to be compared with the top-10 rules per ranking. In each case, analysts were asked a global question on which ranking they preferred, and also to mark actionable rules in each ranking. We also collected feedback in a free-text form.

5.1 Initial Study

In our initial deployment, only a few rules were marked as actionable and most rules were deemed unsurprising regardless of their ranking. After a careful examination of the rankings and of the free-text comments, we found that most rules contained products that had been bundled together as promotional offers, and that most rule antecedents in prod_assoc were "polluted" with frequently purchased items.

For instance, *gas* and *plastic bags* are present in many rules and only confirm what analysts already know: that most customers purchase *gas* and *plastic bags* for their groceries. Similarly, in summer, TOTAL regularly runs offers for multi-purpose *wipes* and for *car washing* services. Other offers are most subtle and formulated as "2 products among": *Evian, Coca-Cola, Red Bull, Lay's Chips, Haribo, Mars, Snickers, Twix, Bounty and Granola*. It is hence unsurprising to find rules associating any two of those items.

As a result, we decided to filter out *gas* and *plastic bags* from the dataset and to remove from transactions items purchased shortly after a promotional offer (identified by their reduced total price).

5.2 Feedback on Ranking Measures

Our second deployment was more conclusive. In summary, we observed that rankings that favor *Confidence* are best to determine which products to promote together, and rankings that favor *Recall* are well-suited for the case where a product is given and the goal is to find who to target. These conclusions resulted from deploying comparative evaluations for 5 products for prod_assoc and 5 categories for demo_assoc.

In the case of prod_assoc, the most preferred cluster was G_1, and an overwhelming proportion of rules in that cluster were marked as actionable. The next most preferred in this same scenario is G_2. Both G_1 and G_2 favor *Confidence*, i.e., $P(\mathcal{B}|\mathcal{A})$, and reflect the case where a product is given and the goal is to find which other products $\mathcal{A}$ to bundle it with in a promotion.

We summarize the feedback we received.

1. **Associations between *Coffee/Coke* and other products:** *Coffee* has a high confidence with *Chocolate bars* and other drinks (*Water*, *Energy drinks* and *Soda*). This association was deemed immediately actionable. A similar observation can be made with the association between *Coca Cola* and *Sandwiches, Drinks, Potato chips* and *Desserts*.
2. **Association between car-related products:** The product *Engine Oil* has a high confidence with the car wash service *TOTAL Wash, Windshield wash* and a product for engine maintenance. This association was deemed immediately actionable. A similar observation was made for *Tire Spray* and *TOTAL Wash, Windshield wash* and different *car wipes* products.
3. **Associations between a product in different categories:** The product *Bounty* chocolate bar has a high confidence with products in the same category (other *Chocolate bars*), but also with different *Biscuits, Coffee* and drinks (*Water* and *Soda*). This association was deemed large scope and immediately actionable.
4. **Associations between products in the same category:** It was observed that the product *Petit Ecolier*, a chocolate biscuit, had a high confidence with other biscuits. According to our analysts, running offers on competing products is risky from a marketing point of view.

These examples illustrate the overwhelming preference for measures favoring *Confidence* for prod_assoc rules, and the need for domain experts in the loop to assess the actionability of rules, beyond automatic measures.

In the case of demo_assoc, the most preferred cluster was G'_5, and an overwhelming proportion of rules in that cluster were marked as actionable. The next most preferred in this same scenario is G'_4. Both G'_4 and G'_5 favor *Recall*, i.e., $P(\mathcal{A}|\mathcal{B})$, and reflect the case where a product category is given and the goal is to find who to target. In the case of demo_assoc, who to target is directly interpreted as which customer segments to target with products in that category. We summarize the feedback we received.

1. *Ice cream* products are mostly consumed in the region around Paris, in the South of France and in stations on the highway from North to South. That is the case for all consumer segments across all ages and genders. This rule led our analysts to look more carefully into the kind of station at which *Ice cream* products are consumed (e.g., on highways or not).
2. *Hot drinks* are less attractive in the South of France.

3. *Car lubricants* are mostly purchased by seniors (regardless of gender and location).

The above examples illustrate the overwhelming preference for measures offering a high *Recall* as a ranking measures for demo_assoc rules, and the interest of domain experts in finding which are the best customer segments to target with products in a specific category.

6   Product Recommendation

Recommendation systems are designed to guide users in a personalized way in finding useful items among a large number of possible options. Nowadays, recommendations are deployed in a wide variety of applications, such as e-commerce, online music, movies, etc. Like many retailers, TOTAL expressed a need for an automatic recommendation system to increase customer satisfaction and keep them away from competitor retailers. The deployment chosen by our business partners is to first design and evaluate recommendations using the synthesized interestingness measures, and then choose the right one for an actual deployment campaign in gas stations and for running personalized promotional offers.

6.1   Recommendation Through Association Rules

Recommendation systems can benefit from association rules extraction [11,26]. As shown in the experimental study by Pradel *et al.* [24], association rules have demonstrated good performance in recommendations using real-world e-commerce datasets, where explicit feedback such as ratings on the products is not available. Thus, it appears necessary to evaluate the performance of recommendations based on association rules mining on our dataset.

Association rules were first used to develop top-N recommendations by *Sarwar et al* [26]. They use *support* and *confidence* to measure the strength of a rule. First, for each customer, they build a single transaction containing all products that were ever purchased by that customer. Then, they use association rule mining to retrieve all the rules satisfying a given minimum *support* and minimum *confidence* constraints. To perform top-N recommendations for a customer u, they find all the rules that are supported by the customer purchase history (i.e., the customer has purchased all the products that are antecedent of the rule). Then, they sort products that the customer has not purchased yet based on the maximum *confidence* of the association rules that were used to predict them. The N highest ranked products are kept as the recommended list. Authors in [11] use a very similar approach but they also consider additional association rules between higher-lever categories where it is assumed that products are organized into a hierarchical structure.

These works present two main drawbacks. First, they require specifying thresholds on *support* and *confidence* which might be hard to adapt for different customers, and which results in the inability to recommend products that are not very frequent. Second, searching for rules where the whole purchase history of a customer is included in the antecedent, might lead to a very low or insufficient number of associations. Thus, for every customer who purchased a single product that fails the minimum *support* constraint the approach cannot compute recommendations. To overcome these drawbacks, we adapt the approach of Pradel *et al.* [24] using bi-gram association rules which consists in computing the *relevance* of the association rules $(l \rightarrow k)$ for every pair of products l and k. In computing relevance of a rule, we do not restrict ourselves to *confidence* and leverage the results we obtained on the synthesized measures to compare how different interestingness measures behave in practice (i.e., in providing accurate recommendations). In fact, as we show in Table 7, for the same anonymized customer, different interestingness measures (in this case: Confidence, Least-Contradiction and Piatetsky-Shapiro) provide different top-5 product recommendations.

Table 7. Purchase history of an anonymized customer and top-5 product recommendation according to different interestingness measures. Product descriptions are kept in French.

Purchase history	Top-5 recommendations using different interestingness measures		
	Confidence	Least-contradiction	Piatetsky-Shapiro
Coca Cola 50Cl	Total Wash 25	Total Wash 25	Café 10
Coca Cola 1.5L	Café 10	Café 10	Fuze Peche 40Cl
Chupa chups	Coca Cola Pet 1L	Chips Lays 45G	Cristaline 50CL
Coca Cola 33CL	Fuze Peche Pet 40Cl	Fuze Peche 40Cl	Mars Legend 51G
Cristaline 1, 5L	Chips Lays 45G	Evian 1, 5L	Evian 1L
PIM'S Framboise Lu			
Sandwish.XXL			
Jamb			
Kinder Bueno 43G			
Total Wash 15			
Snickers 50 g			

More formally, let $\mathcal{U} = \{u_1, u_2, ..., u_m\}$ be the set of all customers and $\mathcal{I} = \{i_1, i_2, ..., i_n\}$ be the set of all products. For a given customer u, $H_u \subseteq \mathcal{I}$ denotes the purchase history of u, the set of all products ever purchased by u. The training stage of the algorithms we evaluate takes as input a *purchase matrix*, where each column corresponds to a product and the customers that have purchased it, and each row represents a customer and the products she purchased.

We denote $\boldsymbol{P}$ the *purchase matrix* of the m customers in $\mathcal{U}$ over the n products in $\mathcal{I}$. An entry $p_{u,i}$ in the matrix contains a boolean value (0 or 1), where $p_{u,i} = 1$ means that product i was bought by customer u at least once (0 means the opposite).

We leverage the purchase history of our customers to extract association rules of the form $i \Rightarrow j$, which means that whenever a customer purchases the product i (antecedent), she is likely to purchase the product j (consequent). Therefore, We use *bigram* rules to compute an association matrix $\boldsymbol{A}$ between each pair of products i, j. The matrix $\boldsymbol{A}$ is computed from the purchase matrix $\boldsymbol{P}$, where each entry $a_{j,l}$ corresponds to the interestingness of the association rule $j \Rightarrow l$.

$$a_{j,l} = interestingness(j \Rightarrow l) \tag{1}$$

The training phase of the approach consists of the computation of all available bi-gram association rules, and stores the corresponding values of the strength on association rules in the association matrix $\boldsymbol{A}$ of size $n \times n$. Once, the association matrix is computed, to generate top-N recommendations for customer u, we first identify a set of association rules that are supported by the purchase history of u. i.e., rules of the form $k \Rightarrow l$, where k is purchased by u. Then, non purchased products are ranked either by their maximum value [24, 26], or the sum of values [11] of all association rules. In our case, the max aggregation was found to give slightly better results. This could be explained by the fact that given a target product purchased by the test customer in the test set (e.g, *cleaning wipes*), if the customer purchased in the past food and drinks products frequently and car wash products (e,g. *windshield washer*) less frequently. Using the sum aggregation will result to a poor prediction for the target *cleaning wipes* even if it is highly associated with the *windshield washer* because of the poor values of associations with other food and drink products that the customer purchased.

Thus, we compute the score of a product j for a customer u as follows:

$$score(u, j) = Max_{i \in H_u} interestingness(i \Rightarrow j) \tag{2}$$

where, H_u is the purchase history of customer u, and i is a candidate product for recommendation. Products are then sorted according to their respective scores and the top-N products are recommended to u.

6.2 Experiments

Protocol. In this section, we present our experimental protocol and the evaluation measures we use in our experiments. The widely used strategy for evaluating recommendation accuracy in offline settings is to split the dataset into training and test sets. The test set is used to simulate future transactions (ratings, clicks, purchases, etc) and it usually contains a fraction of transactions. The remaining interactions are kept in the training set and are fed to the recommendation algorithm to output a list of top-N product recommendations for each user. The accuracy of recommendations is then evaluated on the test set. However, this setting does not reflect well the reality in the retail context as it is time agnostic.

The availability of timestamps in the purchase records enables us to attempt a more realistic experiment. We hence train our algorithm on past purchases and test the results on future purchases. We split the dataset according to a given point in time which acts as our "present" (the time we apply our algorithm).

Purchases that happened before the split point are used for training, whereas future purchases after the split point are used for testing. Customers whose purchase histories are timestamped only after the split point are discarded. For our dataset, we choose 1st January 2019 to be the split date. More specifically, we use purchase records from January 2017 to December 2018 for training and records from January 2019 to December 2019 for testing.

As it is often practiced in the recommendation literature [8,25], for our experiments we discard customers who purchased fewer than 5 products in the training set. An important aspect of our dataset and of all datasets in the retail domain is the tendency to repetitively purchase the same products at different times. It is however much more valuable for the customer and even for the retailer to recommend products that the customer has not purchased recently, or is not aware of. In addition, we noticed that if we simply randomly select N products from the purchase history of each customer as the top-N recommendations, we can reach reasonable accuracy. Thus, after several exchanges with the marketing department at TOTAL, for each test customer we decided to remove the "easy" predictions from the test set corresponding to the products that have been purchased by that customer during the training period. We also select only customers who had more than 10 purchases after removing already purchased products in the test set. This setting makes the task of predicting the correct products harder but potentially more impactful in a real-world scenario.

Evaluation Measures. A recommendation algorithm outputs a sorted list of top-N product recommendations given the purchase history of a target customer. Top-N recommendations are typically evaluated in terms of their precision, recall and F1-score [6,7]. For each customer u, precision measures the percentage of recommended products that are relevant, recall measures the percentage of relevant products that are recommended, whereas, F1-score is defined as the harmonic mean of precision and recall. In our setting, a product i is relevant to a customer u if u has effectively purchased i in the test set.

In our approach, we have a set of test customers with a corresponding target set of products (recall that the target set contains the customer purchases in the test data). For a given customer u, the precision, recall, F1-score and of the top-N recommendations are respectively defined as follows:

$$Precision_u@N = \frac{|R_u@N \cap T_u|}{N} \tag{3}$$

$$Recall_u@N = \frac{|R_u@N \cap T_u|}{|T_u|} \tag{4}$$

where given a customer u, T_u is the target test set and $R_u@N$ is the set of top-N recommendations.

$$F1_u@N = \frac{2.Precision_u@N.Recall_u@N}{Precision_u@N + Recall_u@N} \tag{5}$$

To compute the final performance values, we average all metrics over all test customers.

$$Precision@N = \frac{\sum_{u:test\ customer} Precision_u@N}{Number\ of\ test\ customers} \tag{6}$$

Similar formulas are used to obtain $Recall@N$ and $F1@N$ for all customers:

$$Recall@N = \frac{\sum_{u:test\ customer} Recall_u@N}{Number\ of\ test\ customers} \tag{7}$$

$$F1@N = \frac{\sum_{u:test\ customer} F1_u@N}{Number\ of\ test\ customers} \tag{8}$$

Results. In our experiments, each row of our training purchase matrix contains all known purchases of training customers before the split date at which training and test sets are separated: January 1st, 2019. All algorithms using the different selected interestingness measures are evaluated using exactly the same test customers and the corresponding target sets. The reported performance results are computed following the experimental protocol described in Sect. 6.2 and using the evaluation measures reported in Sect. 6.2.

The values of recommendation accuracy: $Precision@10$, $Recall@10$ and $F1@10$ for each interestingness measure are reported in Table 8. First, we can notice that G_1 achieves the best recommendation performance and performs slightly better than G_2. The performance results confirm our findings in the user study where our domain experts preferred group G_1 and measures that favor confidence for the prod_assoc scenario. Second, we notice that the achieved recommendation accuracy for groups G_1 and G_2 are very close (12.56% and 12.08% for $Precision@10$, respectively). The same occurs with very similar performances for groups G_3 and G_4 (10.95% and 10.56% for $Precision@10$, respectively). These results are consistent with the clustering that we performed using $NDCC$ (Fig. 4b). Since we compute top-10 lists per customer, $NDCC$ gives more importance to associations rules in the top of the lists. This explains the similarities of recommendation performances for G_1 and G_2 as well as groups G_3 and G_4, as the average distance between G_1 and G_2 in the dendrogram in Fig. 4b is 0.15 and the average distance between G_3 and G_4 is 0.17. Then, we notice a really poor performance for measures in group G_5 that are not usable in practice. This is mainly due to the fact that measures having a very low confidence favor rare targets over frequent ones for ranking association rules, which results in recommending mostly irrelevant products. We also noticed that some measures that are in the same cluster may not produce similar recommendation performance. In fact, we also produced recommendations using measures within the same cluster and found that the recommendations were different for some cases. We conjecture that this is due to the fact that the obtained rules for computing recommendations focused on different subsets of purchased products according to different users and exhibit the same phenomenon as the Simpson Paradox. For instance, using Accuracy (G_2)as a ranking measure leads to a poor performance values (0.91% for precision@10), while using *Least Contradiction* (G_2) gives much better results (12.08% for precision@10), even if both measures are in the same cluster.

Finally, we implemented a `MostPop` baseline which is the method that were used so far by our analysts and which consists of a non personalized method that recommends to each customer the set of most popular products that the customer did not purchase yet. We can see from our results that except for measures in group G_5, all others groups of measures perform better than the non personalized baseline. In particular G_1 show an improvement of 53.54% in relative performance.

Table 8. Recommendation accuracy for each representative measure

Measure	Prec@10	Recall@10	F1@10
Lift (G_1)	**12.56%**	**7.03%**	**8.60%**
Least-contradiction (G_2)	12.08%	6.69%	8.20%
Cosine (G_3)	10.95%	6.19%	7.55%
Piatetsky-Shapiro (G_4)	10.56%	6.02%	7.32%
Collective strength (G_5)	0.45%	0.28%	0.26%
MostPop (baseline)	8.18%	4.76%	5.76%

7 Related Work

To the best of our knowledge, this paper is the first to bring a framework for association rule mining to the marketing department of an *oil* and *gas* company, and empower domain experts with the ability to conduct large-scale studies of customer purchasing habits.

The definition of quality of association rules is a well-studied topic in statistics and data mining. In their survey [4], Geng *et al.* review 38 measures for association and classification rules. They also discuss 4 sets of properties like symmetry or monotony, and how each of them highlights different meanings of "rule quality", such as novelty and generality. However, we observe no correlation between these properties and the groups of measures discovered using our framework.

These 38 measures are compared in [14]. Authors consider the case of extracting and ranking temporal rules (*event A→event B*) from the execution traces of programs. Each measure is evaluated in its ability to rank highly rules known from a ground truth (library specification). We observe that the measures scoring the highest are all from the groups identified in this work as G_1 and G_2, which are also favored by our analysts. There are however some counterexamples, with measures from G_1 scoring poorly. The main difference between our work and [14] is the absence of a ground truth of interesting rules for our dataset.

A close work to ours is HERBS [15]. HERBS relies on a different and smaller set of measures to cluster rule rankings. Authors perform an analysis of the properties of measures, in addition to an experimental study. The datasets used are from the health and astronomy domains. Each of them contains at most 1,728 transactions and leads to the extraction of 49 to 6,312 rules. Rankings are then compared between all pairs of measures using Kendall's τ correlation measure averaged over all datasets. The largest group of measures identified, which includes *Confidence*, is similar to G_1.

Our use of the *p-value* (via *Pearson's* χ^2 *test*) in the evaluation of rule interestingness is borrowed from [17]. In that work, the authors propose an exploration framework where rules are grouped by consequent and traversed by progressively adding items to the antecedent. The framework provides hints incrementally to help guess how each additional item would make a difference. Such a framework is suitable to some of the scenarios we consider and could be integrated in a future version of our work.

Other significant works on clustering interestingness measures include [2,5, 29]. In these studies, 61 measures are analyzed from both a theoretical and an empirical aspect to provide insights about the properties and behavior of the measures according to association rule ranking. The number of measures studied in these works is greater than ours. However, our work goes a step further as (1) we provide a user study performed with domain experts from TOTAL marketing department, (2) we show how association rules can be used to perform top-N recommendations, and (3) we show a comparative evaluation of the synthesized interestingness measures according to accuracy measures.

An interesting research area is OLAP pattern mining, which integrates online analytical processing (OLAP) with data mining so that the mining can be performed in different portions of the database [18,23]. However, the focus of our work is not on expressivity nor is it on performance computation. An interesting research direction would indeed be to extend our framework to using the full power of OLAP.

8 Conclusion

We present our framework to enable decision support through mining, ranking, and summarization of association rules. We use large longitudinal TOTAL datasets that comprises of 30 million unique sales receipts, spanning 35 million records. In conjunction with domain expert non-scientists, we studied two scenarios: associations between a set of products and a target product, and between customer segments and product categories. Both of these scenarios led to actionable insights leading to effective decision support for the TOTAL marketers. We empirically studied 35 interestingness measures for ranking association rules and further summarize them in 5 synthesized clusters or groups. Resulting groups were then evaluated in a user study involving a data scientist and a domain expert at TOTAL. We concluded that ranking measures ensuring high confidence, best fit the needs of analysts in the case of prod assoc, and measures that ensure high recall are better in the case of demo assoc. Finally, we discussed how our findings can be used to perform product recommendation using different interestingness measures for ranking association rules.

References

1. Agrawal, R., Imieliński, T., Swami, A.: Mining association rules between sets of items in large databases. In: Proceedings of SIGMOD, pp. 207–216 (1993)
2. Belohlavek, R., Grissa, D., Guillaume, S., Nguifo, E.M., Outrata, J.: Boolean factors as a means of clustering of interestingness measures of association rules. Ann. Math. Artif. Intell. **70**(1–2), 151–184 (2014)
3. Daniel, W.: Applied Nonparametric Statistics. Houghton Mifflin, Boston (1978)
4. Geng, L., Hamilton, H.J.: Interestingness measures for data mining: a survey. ACM Comput. Surv. **38**(3), 9-es (2006)
5. Grissa, D.: Etude comportementale des mesures d'intérêt d'extraction de connaissances. Ph.D. thesis (2013)
6. Gunawardana, A., Shani, G.: Evaluating recommender systems. In: Ricci, F., Rokach, L., Shapira, B. (eds.) Recommender Systems Handbook, pp. 265–308. Springer, Boston, MA (2015). https://doi.org/10.1007/978-1-4899-7637-6_8
7. Herlocker, J.L., Konstan, J.A., Terveen, L.G., Riedl, J.T.: Evaluating collaborative filtering recommender systems. ACM Trans. Inf. Syst. (TOIS) **22**(1), 5–53 (2004)
8. Hu, Y., Koren, Y., Volinsky, C.: Collaborative filtering for implicit feedback datasets. In: 2008 Eighth IEEE International Conference on Data Mining, pp. 263–272. IEEE (2008)
9. Järvelin, K., Kekäläinen, J.: Cumulated gain-based evaluation of IR techniques. ACM Trans. Inf. Syst. **20**(4), 422–446 (2002)
10. Kendall, M.G.: A New Measure of Rank Correlation. Biometrika **30**(1/2), 81–93 (1938)
11. Kim, C., Kim, J.: A recommendation algorithm using multi-level association rules. In: Proceedings IEEE/WIC International Conference on Web Intelligence (WI 2003), pp. 524–527. IEEE (2003)
12. Kirchgessner, M., Leroy, V., Amer-Yahia, S., Mishra, S.: Testing interestingness measures in practice: a large-scale analysis of buying patterns. In: 2016 IEEE International Conference on Data Science and Advanced Analytics, DSAA 2016, Montreal, QC, Canada, 17–19 October 2016, pp. 547–556. IEEE (2016). https://doi.org/10.1109/DSAA.2016.53
13. Kirchgessner, M., Leroy, V., Termier, A., Amer-Yahia, S., Rousset, M.C.: jLCM. https://github.com/slide-lig/jlcm. Accessed 27 May 2016
14. Le, T.D., Lo, D.: Beyond support and confidence: exploring interestingness measures for rule-based specification mining. In: Proceedings of SANER, pp. 331–340 (2015)
15. Lenca, P., Vaillant, B., Meyer, P., Lallich, S.: Association rule interestingness measures: experimental and theoretical studies. In: Guillet, F.J., Hamilton, H.J. (eds.) Quality Measures in Data Mining. Studies in Computational Intelligence, vol. 43, pp. 51–76. Springer, Heidelberg (2007). https://doi.org/10.1007/978-3-540-44918-8_3
16. Leroy, V., Kirchgessner, M., Termier, A., Amer-Yahia, S.: TopPI: an efficient algorithm for item-centric mining. Inf. Syst. **64**, 104–118 (2017). https://doi.org/10.1016/j.is.2016.09.001

17. Liu, G., et al.: Towards exploratory hypothesis testing and analysis. In: Proceedings of ICDE, pp. 745–756 (2011)
18. Messaoud, R.B., Rabaséda, S.L., Boussaid, O., Missaoui, R.: Enhanced mining of association rules from data cubes. In: Proceedings of ACM 9th International Workshop on Data Warehousing and OLAP, DOLAP 2006, Arlington, Virginia, USA, 10 November 2006, pp. 11–18 (2006). https://doi.org/10.1145/1183512.1183517
19. Minato, S., Uno, T., Tsuda, K., Terada, A., Sese, J.: A fast method of statistical assessment for combinatorial hypotheses based on frequent itemset enumeration. In: Calders, T., Esposito, F., Hüllermeier, E., Meo, R. (eds.) ECML PKDD 2014. LNCS (LNAI), vol. 8725, pp. 422–436. Springer, Heidelberg (2014). https://doi.org/10.1007/978-3-662-44851-9_27
20. Pasquier, N., Bastide, Y., Taouil, R., Lakhal, L.: Discovering frequent closed itemsets for association rules. In: Beeri, C., Buneman, P. (eds.) ICDT 1999. LNCS, vol. 1540, pp. 398–416. Springer, Heidelberg (1999). https://doi.org/10.1007/3-540-49257-7_25
21. Pei, J., Han, J., Mao, R.: CLOSET: an efficient algorithm for mining frequent closed itemsets. In: Proceedings of SIGMOD, pp. 21–30 (2000)
22. Piatetsky-Shapiro, G.: Knowledge Discovery in Databases. AAI/MIT, Menlo Park (1991)
23. Plantevit, M., Laurent, A., Teisseire, M.: OLAP-sequential mining: summarizing trends from historical multidimensional data using closed multidimensional sequential patterns. New Trends Data Warehouse. Data Anal. **3**, 275 (2008)
24. Pradel, B., et al.: A case study in a recommender system based on purchase data. In: Proceedings of the 17th ACM SIGKDD International Conference on Knowledge Discovery and Data Mining, pp. 377–385. ACM (2011)
25. Rendle, S., Freudenthaler, C., Gantner, Z., Schmidt-Thieme, L.: BPR: Bayesian personalized ranking from implicit feedback. In: Proceedings of the Twenty-Fifth Conference on Uncertainty in Artificial Intelligence, pp. 452–461. AUAI Press (2009)
26. Sarwar, B., Karypis, G., Konstan, J., Riedl, J., et al.: Analysis of recommendation algorithms for e-commerce. In: EC, pp. 158–167 (2000)
27. Sokal, R.R., Michener, C.D.: A statistical method for evaluating systematic relationships. Univ. Kans. Sci. Bull. **38**, 1409–1438 (1958)
28. Tan, P.N., Steinbach, M., Kumar, V.: Introduction to Data Mining, 1st edn. W. W. Norton & Company, New York City (2007)
29. Tew, C., Giraud-Carrier, C., Tanner, K., Burton, S.: Behavior-based clustering and analysis of interestingness measures for association rule mining. Data Min. Knowl. Disc. **28**(4), 1004–1045 (2013). https://doi.org/10.1007/s10618-013-0326-x
30. Uno, T., Kiyomi, M., Arimura, H.: LCM ver. 2: efficient mining algorithms for frequent/closed/maximal itemsets. In: Proceedings of ICDM Workshop FIMI (2004)

Author Index

Printed in the United States
By Bookmasters